MYSTERY OF THE
POWER
WORDS

DESTINY IMAGE BOOKS BY KEVIN L. ZADAI

Receiving from Heaven

It's Rigged in Your Favor

Praying from the Heavenly Realms

Supernatural Finances

The Agenda of Angels

MYSTERY OF THE
POWER WORDS

SPEAK THE WORDS THAT MOVE MOUNTAINS AND MAKE HELL TREMBLE

KEVIN L. ZADAI

DESTINY IMAGE® PUBLISHERS, INC.

P.O. Box 310, Shippensburg, PA 17257-0310

"Promoting Inspired Lives."

This book and all other Destiny Image and Destiny Image Fiction books are available at Christian bookstores and distributors worldwide.

Cover design by Eileen Rockwell

Interior design by Terry Clifton

For more information on foreign distributors, call 717-532-3040.

Reach us on the Internet: www.destinyimage.com.

ISBN 13 TP: 978-0-7684-5572-4
ISBN 13 eBook: 978-0-7684-5570-0
ISBN 13 HC: 978-0-7684-5569-4
ISBN 13 LP: 978-0-7684-5571-7

For Worldwide Distribution, Printed in the U.S.A.

1 2 3 4 5 6 7 8 / 25 24 23 22 21

DEDICATION

I dedicate this book to the Lord Jesus Christ. When I died during surgery and met with Jesus on the other side, He insisted that I return to life on the earth and that I help people with their destinies. Because of Jesus' love and concern for people, the Lord has actually chosen to send a person back from death to help everyone who will receive that help so that his or her destiny and purpose are secure in Him.

> *I want You, Lord, to know that when You come to take me to be with You someday, it is my sincere hope that people do not remember me but remember the revelation of Jesus Christ that You have revealed through me. I want others to know I am merely being obedient to Your heavenly calling and mission, which is to reveal Your plan for the fulfillment of the divine destiny for each of God's children.*

ACKNOWLEDGMENTS

In addition to sharing my story with everyone through the books *Heavenly Visitation: A Guide to the Supernatural, Days of Heaven on Earth: A Guide to the Days Ahead, Praying from the Heavenly Realms: Supernatural Secrets to a Lifestyle of Answered Prayer, The Agenda of Angels: What the Holy Ones Want You to Know About the Next Move of God, It's All Rigged in Your Favor, Supernatural Finances,* and *Receiving From Heaven,* the Lord gave me the commission to produce *Mystery of the Power Words.* This book addresses some of the revelations concerning the areas that Jesus reviewed and revealed to me through the Word of God and by the Spirit of God during several visitations.

I want to thank everyone who has encouraged me, assisted me, and prayed for me during the writing of this work, especially my spiritual parents, Dr. Jesse Duplantis and Dr. Cathy Duplantis. Special thanks to my wonderful wife, Kathi, for her love and dedication to the Lord and me. Thank you, Sid Roth and staff, for your love of our supernatural Messiah, Jesus. Thank you, Warrior Notes staff, for the wonderful job editing this book. Thank you, Destiny Image and staff, for your support of this project. Special thanks, as well, to all my friends who understand the mystery of the power words and how Jesus would want us to live using them in the next move of God's Spirit.

CONTENTS

PREFACE

OVER THE YEARS, the Lord has dealt with me concerning our words and the importance of speaking our destiny or where we are going in our special path that the Lord has chosen for each of us individually. However, there is another very important aspect to this subject on the use of words. There is a war against absolute truth. By the Spirit, I realize that if we are not careful to uphold absolute truth and the words that represent that truth, we will lose the power and reality of what Jesus taught us.

The enemy desires for the reality of what Jesus obtained for us to fade from our consciences. I have compiled a list of words that we should use often to shake hell and move mountains as we take back what the devil has stolen. The Lord has led me regarding this subject in this season in order to reemphasize the importance of the wonderful truths of the Bible these words represent. I assure you that you will see the fruit of using these *power words* in your life as you allow the favor of your Heavenly Father to permeate your heart and then speak from the supernatural realm.

Kevin L. Zadai, Th. D.

New Covenant - Kingdom Dominion - The Fear of the Lord - Visitation - Habitation - Divine Prosperity - The Blood - Kingdom Dominion - The Fear of the Lord - Resurrection Power - Habitation - Divine Prosperity - The Blood - Repentance - minion - The Fear of the Lord - Resurrection Power - Holy Fir - Divine Prosperity - The Blood - Repentance - New Covenant the Lord - Resurrection Power - Holy Fire - Visitation - Hab The Blood - Repentance - Kingdom Dominion ion Power - Holy Fire - Habitation - Divine Pro - New Covenant - Kingdom Dominion - The Fear of the Lord - Visitation - Habitation - Divine Prosperity - The Blood - Kingdom Dominion - The Fear of the Lord - Resurrection Power Habitation - Divine Prosperity - The Blood - Repentance - minion - The Fear of the Lord - Holy Fir

FOREWORD

I F YOU'RE LOOKING for a lightweight "name it and claim it" book, a book that will teach how "you can have what you say," then this is not the book for you. If you're looking for a book that will teach you how to align your thoughts and words and actions with the Word of God, a book that will help you live a crucified, holy, repentant, yielded, broken, and empowered life in Jesus, a book that will inspire you and take you deeper and higher in the Lord, then this is the book for you. And as you read the Scripture-filled pages that follow and put the teachings into practice, your life will be dramatically changed.

If you know Kevin's story, he speaks of encountering Jesus in Heaven for 45 minutes after dying on an operating table. But how are we to assess suc Crucified Life. But along with an emphasis on living a crucified, holy, disciplined, Spirit-filled life, Kevin also speaks of things like "Kingdom Dominion" and "Divine Prosperity." Aren't these erroneous concepts that have been propagated by misguided teachers? Aren't these things we should stay away from?

3

The answer is absolutely not, since Kevin is not talking about the carnal prosperity gospel, which falsely teaches that Jesus died with the purpose of making us financially wealthy and that you can judge someone's spirituality by their earthly riches. And he is not talking about a "Kingdom now" message in which the Church somehow "takes over" the whole world before Jesus comes. Instead, he is emphasizing the abundance of divine provision for those who do the Father's will, along with the spiritual authority we can walk in to set the captives free, thereby extending the Kingdom of God. Kevin also combats the idea that the closer you are to God, the poorer you will be, reminding us that it's better to be a lender than a borrower and to be out of debt than in debt. Who can argue with this?

As for the concept of "Divine Health," there is no question that some of the saintliest people on the planet are chronically ill. And, if you have actively prayed for the sick, you know that all too often you do not see your prayers answered. But, having written my doctoral dissertation on the subject of the Hebrew word for healing, and having written several major academic works on the subject of divine healing, I came to some simple conclusions. First, sickness, in and of itself is a bad thing. Second, healing, in and of itself is a good thing. And third, God's ideal will for His obedient children, as revealed in the Word, is health and healing. Here, Kevin encourages us to believe God for a greater manifestation of health and healing then we have seen. That should be our dream and goal until we meet Jesus face to face and death is abolished forever.

As for the controversial subject of Jesus' descent into hell, which Kevin discusses in the chapter on Resurrection Power, it is interesting to compare what he writes to the treatment of this subject in the early Church Fathers as well as in various Church traditions (including Eastern Orthodox). And, as always, everything must be examined through the lens of the Scriptures. What did happen between the cross and the resurrection?

In the end, though, this is not a book about theological controversies or doctrinal disputes. It is all about Him and for Him, and this must be our focus as well. As Kevin writes,

> In my prayer time, I check in with God because I want to see what He is up to, what He is saying to me, and what He is doing. I ask, "Lord, what are you doing now? What are you saying now?" In the morning, when I wake up, I ask Him, "Lord, what is your desire? What are you thinking? What is it that you want me to do today?" I am accountable to God, and I keep in contact with Him all the time by speaking to Him and asking Him for help.

God desires that we walk closely with Him, that we learn to live in Him, and that through our lives, many others come to know Him. Our ultimate destiny—yes, "Destiny" is one of those power words too—is to be conformed to the image of Jesus. May we grow into that holy image more and more day by day, making Jesus known to a hurting world, until that day of final transformation comes. This book will help you reach that goal.

MICHAEL L. BROWN, PH.D.
Host of the *Line of Fire* broadcast

Chapter 1

WORDS HAVE POWER

*For the word of God is living and powerful, and sharper
than any two-edged sword, piercing even to the division
of soul and spirit, and of joints and marrow, and is a
discerner of the thoughts and intents of the heart.*

—HEBREWS 4:12

T O MINISTER LIFE to people when you speak to them, you
must use words, but your words must be anointed with power
from the Holy Spirit. Jesus promised the Holy Spirit's coming
on the day of Pentecost when He said,

*If you love Me, keep My commandments. And I will
pray the Father, and He will give you another Helper,
that He may abide with you forever.*

—JOHN 14:15-16

Why is this important? Ministering life to people has to do
with yielding to God's Holy Spirit and speaking the Word of God.
The power of the Holy Spirit is joined together with the Word
because they are the same in Heaven.

The Holy Trinity, the Godhead, consists of the *Word of God*, which is the Son; the *Spirit of God*, which is the breath of God; and the *Father*—and they are all working together. When you speak in this earthly realm, it is important to understand that you must have heavenly power from the Holy Spirit. Jesus promised us that the Helper comes to live with us forever.

> *Jesus answered and said to him, "If anyone loves Me, he will keep My word; and My Father will love him, and We will come to him and make Our home with him."*
> —JOHN 14:23

Jesus promised that the Holy Spirit would come and abide with us and be our Helper. Then He said He and the Father would make Their home in us if we love Him and keep His Word. When you put these two Scriptures together, John 14:15-16 and John 14:23, you can see that as a believer, you have the Trinity living inside you.

When you speak and yield your spirit to the Holy Spirit, you are going to see the manifestation of the power of God. When you fall in love with God and His Word, you will be passionately walking in obedience because that is what God asks of you; He wants you to be obedient to His Word. So, we should want, not only to know His Word, but to also know His acts and His ways.

When the children of Israel were in the desert, Psalm 103:7 says, "[God] *made known His ways to Moses, His acts to the children of Israel.*" I do not want to be a spectator; I want to be a participator. When you fall in love, you are going to obey God, and you are going to obey His Word. When you do that, you merge your spirit with God in a relationship. That relationship is passionate, and it causes you to manifest the power of the Spirit of God in your life.

> *And the glory which You gave Me I have given them,*
> *that they may be one just as We are one: I in them, and*
> *You in Me; that they may be made perfect in one, and*
> *that the world may know that You have sent Me, and*
> *have loved them as You have loved Me.*
>
> —JOHN 17:22-23

What Jesus is showing us here is that once He goes to the Father, the Father is going to love us just like the Father loves Jesus. Then the Father is going to make us perfect and one with Jesus and Him. Jesus explains the glory that He shared with the Father is now going to be given to us, and we can participate in that glory.

As you meditate on John 17:22-23, meditate on the fact that we are sharing in the glory of God. We are sharing in the oneness of the Godhead, and we are sharing in the love that the Father has. The Father loves His Son, and Jesus is saying, "I love You, Father, and You love Me, and the Father loves His children as much as He loves Me." When the truth is spoken, it has to be anointed with this love and this glory. You have to be one in the Spirit of God.

You are going to begin to walk in the power of God so that when you speak, your words have weight behind them in the Spirit. You must realize that satan and all of the demonic spirits down here can hear if you are connected in the Spirit with what you are saying. Your words have power when you connect with the Spirit of God. The Spirit of life that comes out of you must come out in the power of your words.

When I was in Heaven, I saw that Jesus bought us back to the restoration of Adam and even better. We were as Adam and Eve, who walked with God in the garden of Eden and saw Him face to face. When Jesus bought us back, that restoration causes us to be just like Adam and Eve in our inner man. Our bodies will still die because God has pronounced that our earthly bodies will only live a certain amount of years. Our souls—our minds, wills, and emotions—are not redeemed either, and they have to be transformed by the renewing of our minds, which is why we must allow our spirits to dominate our lives.

When your spirit is born again, you have to push out fear, and you have to push doubt away. You have to realize that the change must happen now in your body and your mind. Your spirit is born again, and you are now walking in the power of God. I had to learn to speak from my spirit and not from my head or my soul. If you begin to do that, then you will start to be a partaker of the divine nature because God made you in His image.

SPEAK FROM THE SPIRIT

Your spirit is the only part of you that has been born again. It is the only part that has changed. When you speak from your spirit, your words will have power. If you want the power of God in your life, and you want that manifestation, then you must cross over to where you learn to speak from down in your heart. You must watch the words that you speak.

But I say to you that for every idle word men may speak, they will give account of it in the day of judgment. For

*by your words you will be justified, and by your words
you will be condemned.*
                              —MATTHEW 12:36-37

Jesus spoke this to me in person when I was with Him during a heavenly visitation. I met Him when I died on the operating room table in 1992. Jesus said, "Kevin, you will be held accountable for every idle word that you speak." When I got back, I had to go and look that up because I did not know it was in the Bible, and I loved to talk!

Jesus was instructing me that I needed to tone it down a little bit and be careful about what I say because the tongue is a rudder.

*Look also at ships: although they are so large and are
driven by fierce winds, they are turned by a very small
rudder wherever the pilot desires. Even so the tongue is
a little member and boasts great thing.*
                                        —JAMES 3:4-5

Jesus explained this verse to me and told me that the little rudder is your tongue. We will have to give an account on the day of judgment for every idle word that we have spoken.

Jesus started to teach me, and He told me how everything started. Everything that you see in the universe is everything that is expanding at the same speed that God spoke it. Jesus said, "We decided what We were going to do as a Trinity, and then We spoke. We spoke what We believed in Our Hearts, and We framed the worlds."

Jesus continued and said, "We made man in Our image, and in the same way, man is a speaking spirit; man is a living spirit." Men and women of God have authority on the earth now. If you are born again, you can speak from the Spirit, and it has weight with God because we were made that way. God spoke the worlds into existence. When Jesus framed the worlds, they were formed out of something that did not exist, and so it is with us. We have to speak from our spirits.

Think about the things that you are going through right now and the things that are contrary to your life. From your spirit, you have to speak what is right, and you start to steer your life just as a ship is steered by a little rudder. Your tongue needs to change, and you are going to speak where you are going, and your world is going to be framed by your words. You must believe in your heart and then speak it out. We see this same principle in Genesis 1 when God spoke of creating Adam.

> *Then God said, "Let Us make man in Our image, according to Our likeness; let them have dominion over the fish of the sea, over the birds of the air, and over the cattle, over all the earth and over every creeping thing that creeps on the earth."*
>
> —Genesis 1:26

You are made in the image of God. What does that mean? When God made the worlds, He thought, He believed in His heart, and then He spoke, and man was framed out of nothing. Adam was then standing there, and God brought all of the animals to him. God told Adam to name all of the animals anything he wanted (see Gen. 2:19-20). Whatever Adam named them would be their name. If you see a giraffe, remember that Adam named that giraffe, and it stuck forever.

God gave man and woman authority and dominion over the earth (see Gen. 1:26-30), and God gave them the authority to name the animals. We have authority as men and women of God, and now we can speak in the spirit. We must be very careful about what we say because it is steering us.

Think about being a partaker of the divine nature.

> *By which have been given to us exceedingly great and precious promises, that through these you may be partakers of the divine nature, having escaped the corruption that is in the world through lust.*
>
> —2 PETER 1:4

Many people do not want to think about this verse, and it is because men and women are so fallen that even religious people do not think we could ever achieve what God made us to be. Yet, Jesus Christ Himself told me, "I died, and I redeemed man back to Adam. That means that they are supposed to walk in authority and speak in authority. They are supposed to have dominion." Even in the Old Testament, God blessed Abraham, Isaac, and Jacob, and they had authority on the earth. Abraham was a great man. Yet, when Jesus spoke of John the Baptist, He explained that there had never been anyone greater in the Kingdom and that everyone from then on, even the least in the Kingdom of God, was now greater than John (see Matt. 11:11). If what Jesus said is true, it means that you and me, even if we were the lowest in the Kingdom, are greater than John the Baptist. It also means we are greater than Abraham, Isaac, Jacob, Enoch, and all of those men and women who walked with God because, according to Jesus, John was greater than they.

Jesus then continued with His resurrection power and took us to the heavenly realms (see Eph. 2:6). Now we are greater because of the authority that has been given back to us. If you want to walk in the greater manifestation, you have to do it from down here on the earth. God believes in His heart, and so must you.

> *For assuredly, I say to you, whoever says to this mountain, "Be removed and be cast into the sea," and does not doubt in his heart, but believes that those things he says will be done, he will have whatever he says. Therefore I say to you, whatever things you ask when you pray, believe that you receive them, and you will have them.*
> —MARK 11:23-24

Jesus explained this verse in Mark 11 to me. He said, "The reason I said that was because you need to realize that if you speak from your heart and you believe it, then what you say with your mouth, you shall have it." Jesus said this because we have been purchased back, and Jesus has given us back the authority that Adam and Eve had.

Religious leaders are so used to us being beaten down, but as Christians, we are greater than anyone who came before us because of Jesus Christ. In the Kingdom, we are even greater than those who built the foundation. I do not think that I am greater than Moses, but at the Jordan River, Jesus basically was saying that everyone in the Kingdom from then on is greater.

AGREE WITH THE WORD OF GOD

Right now, you see the discrepancies in your life, such as wanting to participate in the divine nature and not being able to see how you can. I understand that, and I want you to know the discrepancies that you are seeing and experiencing in your life now have to do with how you are talking. You are not speaking the truth. I know this for a fact because, when I began to watch my words, I started to say things that God was revealing to me, and these became the direction in which I started going. I started to sense from the Word of God that there were certain areas which I needed to apply to my life. I began to meditate on those Scriptures, and then, all of a sudden, I started to receive guidance for my own life.

As I meditated on the Scriptures in the Bible that were from the Lord concerning me, in a flash, the Lord started to show me what would happen three months in the future. I was not even thinking about my future; I was just meditating on the Word of God. That is how it comes. You start to connect with what the Spirit of God is saying through the Word of God, and then, suddenly, there are no discrepancies in your life because you agree with the Word of God. At that very moment, you will start to see into the future. I have taught this to many people, and they tell me that they are starting to see and are starting to hear God's voice in a greater way.

And it all has to do with your words. I found that as soon as I began to correct my words and learned to stop saying certain things, then the curse stopped in my life, and I began to have revelation. I started to move forward, and most importantly, I stopped being a victim. I started to see that satan and all those devils became the victims instead. Everywhere I would go, those devils would be rushing to get away from me instead of rushing to come and get me.

The thief does not come except to steal, and to kill, and to destroy. I have come that they may have life, and that they may have it more abundantly.

—JOHN 10:10

This physical world is fallen, and satan is the god of this world. He controls everything down here. That is why you have poverty, sickness, discrepancies, disappointments, and all the killing, stealing, and destroying. Jesus said He came to give you life and give it to you more abundantly. Participation in that abundant life has to do with speaking the truth in love. You speak the truth in God because God is love. So, you speak the truth in God, and out of your spirit, you begin to live off the words, the fruit of your lips. You start to speak where you are going.

You begin like this: You start with the Word of God, you meditate on it, and then you start speaking it. Suddenly, prophetically, it will all start stirring in you, and you will begin saying things about your future and then you will know what you are supposed to do. All of those decisions you have had to make that you have been wondering about for months, the Spirit of God will unexpectedly show you what to do. Operating like this in the Spirit of God needs to happen in your life.

So many people need to move into this mode of operation, where they walk in the Spirit, and they talk in the Spirit. You can, however, still go about your day. I worked for a company for thirty years, and I was still able to pray in the Spirit silently and meditate on the Word of God *and* operate in the supernatural. Even though it was not easy at times because I was at a secular job, I still learned how to do this. I learned to live out of my spirit.

Additionally, after seeing so many discrepancies and experiencing so much disappointment and heartache, the Spirit of the Lord wants you to be healed as well. Healing is going to come to you when you start to meditate on the Word of God. You need to let go of any hurts or offenses that may be entangling you and preventing you from running your race. Hebrews 12:1 encourages us:

> *Therefore we also, since we are surrounded by so great a cloud of witnesses, let us lay aside every weight, and the sin which so easily ensnares us, and let us run with endurance the race that is set before us.*

Let go of the hurt right now, and let the Word of the Lord, the fear of the Lord, come into you and your life. The Word of the Lord will bring you the correction that is needed, and the fear of the Lord will bring you the wisdom of God. And the Spirit of God will want to speak through you.

I want to encourage you. You have to watch your words. The power of the Holy Spirit is present at all times to do what God has written about you in your life. The proper procedure is this: You first meditate on the Word of God, and then when the Spirit of God starts to bubble up within you, speak that Word. Then no matter what you feel or what you see or what happens, you stick with that Word. God is going to start to lead and guide you because "[His] *Word is a lamp unto* [your] *feet and a light unto* [your] *path"* (Ps. 119:105).

Did you know that in other countries where the Word of God is not spoken as much, there is a lot more demonic activity? In the United States, we have so much Word going forth that it is hard for satan to take over completely. That also explains why the

United States does not have a lot of demon possession. It is harder for demons to operate because of the light of God.

In the United States, the demons mostly operate in people's emotions and their minds. When more people have the gospel, there is more light, and demons cannot fully possess them. Many people in the United States have been exposed to the light of the gospel and God's Word being preached.

You need to make your environment one where you incubate with the Word of God and the power of God, and then you speak it. It is not wrong for people to want to prophesy, and you do not have to be a prophet to prophesy. You can prophesy because you are speaking forth the mysteries of God (see 1 Cor. 2:7). You can pray that you interpret what you are praying in the Spirit (see 1 Cor. 14:13-15). If you are speaking in tongues, you pray that you can interpret, and then you should speak out the interpretation.

HOOK UP TO THE POWER

Interpreting my tongues is how I developed my relationship with God in this area. I started to pray in the Spirit a lot, but then I would have these words come up in English, in my known language, and I would want to speak those things. As I started to speak those things, the power of God was so strong that I felt it go out like a missile.

Then the Lord began showing me that this is how the power words work. The power comes when you hook up with the Holy Spirit and the Word of God prophetically. That power is going to come forth, and it is going to come forth in your words.

You need to pick a few of the powerful words that are in God's Word and meditate on them. Meditate on them until they start to take root in your heart and you start to feel the anointing. For a long time, I meditated and focused on the end part of John 15:5, *"For without Me you can do nothing."* I thought about that for a while, and then the reality of it started to hit me. Now when I say that verse as I speak or teach, it is so powerful, and that is because my spirit received the revelation of it. It then became part of me.

When you begin to meditate on different Scriptures, they start to translate over into your speech, and you become careful with your words. I often repeat what Jesus said to me in Heaven. He said, "Kevin, if you go back for Me, you cannot fail. You *will not* fail." Jesus told me that my going back would be extra credit. Now when I speak those words, even though they are not exactly in the Bible, they have power. The power comes because I encountered Jesus, and He spoke them to me.

The same thing happens to you when you are praying. Suddenly, you start to realize, "I think I am due for a promotion at my job," or "I think it is time for me to look at another career," or "I think it is time for me to move." You start to feel those things, and it is the Spirit nudging you in a certain direction. You can begin to pray those things out. You can also start to pray things in line with Scripture verses such as, "I hear the voice of my Shepherd, and the voice of a stranger I will not follow" (see John 10:4-5). You are then incorporating Scripture in your prayers. You may pray, "I want to know the perfect will of God for my life. I am going to present my body as *'a living sacrifice, holy and acceptable to God, which is* [my] *reasonable service'"* (Rom. 12:1). And, "I am going to be able to discern *'what is that good and acceptable and perfect will of God'* for my life" (Rom. 12:2).

As you start to quote and pray these verses, one day, as you are praying in the Spirit, your answer will come out in English. I have had this happen. In my native tongue, I might hear "Promotion is coming," or "You are going to get a new job," or "You are going to move, and this is what is going to happen." As I began to experience this and began to speak these words from the Spirit, I was so surprised. It was not long after speaking these things that they began to happen in my life.

Even though many of the things I have spoken looked contrary to my current situation, they have started to happen. I did get a promotion, I did change jobs, or I did move. The Holy Spirit wanted to say it first before He did it. God's Spirit wants to say some things that are what we call *prophetic.* They are forward-looking, but to the Spirit of God, they are the reality right now. God already sees your future, and He has already written a book about you (see Ps. 139:16 TPT). Be encouraged and continue to connect with God.

When I was with Jesus, He was very selective about what He said to me because Jesus manifests everything that He says. Imagine if you got everything that you said, how would you talk? You would stop and think about your words because you would understand just how very powerful they are. Jesus taught me about the power words, and He showed me that when you hook up with the Holy Spirit, you have authority on the earth, and the demons know it. Jesus said to me, "You need to choose your words, choose your battles, choose what you do and what you say, and be wise." I am always careful now to listen to my spirit down inside of me, and

I never say something off the cuff. I always wait until I hear what the Spirit is saying, and then I say that.

When I was in Heaven with Jesus, He took me to different places and showed me the demonic activity and how it works. I saw that a person who has hooked their spirit up with the Holy Spirit begins to speak from the Spirit and not from their soul. When that happens, it can vibrate the building spiritually. We were in a restaurant, and when I was speaking, it vibrated, and the demons could feel it. They knew that someone had just entered the building who was speaking from the Spirit. The demons knew I was not speaking from my own mind or relying on my own understanding. It is so powerful to connect with what God is saying.

Many people tell me that they cannot determine if it is their voice or God's voice that they are hearing. They cannot discern because they want "this, this, and this." As Christians, we are not taught that we are supposed to live a crucified life and that our lives are not our own. If you want to know if it is your voice or God's voice, you must live a crucified life. You have to say, "This is not my life, and my life is not my own. It is God's now" (see Gal. 2:20).

Hebrews 4:12 says,

> *For the word of God is living and powerful, and sharper than any two-edged sword, piercing even to the division of soul and spirit, and of joints and marrow, and is a discerner of the thoughts and intents of the heart.*

We know this means that the Word goes in and it cuts. The Word of God is so powerful that it splits between your soul—your mind, will, and emotions—and your spirit, and that it will separate them. The Holy Spirit will show you what is of your soul and what is of your spirit. The Word of God is very powerful. When you are praying in the Spirit, and when you are quoting the Word of God, that sword is being effective. Whatever it is that you are going through, I want to encourage you right now by the power of the Holy Spirit. The Spirit of God and the Word of God together are very powerful.

Chapter 2

THE FEAR OF THE LORD

The fear of the Lord is the beginning of wisdom, and the knowledge of the Holy One is understanding.

—PROVERBS 9:10

P OWER WORDS ARE the words that satan is fearful of when Christians use them. The Lord gave me these 23 power words and told me that we should use these words often. The first power word is called *the fear of the Lord.* A lot of people have their own ideas about what the fear the Lord is. The fear of the Lord is not like being afraid of the dark or having a negative fear. I am talking about a good healthy fear, having respect and honor. It's a fear that causes you to fall before God knowing that He is God and you are not, that God is holy, He has made you holy, but you cannot get there on your own. This kind of fear is more about overwhelming awe and respect for God. It is encountering the holiness of God, shaking and fearful, but it is not like being afraid of the dark or afraid of the devil.

The fear of the Lord is not something satan wants Christians to have in their lives. This fear is the beginning of wisdom, and the knowledge of the Holy One is understanding. Lucifer used to walk in holiness, and he understands that the fear of the Lord is very important.

In Ezekiel 28 and Isaiah 14, you can read a little about what lucifer was like and how he knows the fear of the Lord. After lucifer fell, he became determined to try to lead men away from God, and one of the ways he does that is to get people away from the fear of the Lord. It is one of those words that satan fears, but Christians should use often.

When the fear of the Lord comes into your life, you start to have awe and respect for God's Word. You begin to have reverence and respect for God in worship, in your life, and at your job. Wherever you go, you will represent God in a way that people will want to know why you are the way you are. You can tell them it is because you are a Christian. However, they must be able to see the power and manifestation of God in your life.

When you pray, you should pray from a place of power, from a place of respect and awe of God. Your walk with God is a part of this. You must discern that you need the fear of the Lord in your life. The loss of the fear of the Lord is something the Lord has warned me is happening in churches and people's lives individually. We need to have that corporate time together where we fear the Lord when we worship Him. This causes us to bring that fear of the Lord into our personal lives.

In Heaven, I saw the fiery stones of holiness that were in the throne room of God (see Exod. 24:10). The stones were more than a meter thick of pure sapphire. There were tongues of white fire coming up and going through them. The white flames were beautiful coming through the blue sapphire stones, and they were all over the throne room. Lucifer walked on these fiery stones before he fell (see Ezek. 28:14). When I was in Heaven, I walked on them.

As Christians, we are called to be holy, and God has asked us to be holy as He is holy. *"For Scripture says: 'You are to be holy, because I am holy'"* (1 Pet. 1:16 TPT). Jesus Christ bought us back *positionally* into the family of God and the position of holiness through His blood. However, *relationally*, we need to walk it out every day. It is not just about your position in Christ. Your relationship with God needs to be displayed, as well. What would that look like in your life?

COME OUT FROM THE WORLD

The apostle Paul said to come out from the world—come out and stand out, and be separate from the world.

> *Therefore "Come out from among them and be separate, says the Lord. Do not touch what is unclean, and I will receive you."*
> —2 CORINTHIANS 6:17

We are not to act like the world, and we are not to talk like the world. God wants His people to come out from among the evil and separate themselves, and the fear of the Lord will do this. It will cause you to choose good when you have a choice between good and evil. That choice is called *temptation*, and it happens every day with you and me. God wants you to be able to choose good, and the only way you can do that is if you fear God because God is your Commander.

God is the one who has started your faith, and He is going to finish your faith, and you have to love and respect Him (see Heb. 12:2). There is a healthy fear of the Lord that would say, "No, I am not going to do this; I am going to stand out and be separate from the world." This attitude enables you to walk away from temptation. Jesus feared God, and it was the only way that He could walk away from temptation (see Matt. 4:1-11). When Jesus was tempted in the desert, He spoke the Word of God, and we must do the same thing as He is our example.

God is all-powerful, but He has also made you His child, which means that you have inherited all the benefits of being a child of God. What does that mean? God's Word stands forever, so whatever He has spoken is going to be true forever. If you adhere to God's Word and you fear God and speak His Word as Jesus did in the desert, then you can walk away from temptation. It is a healthy fear that enables you to do that. Do you know that God has better plans for you than anything you imagine you are missing out on now?

You know that you need to come out from among the world and separate yourself, but you still have things to do in the world. You still have to go to work, you have to go shopping, and you have to participate in all of these things. You are out in the world, but you are not part of it. You keep yourself separate from the world, and that means having a healthy fear of the Lord. It has to do with holiness.

The ministry of the Holy Spirit is to promote Jesus. In Jesus' ministry on the earth, He was being promoted by the Holy Spirit. However, Jesus Himself was promoting the Father in Heaven. When the Holy Spirit comes into your life and you begin to walk in the Spirit, the Holy Spirit promotes Jesus, and He begins to separate you from the world. When you lift Jesus up and you testify of Him, the Father is glorified. As you start to participate in this relationship through the ministry of the Spirit, you become a partaker of the divine nature. You are now walking in the Spirit, and the fear of the Lord causes you to stay in line with the ministry of the Spirit.

The Lord showed me that this process sometimes never happens in believers. Some people live their entire lives, and they never really walk in the Spirit in power and synchronization in ministry. Do you know that as believers—as Christians—we all have a ministry? We are all called to minister because we minister according to what the Spirit is doing in us and through us. God has given us all gifts individually. We all have gifts, and the Spirit willingly manifests these gifts from God in our lives. That is why we have to walk in synchronization with the Spirit of God.

Jesus showed me that a lot of people never get to this place, and that holiness is the key. Holiness is something that people do not understand. If you do not fear the Lord, you are not going to walk in separateness and holiness. You do not understand that the beginning of wisdom and understanding of all things is the fear of the Lord.

HOLINESS IS OWNERSHIP

Once you start to walk in holiness, you must realize that holiness is not just about behavior. Jesus told me that holiness is *ownership*. Holiness means that Jesus bought you back for the Father, and He separates you from the world. Jesus has you on display in front of this whole generation as a manifestation of His love and His power to the people around you. God owns you now, and He takes you and places you as His private possession, and God allows you to display the divine nature.

When you are a partaker of the divine nature, you do not have to be like the world. It is the world that should want to be like you. You should be the pacesetter and the trendsetter. Christians should be the ones who are the cutting edge, and this is because holiness is ownership. Start to realize that you live in God's house and that God owns you. God has taken you as His private possession and stock for His display, and He loves you. Christians are called to be separate from the world, and if you start to realize that then you are going to start to walk in power.

The book of Acts records many instances where people walked in the Spirit, and they saw mighty miracles. It was recorded that the Church grew by thousands and thousands, sometimes in a single day (see Acts 2:41; 4:4). There were people like the apostle Peter, who started walking in the Spirit when the Holy Spirit came on the day of Pentecost. As Peter was led by the Holy Spirit, he started to see things happen that he had not seen in his life while he was with Jesus. One amazing account said that whenever Peter's shadow fell upon someone in the street who was sick, they would get healed (see Acts 5:15). As a result, people brought the sick on beds into the streets so that Peter's shadow would fall on them. You might want to know what happened to Peter. He started to walk in the synchronization of the Spirit of God and the fear of the Lord.

The fear of the Lord even caused Ananias and Sapphira to drop dead at Peter's feet when they lied to the Holy Spirit (see Acts 5:1-11). Peter had allowed the Holy Spirit to synchronize his spirit with Heaven, and that enabled Peter to begin walking in the fear of the

Lord. After Ananias and Sapphira fell dead, their bodies were carried out, and great fear spread throughout the Church and the city when the people heard of these events. I can guarantee you there were not many people lying to the Holy Spirit in the Church after that.

Once we start to realize that the fear of the Lord is what is causing us to be separate, then we will not want to be like the world, and we will fear God.

> *And do not fear those who kill the body but cannot kill the soul. But rather fear Him who is able to destroy both soul and body in hell.*
> —MATTHEW 10:28

In this verse, Jesus is telling us not to fear those who can kill our bodies, as a man can, but to fear Him who can destroy both soul and body. Jesus was talking about His Father. We are redeemed, and we need to walk as though we are redeemed.

Through Jesus Christ, we have inherited many benefits that God has given us. We have many wonderful promises that God gave us so that we can be partakers in the divine nature. All of these things were bought by Jesus Christ, but we are also *co-heirs* with Jesus. Down here on the earth, satan thinks he is running things. Believers must start to realize that God has given them the keys to the Kingdom, and He has given them the name of Jesus. We need to realize that we have been bought at a price, and we are in the world, but we are not of it. God does not take us out of the world for a reason. We need to start to realize that satan does not have to run things down here and that we can stop him from doing his works. We need to start doing the works of Jesus and manifesting His ministry.

Most assuredly, I say to you, he who believes in Me, the works that I do he will do also; and greater works than these he will do, because I go to My Father.

—JOHN 14:12

Jesus told us that we would do even greater works than He did. What does that mean? It means that you are going to fear the Lord and be separate. You are going to get in sync with Heaven and start to walk in the Holy Spirit and power. That means that your words mean something, and when you show up, devils start to scream. Those demons want to get out, and that is because they know you have separated yourself. There is a power that is going to be revealed in these last days, and the sons of God are going to be revealed. That power that is going to be made manifest has to do with dominion and authority, and it has to do with the fear of the Lord. The fear of the Lord is a very important thing.

MADE STRONG IN WEAKNESS

You are going to experience times when your flesh will be weak, and you are not going to feel the power of God. The apostle Paul understood this weakness. He would get excited when he was weak because Paul said that was when the Holy Spirit would come in and make him strong.

And He said to me, "My grace is sufficient for you, for My strength is made perfect in weakness." Therefore most gladly I will rather boast in my infirmities, that the power of Christ may rest upon me. Therefore I take pleasure in infirmities, in reproaches, in needs, in persecutions, in distresses, for Christ's sake. For when I am weak, then I am strong.

— 2 Corinthians 12:9-10

Paul gloried in his weaknesses because he knew that was when the power of God was going to be revealed. Paul walked in the crucified life, and that was when the power of God came and was made manifest.

Holy fear keeps you in a place that you need to be. Even though you might suffer weakness, it causes revelation to come because, in that weakness, the Spirit of God comes in power. People are perishing all around us because of the god of this world, and revelation is all veiled to them. The world does not see it, and even though you feel weak, the Spirit of God can come in and make you strong.

But even if our gospel is [in some sense] *hidden [behind a veil], it is hidden* [only] *to those who are perishing; among them the god of this world [Satan] has blinded the minds of the unbelieving to prevent them from seeing the illuminating light of the gospel of the glory of Christ, who is the image of God.*

— 2 Corinthians 4:3-4 AMP

The Spirit of God also unveils so that you can see into the spirit. You can understand that this weakness is not a permanent thing and is actually your friend. You begin to learn that when you feel weak, it is a definite sign that your breakthrough is coming.

When I was in Heaven and did not think that I was coming back, I saw that every time I was attacked by satan and felt weak as a result, the next step was a supernatural event. Once I understood this, I chose not to yield to the flesh but chose to walk in that weakness. This allowed the Holy Spirit to come in and make me strong, and then I became empowered.

It is in your weakness that the Spirit of God comes in and takes hold of you and strengthens you.

> *Likewise the Spirit also helps in our weaknesses. For we do not know what we should pray for as we ought, but the Spirit Himself makes intercession for us with groanings which cannot be uttered. Now He who searches the hearts knows what the mind of the Spirit is, because He makes intercession for the saints according to the will of God.*
> —ROMANS 8:26-27

Holy Spirit even causes you to pray out the mysteries of God and His will for your life. When you do not know what you should do, and when you do not understand what is going on, Paul said the Spirit will come in as your Helper. The Holy Spirit will lift you up and empower you in your weakness. He will cause the will of God to be prayed so that you can participate in the divine nature. The fear of the Lord can cause you to feel weak in yourself because you fear God and you feel undone. However, at that moment, when you feel your weakest, that is when the power of God will come in and anoint you.

Be happy when you feel weak at times because it is an opportunity for the Holy Spirit to come in and lift you up and make you strong. It will happen every time because the Holy Spirit is faithful. God does not want you to pump yourself up with pride saying, "I can do this," using your mental capacity. God wants you to be built up in the inner man by the power of the Holy Spirit.

You can pray in the Spirit, and you can build yourself up in the Word of God, and then you rely on the Holy Spirit to come in and strengthen you (see Eph. 3:16).

The world knows how to pump themselves up with pride, but *"pride comes before a fall"* (see Prov. 16:18). When people build themselves up mentally, saying that they can do something, there is no spiritual activity. They are setting themselves up for failure. The god of this world, satan, wants people built up in pride with no fear of the Lord so that they fail. Often, people do not understand what happened to them because, according to the world, their confession was right. They were pumping themselves up, but there was no spiritual activity.

There is a mental and psychological event that does take place when you act and speak positively, building yourself up vocally. I am not talking about that; I am talking about a spiritual experience. You can feel weak in your heart because you feel like satan is tempting you, and then you yield to the Spirit of God. That's when the Holy Spirit comes in, and He lifts you up, and He walks you out of it.

Paul said, no matter what situation you are in, God will not tempt you beyond what you can handle.

> *No temptation has overtaken you except such as is common to man; but God is faithful, who will not allow you to be tempted beyond what you are able, but with the temptation will also make the way of escape, that you may be able to bear it.*
> —1 CORINTHIANS 10:13

God will always provide a way of escape for you. Remember that God is faithful in your weaknesses.

The Way to Life and Satisfaction

When you fear the Lord, evil will not visit you.

> *The fear of the Lord leads to life, and he who has it will abide in satisfaction; he will not be visited with evil.*
> —Proverbs 19:23

This means that God has come in and fenced you in and protected you. The one who fears the Lord will live satisfied, and I know you want to be satisfied. The way you do it is by fearing the Lord and Him only.

As a believer, I thought that I did fear God. I am telling you that I got a dose of the fear of the Lord on certain occasions, to the point where I thought I was going to die. There was such a strong presence of the Lord, and I felt I did not fear the Lord like I should at that moment. Surprisingly, just before that happened, I thought I was fine. I have found that God is so great and His power so great that when you encounter Him, He will take you to the next level.

Every time that I have had an angelic visitation, I have encountered the fear of the Lord because they are fearful. God's angels are full of the holiness of God. When they stand before you to give you a message, they have just come from the presence of Father God, and they are full of holiness. They truly are holy angels.

Many people say they want an angelic visitation, but I never pray for an angel to come because the power, presence, and holiness on those angels are not easy to encounter. Their holiness is so strong that it changes you, and you will be held accountable for those angelic visitations.

The fear of the Lord leads to life, and that is what we all want—we want life.

> *The thief does not come except to steal, and to kill, and to destroy. I have come that they may have life, and that they may have it more abundantly.*
> —JOHN 10:10

Here Jesus is saying that He has come to give you life more abundantly. It is not just life; there is abundant life. It is good to let God graduate you to the next step into the abundant life, and this is part of the fear of the Lord.

> *I will invite the poor and broken, and they will come and eat until satisfied. Bring Yahweh praise and you will find him. Your hearts will overflow with life forever!*
> —PSALM 22:26 TPT

You need to have more of that abundance in your life. One of the things that you can do is ask the Holy Spirit to reveal the fear of the Lord to you.

> *But whoever drinks of the water that I shall give him will never thirst. But the water that I shall give him will become in him a fountain of water springing up into everlasting life.*
> —JOHN 4:14

There is a trend here with these verses, and they are all talking about being satisfied. Most people I meet are not satisfied, and to tell you the truth, up until just a few years ago, I was not either. It all began to change when I tapped into the fear of the Lord and started to allow God to take me into the abundant life. It is a process.

The fear of the Lord is part of the process of the secret place too.

> *No evil shall befall you, nor shall any plague come near your dwelling; for He shall give His angels charge over you, to keep you in all your ways.*
> —PSALM 91:10-11

When you are in the shadow of the Most High, you are going to encounter the fear of the Lord because you are so close to Him. Most people do not abide in the shadow of the Almighty.

The fear of the Lord leads to life and more abundant life. The fear of the Lord leads to satisfaction. You will not have visitations from the evil one when you fear the Lord because God will block that for you. The Word of the Lord is true, and you do not have to wait to get to Heaven to encounter the fear of the Lord and to believe it. You can encounter it in your life right now. God wants us to have a healthy fear of Him.

Proverbs 22:4 tells us that we will have "riches and honor and life" if we are humble and fear God. Jesus died and thereby secured the new covenant with us, and it has better promises. Even though this verse is in the book of Proverbs and is under the old covenant, you have to know that what Jesus died for is even greater. Here in the old covenant, you are promised riches, honor, and life if you are humble and fear God. How much better is it going to be in the new covenant? Be humble and fear the Lord, and this is His promise to you.

Yes, God is going to prosper you.

Only if you carefully obey the voice of the Lord your God, to observe with care all these commandments which I command you today. For the Lord your God will bless you just as He promised you; you shall lend to many nations, but you shall not borrow; you shall reign over many nations, but they shall not reign over you.
—Deuteronomy 15:5-6

You are going to be full of the wealth of God when you reverence the Lord with obedience. Riches are guaranteed when you walk in the fear of the Lord.

The Beginning of Wisdom

I want to encourage you to spend time meditating on the following verses that talk about wisdom:

You will find true success when you find me, for I have insight into wise plans that are designed just for you. I hold in my hands living-understanding, courage, and strength. I empower kings to reign and rulers to make laws that are just. I empower princes to rise and take dominion, and generous ones to govern the earth. I will show my love to those who passionately love me. For they will search and search continually until they find me. Unending wealth and glory come to those who discover where I dwell. The riches of righteousness and a long, satisfying life will be given to them. What I impart has greater worth than gold and treasure, and the increase

*I bring benefits more than a windfall of income. I lead
you into the ways of righteousness to discover the paths
of true justice. Those who love me gain great wealth and
a glorious inheritance, and I will fill their lives with
treasures.*

—PROVERBS 8:14-21 TPT

Wisdom is personified here in Proverbs. The beginning of wisdom is the fear of the Lord. When you fear God, wisdom comes, and then you have understanding, and that is what you get if you have wisdom.

You need to appropriate what is being said in Proverbs 8. The fear of the Lord is the beginning of wisdom, and if you gain wisdom, you gain everything that you just read in this chapter.

Chapter 3

REPENTANCE

*Therefore bear fruits worthy of repentance, and do
not begin to say to yourselves, "We have Abraham
as our father." For I say to you that God is able to
raise up children to Abraham from these stones.*

—LUKE 3:8

I N THE WORLD, people are self-sufficient. They think that
they are getting along fine and can do all things on their own.
However, they do not realize that they are being empowered by
the spirit of this world, and that in reality, they are powerless. This
sense of self-sufficiency has even made its way into the ranks of
Christianity, but Jesus said,

*I am the vine, you are the branches. He who abides in
Me, and I in him, bears much fruit; for without Me you
can do nothing.*

—JOHN 15:5

When we turn from our ways and turn to Jesus and focus
on Him, this is called *repentance*. We are turning away, turning

around. We are turning back and getting on track. Repentance is when you repent of your ways, you repent of your self-sufficiency, and you rely on God. Your focus is something that needs to be adjusted every day. When I find myself focusing on other things and realize that I need to focus on Jesus alone, I repent and turn back to Him. I repent every day. Satan, however, does not want anyone to repent.

In a visitation, Jesus told me that true repentance is not just the turning of your ways or the way that you walk. Jesus told me that any time a Christian has focused on something other than Him, that person needs to turn back to Him, and this is called *repentance* as well. Repentance is part of the daily activities of a Christian.

Usually, as long as everything goes right in a person's life, whether they are Christian or not, they do not feel the need to repent. However, God says that they are lying through their teeth.

> But their repentance lasted only as long as they were in danger; they lied through their teeth to the true God of Covenant. So quickly they wandered away from his promises, following God with their words and not their hearts! Their worship was only flattery.
> —PSALM 78:36-37 TPT

Only when something bad happens do people seem to want to repent, turn, and make their hearts right with God. We should be following God with our hearts in repentance all the time.

It is about a relationship with God and not a system, a position, or a mindset. We cannot think that we have repented once and do not need to repent ever again. In Psalm 78, God is saying that everything was fine until they got into danger. They ran to God in repentance, but they lied through their teeth. Then quickly, they wandered away from His promises, following God with their words but not with their hearts.

That is what is happening in the Church today. I am seeing believers who are beginning to wander off, but they do not seem to know it. They are wandering because they have not taken advantage of God's promises. They wandered away from God's promises, and their words did not match their hearts. When your words do not match your heart, then you need to repent. You cannot just say things with your mouth and then have something else in your heart. That is where repentance needs to begin to happen.

I saw that repentance was one of the words that satan was going to be extracting out of the Body of Christ. It is going to be taken out of our vocabulary in the last days. Satan knows the only way that he can get people off track is to get them to a place where they see no need to repent. Satan does not want anyone to be repentant or to be sorry that they have strayed from God. He does everything he can to keep them from even realizing it.

God wants us to follow Him because we *want* to follow Him. God loves us, and He chose us, and He sent Jesus to die for us before we were born. Jesus purchased us back to the Father, but He wants us to serve Him out of our hearts, not just out of our mouths.

A HEART MATTER

Jesus reminded the scribes and Pharisees of what the prophet Isaiah said in the Old Testament. He said,

*These people draw near to Me with their mouth, and
honor Me with their lips, but their heart is far from Me.*
—MATTHEW 15:8

Jesus saw that their behavior was repeating itself in the New
Testament. They honored God with their lips, but their hearts
were far from Him.

People give God lip service. They can say the right things, but
their hearts are not in what they say. That is what being positional
is all about. Being relational is when your heart matches your
words, you passionately love God, you *want* to serve Him, and you
are sorry when you stray.

I am not seeing as many believers in the type of relationship
with God that causes them to be really sorry when they have
strayed from Him. Some may be sorry that they got caught. Some
are sorry that it cost them because they did something wrong. I do
not see them fearing God and turning back to Him to follow Him
with all their hearts, and it is a heart matter.

Jesus said that hell was made for the devil and his angels (see
Matt. 25:41). There is no reason for a man to go to hell. God never
designed hell for man. God always wanted and planned for man to
repent. If that is the case, then why are we trying to stay so close
to the world instead of getting closer to God? Why is that? We are
wandering away, and our hearts are not matching what we are saying. We need to turn our hearts back to God and repent.

You should check your heart every day. Every day the spirit of
this world is working against you to keep you from having a relationship with your Heavenly Father. I check my heart and turn back
to God daily. I saw when I was in Heaven that I had to be actively

working at coming against the world system every single day. I saw that I had to be consciously working and plowing, or I would find myself going downstream very quickly. The current of the world and the spirit of the world are going downstream as fast as they can. I saw that if you were not actively swimming against the flow, then you were being swept away. You must diligently turn to God daily.

Only a fool would mock repentance, but favor rests on those who are God's lovers as Proverbs 14:9 affirms, *"Fools mock the need for repentance, while the favor of God rests upon all his lovers"* (TPT). You want favor because you are a child of God. Here, lovers of God are equated with repentance.

You should think about what Jesus said in Matthew 3:8—*"You must prove your repentance by a changed life"* (TPT). In other words, you may say you repent, but you prove it by a changed life. I have seen this happen. People will say, "You know I'm sorry, and I repent." Yet, the very next day, they do the same wrong again. There is a huge disconnect between their hearts and their mouths because true repentance brings a behavior change. According to what Jesus said in Matthew 3:8, you should have a changed life. If a person really means what they say, they will not continue to do that very thing they did before, and that is true repentance—a changed life.

Jesus spoke to the Pharisees and the Sadducees, calling them snakes and offspring of vipers.

> *You are nothing but snakes in the grass, the offspring of poisonous vipers! How will you escape the judgment of hell if you refuse to turn in repentance?*
> —MATTHEW 23:33 TPT

Jesus said that they were going to go to hell because they refused to turn and repent.

Jesus told us that we are supposed to preach repentance and forgiveness of sins, and then people will turn to Him.

> *Now you must go into all the nations and preach repentance and forgiveness of sins so that they will turn to me. Start right here in Jerusalem.*
> —LUKE 24:47 TPT

We are to start right now in our hometown. There is also the idea here that we are supposed to speak these things in ministry and preach to people. We are to get them to turn away from sin and turn to God.

THE GOODNESS OF GOD

One of my favorite portions of Scripture reads:

> *And do you think this, O man, you who judge those practicing such things, and doing the same, that you will escape the judgment of God? Or do you despise the riches of His goodness, forbearance, and longsuffering, not knowing that the goodness of God leads you to repentance?*
> —ROMANS 2:3-4

I want to emphasize the fact that I believe there are two basic ways that stir people to repent. One way is you can preach that sinners are going to hell if they do not repent and turn to God. That fear of going to hell will sometimes bring a person to the altar to repent. However, in Romans 2, there is another way, and it says that when people have the goodness of God revealed to them, it causes them to repent. There is a repentance that can come because of the revelation of the goodness of God, and this goodness leads people to repentance. That is one reason why people come to the altar, and they give their lives to Jesus. I see these as two ways of preaching the gospel.

There is a positive way of preaching the gospel, and I think it makes a true convert or a person who has realized that God is good. The one who has a revelation of God's goodness and His love, repents. A person who repents only to escape hell when they become a Christian, has no depth. They do not have the revelation of the goodness of God. It can take people years to come to the place where they realize that God is good and that they have received much more than an escape from hell. Jesus did so much more for them. They have inherited all the benefits of being a Christian and what God through Jesus Christ has bought and given to us. God is showing us how good He is in these days. Many people are coming in because they realize that they are in sin and need to repent and turn to God.

The threats of going to hell do bring people to repentance; however, Paul showed us a better way, and that way is love (see 1 Cor. 13). The revelation of this love should bring people to the place where they make a decision for Christ. In John 3:16, it says,

> *For God so loved the world that He gave His only begotten Son, that whoever believes in Him should not perish but have everlasting life.*

Remember, people have free choice, and some people no matter what you do or say, they are not going to repent. Jesus walked in love in His ministry, and He had compassion for people, but He always told them the truth. That love and compassion of Jesus Christ caused people to be healed, and it caused people to repent. It's still doing that today.

COURSE CORRECTION

Psalm 89:14 (TPT) talks about God's throne.

> *Your glorious throne rests on a foundation of righteousness and just verdicts. Grace and truth are the attendants who go before you.*

We see here that there are layers to God's throne of righteousness, justice, and truth, and that throne is what God sits on. In Heaven, there is absolute truth. God has absolute rule, and He judges rightly and justly. Such judgment is part of the foundation of His throne. God bases everything that He has ever said on truth, but it is absolute truth. With that in mind, God has already announced certain things, and He has certain requirements, and those have to be met.

In the Old Testament, God's requirements used to be met by obeying God's law. Now in the New Testament, it is through the blood of Jesus that they have been met, and it is by our faith in Jesus' blood. God is truth, and He has spoken certain things. No matter how much we might disagree with something that God has said, God is right, and we are wrong. When the truth comes in, it sets people free, *"Therefore if the Son makes you free, you shall be free indeed"* (John 8:36). It also judges people.

Remember that God chose us, and we did not choose Him (see John 15:16). Once the truth is presented, then we have to allow the

Word of God to judge us. When we read the Bible, we allow that righteous Word, which is the Bread from Heaven, to judge us. We have to measure up according to what the Word of God says. God spoke that Word from His throne in Heaven, and it is absolute truth. We must never allow our own opinions to come in and rob us of the truth of repentance.

Wherever you are, especially in your house, your environment, everything about you must have the Word of God present. In my environment, I have the Word of God playing audibly, and I have teaching going on the TV sets around my home. I am constantly, silently praying in the Spirit. When I sit and meditate on the Word of God, it is structured in the sense that I pick certain passages on which I want to meditate. It is not about the quantity of Scripture but the quality of my time meditating on those certain verses. I want the truth that I glean from these Scriptures to come into my spirit and then cause me to change my heart. That change of heart is an act of repentance. It is because I acknowledge that there are shortcomings in my understanding, in my mind, and the way I walk that the Word of God brings correction. My heart changes, and I shift.

If you judge yourself this way, then you will not be judged.

> *For if we would judge ourselves, we would not be judged.*
> *But when we are judged, we are chastened by the Lord,*
> *that we may not be condemned with the world.*
> —1 CORINTHIANS 11:31-32

If you allow the Word of God to judge you, it steers you, it corrects you, and it brings you back in line. Once that happens, that is repentance, too, because you have made an adjustment.

You are admitting that you did not discern your error. You realize that what you have been doing was wrong and now you see it because of God's righteousness that is brought forth through the Word of God. God's Word brings forth correction, and it brings repentance.

You know that you are not going to hell because you repented once at an altar and then gave your life to the Lord. However, you still need to turn your focus back on the Lord regularly. Repentance is sometimes just a course correction that is needed for your focus and your direction. Sometimes, you walk away from where you are supposed to be going. When you bring a course correction, it brings you back into line, which evidences that you have repented. You have turned from your way to God's way because God showed you that you were getting off track.

Allow the Word of God to judge you by being in the Word of God all the time. Let it be on your TV and audio devices, and pray in the Spirit. I am constantly meditating on a verse. Pick a verse for the day, and you can read through it systematically. What I do is I go through a chapter or possibly more. As an example, let's say I read John 14-17. I look at those verses and then take one verse at a time, meditating on it. I take just one verse every day, and I think about it all day. I create my environment based on what I can control, which is what I hear and what I see. Then I use that verse that I have read during the day, and I start to allow the correction to come.

When you get to Heaven, you are going to realize that a lot of things that you believed were wrong. What you did not know stopped you from prospering and being in good health. It also stopped you from doing the ministry of Jesus on the earth.

When I was with Jesus, when I died, I was complimented and rewarded for what I had done on the earth. However, I was aware of and saw the things that I *could* have done in my time on the earth. They were so evident to me, but Jesus never said a word about them. I was standing before the Word of God, who is Jesus Christ, and that Word, as I was in His presence, started to judge my heart. I did not feel condemned in any way, but it showed me where I should have been on the earth and where I ended up. I still received rewards for all the things that I had done, but I realized that I could have done so much more than I did. I saw all that in a flash. Jesus was so kind to me, and He never mentioned these things to me, but I saw them.

I saw that I should have emphasized repentance more in my life, and I should have allowed the Word of God to correct me because all the truth that I was shown in Heaven was available to me on the earth. I was shown all this amazing truth that we could be operating in down here. We could be working with angels, praying in the Spirit all the time, praying in tongues, and operating in the resurrection power of God.

I saw that we were not being limited by God down here but by the spirit of this world. That spirit was limiting us and our own understanding. The most important thing I saw in Heaven was that in my earthly life, I needed to repent more and keep turning back to God. I had not seen that as so important in my life. I was told that once I repented at the altar and gave my life to God, I did not have to repent anymore. That was wrong because there are always going to be course corrections. You are always going to need to turn back to line up with what God has for you.

There will be days when you do not walk in the perfect will of God, and sometimes you will walk in just the permissive will of

God. There will be times when you will make decisions and not check in with the Holy Spirit and ask God for guidance. You will just go and make decisions, and then, later on, you will see that they were not good decisions. These decisions may not dramatically affect your life, but they will not have been God's perfect will for your life.

When I was in Heaven, I saw that you must have a repentant heart and allow the Word of God and the Spirit of God to judge you in your heart. You must, by the Word and the Spirit, discern the right way to go in any situation. Sometimes, you may choose to lean on your own understanding or to do something even out of rebellion as a Christian. What you have chosen to do is go your own way, and you need to repent. Once you get on that path of independence, you are going to start to feel alone, and you are going to experience grieving in your heart. That is because the Holy Spirit is not going with you on that path, and He does not agree with what you just decided to do.

As you mature in the Lord, you will recognize that something is wrong. You will learn to stop and reconsider what you just did. When you seek the Lord, He will say, "I never told you to go that way," or "I never told you to do that." You will have to backtrack to get back on track with God, and that is true repentance. I find that repentance is something that happens all the time, and there have been constant course corrections in my life.

The more I pray in the Spirit, and the more I meditate on the Word of God, then when I fast and pray, I find corrections coming. God disciplines those He loves (see Heb. 12:6-11). God is treating us as sons and daughters because the Holy Spirit wants to keep us on the perfect path that God has chosen for us.

Your decisions are not going to affect you alone. If you make bad decisions, you are not the only one who suffers. Everyone around you is affected. If the Lord told you to do something, and you decided you were not going to do that you have turned from the perfect path. You have started to go in another direction. If you were supposed to do something for someone and you did not do it, then you went down the road of disobedience. That person who you were supposed to help is also affected by your disobedience. Then everyone that person was supposed to affect is affected because you did not help the individual. You did not do what God told you to do, and it affects people whom you may never meet. I saw this in Heaven, and it had a long domino effect.

Obedience is part of the fear of the Lord. By repenting for disobedience, there is constant course correction, and it will cause you to affect people in your generation. I saw that by the end of my life, I could affect so many people just by being obedient once. One single thing that God speaks to you to do, and it might be something so silly like you are supposed to give five dollars to a child. Or you are supposed to mow someone's lawn or give people time when you do not have time. You need to be obedient to what the Lord tells you to do.

You might find out that the person you helped was key to something that God was doing for a whole group of people. Because you helped that child, when he grew up and became governor of your state, for example, it affected a lot of people. He was praying for five dollars and asking God to help him. When you gave him the five dollars, that child grew up and became governor and always remembered that God was faithful in his finances. You helped him grow up to be a mature Christian and have a revelation of the faithfulness of God.

God showed me that we always need to repent when we get off track. We need to repent when we disobey God in our finances and in our time and everything that we do in our lives. If we get off track, if we do not learn how to turn back, we are affecting other people as well. Just tell the Lord, "I am sorry, Lord, I repent. I want to get back on the path. I want to do everything that You have for me because I know it affects me and other people, in the name of Jesus."

Chapter 4

SPIRITUAL HUNGER

*Blessed are those who hunger and thirst for
righteousness, for they shall be filled.*

—MATTHEW 5:6

S PIRITUAL HUNGER IS another one of those words that satan
fears because God wants us to be hungry for Him. Jesus hun-
gered all the time for His Father and was always talking about
His Father. Jesus only did what He saw His Father doing and only
said what the Father was saying. Jesus never used His own words
because He spoke by the Spirit of God, and He only spoke the
words that the Father had given Him (see John 12:49).

In Matthew 5:6, Jesus said, *"Blessed are those who hunger and
thirst for righteousness, for they shall be filled."* Spiritual hunger is
something that God provided for us. When we hunger and thirst
for Him, He is going to fill us, and it is His promise to us. In this
verse, Jesus was talking about righteousness. Righteousness is our
hungering for right standing with God and hungering for the

things of God. The Lord wants to move by His Spirit and wants to right the things that are wrong.

When righteousness comes in, it corrects things that are wrong. Spiritual hunger is the catalyst for everything that you are going to encounter in this life. Things are not going to come to you all the time. Many times, you are going to have to search for them, and you are going to have to seek God. This all will be driven by hunger.

Jesus was often speaking to the religious leaders of His day, the Pharisees, and pointing out that they were not hungering after God. The Pharisees were just acting the part in the system that Moses had given them. Their hearts were not in it because their hearts were far from God (see Matt. 15:8-14). That mindset caused the Pharisees to confront Jesus continually.

Jesus was hungry to do the Father's will, and He only wanted to manifest His Father in everything that He did. In Matthew 23:15, Jesus exclaimed,

> *Woe to you, scribes and Pharisees, hypocrites! For you travel land and sea to win one proselyte, and when he is won, you make him twice as much a son of hell as yourselves.*

Jesus was calling the Pharisees "sons of hell"! The Pharisees were not seeking God, and they were not hungry for the things of God. You have to hunger after God, and when you do, God will fill you. If you are not hungry, then you will not seek after God and His ways.

Even in the New Testament, it says that we cannot just believe in God. We have to believe that He is a rewarder of those who diligently seek Him.

> *But without faith it is impossible to please Him, for he*
> *who comes to God must believe that He is, and that He*
> *is a rewarder of those who diligently seek Him.*
> —HEBREWS 11:6

Believing in God does not have any action to it, whereas diligently seeking God is active; it is showing God that you are hungry for Him.

I saw when I was in Heaven that many people mentally agree with the Word of God, and that is called *mental assent.* You hear the Word of God, and you say, "Yes, I believe that," but in your heart, there is no transformation. A lot of people will mentally agree with something, but that is not what will bring about the manifestation in their hearts and lives. Spiritual hunger is much deeper than that as it comes from within your spirit.

Spiritual hunger has to do with your spirit while hunger that your body experiences is something that happens in your flesh and your mind. If you are hungry for knowledge and wisdom, you can memorize books, and you can become a lawyer, a physician, or a pilot. You can discipline your mind to study and recall things, but that is all up in the mental realm. What I am talking about is that *"God is a Spirit, and those who worship Him must worship Him in spirit and truth"* (John 4:24). Hungering and thirsting for righteousness is something spiritual.

When you actively hunger and thirst in the spirit realm, then that is where you will start to have manifestation. I want to see manifestations at the end of this age. I want to see people having a manifestation of God's goodness, a manifestation of God's power and understanding. You want to gain understanding, but you want it to be spiritual. You want it to be something that is in your heart, and then it is going to manifest in the physical. Many times, we will not see the manifestation in the physical first because we have to believe for it, and that is why we have faith. And *"faith is the substance of things hoped for"* (Heb. 11:1). Faith is a spiritual thing first, and then it comes into the physical realm as a manifestation.

If Jesus starts your faith and He finishes your faith, then He is going to be in there with you the whole time.

> *Looking unto Jesus, the author and finisher of our faith, who for the joy that was set before Him endured the cross, despising the shame, and has sat down at the right hand of the throne of God.*
>
> —HEBREWS 12:2

Jesus' being with you will cause you to hunger for more because you will always want to know what is next and to see what is going on around you. That hunger is going to cause you to seek God fervently. Then you will have an encounter with God, and you will have a manifestation of God.

PREPARING THE WAY FOR YOUR FUTURE

God, through Jesus Christ, is actively involved in your daily life. God has already written your future. He has gone to your future, and He is waiting for you to show up there.

You've gone into my future to prepare the way, and in kindness you follow behind me to spare me from the harm of my past. With your hand of love upon my life, you impart a blessing to me.

—PSALM 139:5 TPT

God is also behind you, and He is protecting you from your past. God is keeping you from the hurt of your past because He wants you to forget about the past, and He wants you to think about your future. Until you get to where you are going, God is placing His hand of love upon you, and He is imparting a blessing to you, so you have nothing to fear. You have your past, your present, and your future, and God is in all of them. You should be spending all your energy on seeking God.

Jesus showed me that He inspired David and other psalmists to write by the Holy Spirit because they were writing about Jesus. Jesus said to me, "I had David write Psalm 16 by the Spirit before I even came in the flesh to walk among men." He said, "I used Psalm 16 when I was in the belly of the earth. I was rehearsing Psalm 16 and Psalm 22, and those psalms were talking about Me." The Spirit of God already knew what Jesus would need when He was on the earth. As people like King David were writing their psalms, you can see that they were writing exact quotes that Jesus spoke when He was on the earth.

Jesus was hungry for God the Father even though He was the Son of God. While He was in the flesh, Jesus walked as a man would on Earth. Jesus would seek God by praying at night in the mountains because He needed to know God's will. Even though Jesus was the Son of God, He came as a man and sought God.

One night, Jesus prayed all night on the mountain, and when it was day, Jesus picked His disciples (see Luke 6:12-13). Jesus was asking His Father for guidance even though He was the Son of God, and that is what we must do. We must seek God and hunger and thirst after Him.

> *Here's the one thing I crave from God, the one thing I seek above all else: I want the privilege of living with him every moment in his house, finding the sweet loveliness of his face, filled with awe, delighting in his glory and grace. I want to live my life so close to him that he takes pleasure in my every prayer. In his shelter in the day of trouble, that's where you'll find me, for he hides me there in his holiness. He has smuggled me into his secret place, where I'm kept safe and secure—out of reach from all my enemies. Triumphant now, I'll bring him my offerings of praise, singing and shouting with ecstatic joy! Yes, listen and you can hear the fanfare of my shouts of praise to the Lord!*
> —PSALM 27:4-6 TPT

In this psalm, you can see that David wants to live in God's house; in fact, he craves to be there. David is asking where God is so he may meet with Him. He wants to know where God is so he can live in God's house with Him. That is the passion we should have, wanting to live in the house of God all the time and craving after Him.

The enemy is stealing our hunger for God. The enemy is causing you to live from your mind's perspective, mentally agreeing with the Word of God only. Christians are becoming ineffective, and they are not seeing answers to their prayers. Satan is starting to move in and do things at an alarming rate with believers, and this is not God's will. Jesus asked me to emphasize all of these power words, and especially this one about spiritual hunger. In the last days, it says, *"And because lawlessness will abound, the love of many will grow cold"* (Matt. 24:12). Many will fall away, their hearts will grow cold, and they will not follow after God anymore.

I am combating believers' growing cold and falling away by emphasizing the fact that King David wrote about craving and desiring God passionately. He sought God all the time. King David even instituted 24-hour worship in the tabernacle and had minstrels and worship teams playing there all the time. He eventually had 24-hour worship in the temple as well.

> *But let all who passionately seek you erupt with excitement and joy over what you've done! Let all your lovers rejoice continually in the Savior, saying, "How great and glorious is our God!"*
> —PSALM 40:16 TPT

I like how the Passion Translation uses words like *passionately seek* and how they *erupt in excitement and joy over all that God has done.* You need to do this, too, and it is one of the things that will cause the river that is flowing out of you to flow even more. Jesus talked about the rivers of living water that are coming out of your belly and flowing out of you into eternal life (see John 7:38 KJV). You can release those rivers daily by passionately seeking after God. As you seek Him, you erupt into worship and praise every time He does something good for you, and this honors God.

God visits us, and He talks with us, and we receive from Him in these times, but we have to seek after Him. You must become accustomed to the fact that God is good, and when He speaks, He will say and do good things for you. God is not waiting to harm you, because He is satisfied with the blood of His Son. God is not hovering over you, waiting to correct you or slap you every time you do something wrong. God is pleased with what His Son has done. We live, not in the flesh, but in the Spirit, and the blood of Jesus cleanses us from all sin (see Rom. 8:1; 1 John 1:7).

The reason that God may not be talking with you or moving with you could be that your passion and your seeking after God have dropped off. Once you start to seek God and call out to Him, you are going to start to receive wisdom and knowledge from Him, and you are going to hear His voice.

King David pursued God all the time, and when he would seek God, David would receive battle strategies from Him. God would tell him when it was okay to go up and whether David would win the battle, and God guided David. David always sought God, and he always got an answer from God.

EAGER TO HEAR THE FATHER

The fruit of spiritual hunger is that you are going to find what you seek after as we read in Jeremiah 29:13, *"And you will seek Me and find Me, when you search for Me with all your heart."*

You need to hear God's voice every day, and that is a result of spiritual hunger. You will hear God's voice, but you have to be open to it. Did you ever notice that when something in which you are interested is being spoken, you will listen very carefully?

If someone tries to interrupt you, you ask them to wait because you are so eager to hear what is being said. If you are interested in God your Father, then you will seek after Him, not letting anything hinder you from hearing His voice. You will be amazed at the things that you will hear when you set your ear to hear Him.

There are so many voices in the world, and yet God is still speaking as one of those voices. In Heaven, I saw that there were so many voices down here on this earth. For some reason, believers were not turning down the voices of the world. They wanted to hear God's voice, but they had all these other influences in their lives. The Lord showed me that if His children would start to turn down and tune out the voices of the world, they could eliminate the clutter. Then they would hear God's voice loud and clear. I could see that God was speaking loudly, but many people's environments are not conducive to God communicating with them. People were having trouble hearing God's voice.

When you seek God, your spiritual hunger will cause you to start turning down and eliminating those things that are trying to take your attention away from God. You will begin to tune out the voices in your life that are too loud—voices that are preventing you from hearing the voice of God. You must spend time in the secret place with the Lord, not allowing yourself to answer your phone or the front door. I have gotten to the place where I can go for hours without being interrupted, and I can clearly hear God's voice. I can go outside, and I can still hear God's voice even though there are other voices around me. This has happened because I chose to tune in to God's voice. Now God's voice is more dominant in my life than it has ever been.

King David sought God, and even as a shepherd boy out on the hills, he spent quiet times in the presence of God. He was allowed to hear God's still small voice. God mostly speaks through the still small voice and not from a loud voice where you hear it audibly. Most of the time, God is going to speak to you by His Word or in your spirit with a still small voice. That means you are going to have to be in an environment where it is quiet.

Another thing that can cause spiritual hunger is ministering to other people. When I am earnestly seeking God and wanting to know what He is saying to me, I will go out, and I will give things away. I used to minister to the poor and the needy on the streets. I would go out and minister to those people and give them food. I found that if I would go and help somebody else, then God would answer me. I was seeking God by helping other people. You can do that too.

You could go to your local church and serve as a volunteer. When you start to minister to other people, it is a form of seeking God. Your spiritual hunger will cause you to want to do things for God. I started to participate in the outreach of a local church, and I started to become involved in teaching, even Sunday school. Then I asked if I could be on the worship team, and so I would practice and come and play an instrument during the worship time.

While I was worshiping, God would start to speak to me. He would give me instruction that I needed to know and that I could not hear at other times. It was in the process of going out and ministering to others and my being used of God that God spoke to me. Spiritual hunger will cause you to want to minister to other people.

Seed Sown in the Heart

The most important thing regarding spiritual hunger is matters of the heart. Jesus talked about this in Matthew 13 in the parable of the sower, which is the parable of the soils. Jesus spent a lot of time in this parable talking about the different types of soil. There were four types. He said that the soil represented the condition of a man's heart. Jesus listed the four of them, and out of the four, only one yielded a crop.

There was only one soil, the good soil, that when the seed, which was the Word of God, fell there, it produced a crop. In that one soil that generated a crop, there could be a difference of a thirty-, sixty-, or one hundredfold return on what was sown. There was only one soil that worked while the other three all had problems. One soil was hard, and so its seed could not take root. There was a rocky soil, and there was one that had thorns and thistles. Each soil represented a problem of the heart, which meant that the seed could not take root and produce a crop there.

What might be happening with your spiritual hunger in your heart? Maybe you feel like you just don't have the passion. You cannot seem to follow through with your desires in seeking God, and this is a condition that needs healing. Jesus spoke to me about the healing of the soul and how just about everyone has these issues within their souls. It is not a problem with your spirit because your spirit is born again.

Jesus taught me, and He said, "There are different ways for Me to heal a person's soul." He told me that I needed to be healed in my mind, will, and emotions, which is my soul. Jesus said that my soul was obstructing the beauty of my spirit, and it was also hindering me from operating in the fullness of the Spirit of God on this earth.

So, because I had been hurt, I did not seek God as passionately as I should have because of all the discrepancies and disappointments that I had in my life. I thought God had allowed these things to happen to me, and I was blaming Him for some of the things that had happened in my life. I had questioned why God had not stopped certain things or why He had let them happen. I had to realize that God was not at fault for those things happening.

I had allowed God to heal my heart through the born-again experience. But as Jesus went through this with me, I saw that my soul—my mind, will, and emotions—needed to be healed. As Jesus took me through this process, He said, "Kevin, I could do a miracle. I could wave My hand over you and just pull that hurt out of you, out of your soul." Then He said, "Or you could build yourself up in the Word of God, rehearsing the Word of God, the truth, and renewing your mind. Then your soul would be healed." He continued, "Or you could pray in the Spirit and build your spirit up on your most holy faith, keeping yourself in the perfect love of God (see Jude 20). Your spirit would become so strong that it would overthrow your soul and make it do the right thing." Then Jesus told me the last way I could be healed. He said, "Or you could get godly counseling, and a person could help you walk through that hurt and emotion."

So that was number four, and I wondered which one Jesus was going to use to heal me because I knew that I needed help, but Jesus never told me. It was amazing because, in the end, God used all four of those. First, Jesus healed me by touching me with His hand. Then He healed me by showing me that the Word of God was true and that everything else was a lie, and I renewed my mind by reading and meditating on it. I also prayed in the Spirit all the time. My spirit became so strong that it overthrew my soul and overcame my hurts, and they were pushed out. Lastly, I had godly people counsel me, and they walked me through my hurt. My spiritual fathers spoke words of healing to me and walked me through it all, and I was healed.

Whichever way that Jesus chooses to heal you, the hurts that you carry are hindrances to your spiritual hunger. Jesus is saying that you need to get the rocks out of your soil, and you need to get the thorns out of your soil. You need to get the hardness of your heart broken up so that you can have good soil so that when the seed is planted, it will bring forth a crop.

What is happening right now among Christians, and you will notice it among your friends, is that there are hindrances to their walks with God. They love God, and they want the supernatural. However, there seems to be some sort of gap between what they want and what is happening, and it comes down to matters of the heart. You cannot seek God with all your heart if you have issues and problems and discrepancies. If you think that God caused certain bad things to happen to you when He did not, then you need to be renewed in your mind about that. You need to be counseled and told that God has not done those things.

Jesus showed me that we have had bad things happen to us because we did not allow the Holy Spirit to guide us and lead us into the truth. There were times in my life when things happened to me that were bad. They were permitted to happen to me, but they were not from God. Yet, God let them happen because of my own free will. I had chosen to go in a certain direction, and because of that, I suffered the consequences of it. As I grew and matured, I realized that I did not have to have these bad things happen to me any longer. I think I was healed because I matured and my spiritual hunger became very strong and unhindered—so strong, in fact, that I actually started to walk in synchronization with Heaven, and you can have that too. I encourage you right now by the Spirit of God that you can have this walk with God.

When I was in Heaven, I saw that it was not going to just be about me. Yes, I was on an operating table and died and went to Heaven, met Jesus, and was sent back. Jesus sent me back to tell everyone that we are all supposed to walk in this walk of power. We are all to walk, having the knowledge of God and the understanding. After you have encountered the power of God and you have repented, then you will turn back to God with the fear of the Lord in your life. Then spiritual hunger is going to cause you to walk in the supernatural. I am guaranteeing this will happen.

I saw that if you do these things, the manifestation of your faith will happen because God wants it to happen. If it is not happening, it is because there is a hindrance, and it is not God's fault. Let's allow the Lord to heal us so that we can passionately seek God. Spiritual hunger is a very important thing in these last days.

Chapter 5

THE HOLY ALTAR

I beseech you therefore, brethren, by the mercies of God,
that you present your bodies a living sacrifice, holy,
acceptable to God, which is your reasonable service.

—ROMANS 12:1

THE LORD TOLD me that the holy altars are coming back into the Church and into the lives of believers. The holy altar is one of those things that we think of as being in the Old Testament. All the patriarchs and everyone that God used in the Old Testament had altars where they would go and worship and make sacrifices. Now in the New Testament, we are supposed to present our bodies as living sacrifices, holy and acceptable unto the Lord. We are supposed to present them on the altar, and we are supposed to acknowledge God in all our ways.

Even today, in this dispensation, we should still have altar times. We should have memorials that we set up to the Lord where we kneel and acknowledge God in our lives. We have holidays, we have birthdays, and we have all these things we celebrate, but we should celebrate meeting with God. One of those places to meet Him at is the holy altar.

Romans 12:1 says this, *"You present your bodies a living sacrifice, holy, and acceptable to God, which is your reasonable service."* Now is the time in this dispensation, this age, and in this generation to bring back the holy altar. I believe I was sent back to bring this power word back into our vocabulary and into our lives.

The apostle Paul said,

> *Or do you not know that your body is the temple of the Holy Spirit who is in you, whom you have from God, and you are not your own?*
> —1 CORINTHIANS 6:19

Your body is not your own anymore; it is God's, and it is a temple of the Holy Spirit. We need to honor God with our bodies, and if they are the temple of the Holy Spirit, then they become altars as well. When you kneel, and when you fall to your knees, there is the idea of submission and the sense of worship. This awareness of the holy altar needs to be brought back to the Body of Christ.

God showed me this will happen at the end times. It will not be that long before you start to see altar time again and deep worship. You will start to see people coming forward and kneeling before God. They will lay their whole bodies down before Him as a sign of deep spiritual worship at the holy altar. I saw that the services were going to get longer and longer. People will be moved to come forward to be ministered to by the Lord because the glory of the Lord is coming back into our services. I saw services where the cloud of God's glory will come in. People will start to come up to the front and present themselves to God in deep, spiritual worship.

THE GOVERNMENT OF THE CHURCH

In the following verses, we can see the government of God on the earth and the people who are set in the Church in authority by God:

> *And He Himself gave some to be apostles, some prophets, some evangelists, and some pastors and teachers, for the equipping of the saints for the work of ministry, for the edifying of the body of Christ.*
> —EPHESIANS 4:11-12

These are selected by God to bring us together in the unity of the faith in this end time. The Body of Christ needs to re-emphasize the true fivefold ministry of the Church. Then we need to submit to the authority that these men and women carry. God has instituted His government into the Church, and we need to honor that.

The apostle Paul said that he was an apostle, but he said that he carried the marks of Jesus Christ on his body. The marks of an apostle to Paul meant that he had partaken in the sufferings of Jesus. A lot of people today claim to be apostles and prophets, but they do not have any track record. They do not bear the marks of Jesus, as Paul did. In other words, Paul suffered for his position in the fivefold ministry. Today, many people want that title, but they do not want to partake in the sufferings of Jesus Christ.

Most apostles and prophets that I know do not want to be apostles and prophets. To be an apostle or prophet means to face a lot of persecution, a lot of warfare, and a lot of things that go with that title spiritually. The true apostles and prophets take their position very seriously. It is not something where you can print a certificate, and then you are an apostle. Being an apostle or a prophet is something that is a lifelong calling of God, and people who qualify for these positions are put through a training process. I would rather preach as a pastor or be an evangelist or teacher than claim to be an apostle or prophet.

God places an authority on apostles and prophets, and because of that there is a lot of accountability placed on them too. However, a pastor, an evangelist, and a teacher are just as important in authority as the apostle and prophet. Many people seem to choose and migrate toward the apostle and the prophet, but they do not want to pay the price that it takes to walk in that authority and be accountable for it. James said, *"Let not many of you become teachers, knowing that we shall receive a stricter judgment"* (James 3:1). We need to think these things through.

The holy altar is coming back to the Church, where we kneel in submission to God. We must remember that God set the fivefold ministries in the Church, and we are also to submit to their leadership only if they are the true fivefold. We are not to submit to someone who wants to be in control of people. We are to submit to the true authority and government of God.

RETURNING TO THE ALTAR

Abraham was called by God to leave his country and go to another country that he knew nothing of.

And he moved from there to the mountain east of Bethel, and he pitched his tent with Bethel on the west

and Ai on the east; there he built an altar to the Lord
and called on the name of the Lord.

—GENESIS 12:8

Abraham had no idea where he was going. He just left, and when he got to Bethel, the Lord had him build an altar and meet with God there. This altar became very significant because, later on in Scripture, we find that Abraham often returned there. Still, later it shows that Jacob, his grandson, ended up there as well. This altar continued to be a place of visitation and a place of honor to God.

And he went on his journey from the South as far as
Bethel, to the place where his tent had been at the begin-
ning, between Bethel and Ai, to the place of the altar
which he had made there at first. And there Abram
called on the name of the Lord. Lot also, who went with
Abram, had flocks and herds and tents.

—GENESIS 13:3-5

Now, this is a very interesting verse because Abraham returned to this altar, and he remembered that he had built it and had met God there. It is very important for us to see that God honored Abraham's altar. When Jacob, Abraham's grandson, was passing through that region, he fell asleep on a rock and had a vision. Jacob saw a ladder, and we know it as Jacob's ladder. He saw angels ascending and descending on the ladder (see Gen. 28:10-22). When Jacob woke up, he said, *"Surely the Lord is in this place, and I did not know it"* (Gen. 28:16). We know from Scripture that Jacob should have known this from his grandfather and his father Isaac because they both had been there. They all had honored God in this same place in Bethel. Abraham had built that altar and made a covenant right there with God.

The same thing happened with Moses. Moses stood in the gap for his people when he was on the mountain of God, which was a type of altar. In the same way, Abraham stood in the gap between Lot and his family when God was going to judge Sodom and Gomorrah. Lot was there when Abraham built that altar in the Scripture (see Gen. 13:1-5). God affirms man's building of altars. He makes covenants with people, and He remembers their memorials.

In Genesis 28:10-22, when Jacob was there in Bethel, he should have known that his grandfather Abraham had built that altar and his father Isaac had been there as well, but he did not remember it. Jacob did not understand, first, that God had an inheritance for him; second, that he had a heritage; and third, that his inheritance and heritage had to do with the Lord and Bethel. Jacob had accidentally found himself in that place and then had the vision of the angels. Again, Jacob should have known all along, however, about this altar in Bethel.

It probably would have worked out better for Jacob if he had purposely gone to that altar, honored God, and then went into the Promised Land. Instead, Jacob had to wrestle with an angel, causing him to limp the rest of his life. Jacob went through a lot of trouble because he did not go the way that God had established. God's way was through His covenant and Bethel. This altar was very important to that covenant with God. Jacob's grandfather had done the right thing by building the altar, and his father, Isaac, had followed through going there. When Jacob came to this place in the third generation, he had no knowledge of it.

The Lord told me that is where we are right now in this generation. That is why He wants me to speak about the holy altars and to bring them back into the services. It is where we come forward and acknowledge God. We remember when we gave our lives to the Lord, and we remember the times when God met with us. We come up to the altar at the end of a service, and we respond to the message. The Lord is saying that this is going to happen again, and we are going to start responding from our hearts to the Word of God when it is spoken.

You can also have an altar in your house, or anywhere that you designate it, but in a church service, you should respond to the message. You should be able to come forward, but because of the restrictions that we have with time, we have eliminated a lot of these things. The altar time seems to have been one of those things that have been eliminated. Because of time constraints, we do not have altar calls like we used to. In the old days, people used to come up after the service and meet with God for hours, and services would go on for long periods of time. The Lord is showing me that altar time is coming back.

In this verse, God reminded the patriarch Jacob that He still remembered what Jacob's father and grandfather did.

> *I am the God of Bethel, where you anointed the pillar and where you made a vow to Me. Now arise, get out of this land, and return to the land of your family.*
> —GENESIS 31:13

God was saying that He was the God of where Jacob's family had made that altar. I believe God was talking about Abraham.

Later on, we find out that God did appear to Jacob in Bethel.

Then God said to Jacob, "Arise, go up to Bethel and dwell there; and make an altar there to God, who appeared to you when you fled from the face of Esau your brother."

—GENESIS 35:1

God wanted Jacob to return to that altar and acknowledge that was where their meeting place was and where the covenant was made. Jacob ended up back there at the altar, and he had an encounter with God.

Interestingly, after Moses died and Joshua was appointed to take over for Moses, Joshua came to this area of Bethel as well.

Now Joshua sent men from Jericho to Ai, which is beside Beth Aven, on the east side of Bethel, and spoke to them, saying, "Go up and spy out the country." So the men went up and spied out Ai.

—JOSHUA 7:2

God sent Joshua right to the same area where the altar was made by Abraham. God caused Joshua to set up a camp there, and Joshua sent the spies to spy out the land. I think it is interesting that all this happened in the same area where Abraham made a covenant with God. God appeared to him there, and then all the sons, from then on out, had encounters with God there.

As Joshua was about to go into the Promised Land, God told Joshua to set up a camp there and send the spies into the land from that place. I believe that God was honoring the altar that was built there. I think that in this day and this hour, we need to bring the altar time back. We need to acknowledge God and set up memorials in times where we acknowledge what God has done and said in our lives. Then we use that altar as our command post, as our launching place for the next phase of our lives.

You will find God bringing you back to what He has already done for you. You need to acknowledge what God has already done, and when you do that, then He is ready to promote you from there. I have seen this in my life many times before a promotion comes. God always wants me to acknowledge the things that He has already said to me and the things that He has already done for me. I do not think it is any different for you.

In Joshua 8:30, we see that *"Joshua built an altar to the Lord God of Israel in Mount Ebal."* He continued what his forefathers and all the people before him had done. God wanted Joshua to honor Him, so Joshua built the altar.

Bethel is mentioned again in Elijah's day with Elisha.

> *And it came to pass, when the Lord was about to take up Elijah into heaven by a whirlwind, that Elijah went with Elisha from Gilgal. Then Elijah said to Elisha, "Stay here, please, for the Lord has sent me on to Bethel." But Elisha said, "As the Lord lives, and as your soul lives, I will not leave you!" So they went down to Bethel.*
> —2 KINGS 2:1-2

It is interesting that Elijah reported to Bethel because the Lord led him there, and then Elisha followed him because Elisha was going to get his mantle (see 2 Kings 2:1-15). Bethel keeps being mentioned because it all started with Abraham building an altar and sacrificing to the Lord, and then making a covenant with the Lord there. Building this altar is what Father Abraham did, who is the father of us all as well as our example. It is time to bring back these times of worship, acknowledging God in all our ways and spending time waiting on Him.

Get ready to respond to times of deep spiritual worship where you come forward at the end of a service or even during the service. The Lord will start to move in great ways. It is already starting to happen in our services, where it seems to come to a point where people have to respond and come forward. This response has all of the characteristics of a new move of God.

I have studied in great detail every move of God that I could find, and every man and woman of God in those moves. What I have found over the years, studying each move, is that the altar comes back and there are times of waiting on God. Times of laying yourself down and crucifying the flesh and saying, "God, You know we need You, and we are crying out to You, God," and *this* is the holy altar. Your personal life can affect a whole congregation. If even one person comes up and kneels at the altar, it seems to give permission for other people to do the same.

THE HOME ALTAR

It all starts in your personal life, and that is why I believe you should have a place that you call your secret place. Your secret place is where you can retreat to be with the Lord. It's where your altar is. The secret place could be your altar time. You should spend at least ten minutes a day where you shut yourself off, detach yourself, and have no input from the world. You sit, waiting on God, and you meet with Him there.

I picture laying myself on the altar and being a living sacrifice, and I let the flesh be completely overcome. The Lord is telling you that you need to make an altar. You need to have a secret place so that He can meet with you there, and you can have a place to return to Him.

There is a special season coming to your life right now where God wants to meet with you and give you instructions and understanding. It is going to be at the altar that you have made in your house where you can meet with God without any hindrances. The Spirit of the Lord is saying that He wants you to do this. You must close yourself off and let everyone know that there can be no interruptions. I get very strict about this, and I do not let anyone even come near my door when I shut it. I turn my cell phone off, and I let that altar time be God's alone.

I know that you might not be able to do this right away, but I tithe each of my days to the Lord. For every twenty-four hours, I tithe two and a half hours to God every day so that God gets two and a half hours of the twenty-four hours that He gives me. I believe that God is going to take care of me now. I will live longer than most people because I am tithing each of my days to the Lord, and He is going to preserve my body.

That should be your goal, to tithe 10 percent of the time that God gives you. God gives you twenty-four hours a day, and you sleep about six to eight hours of that. The rest of your day is spent working and doing what you want. I am recommending that you give God two and a half hours of your day and let that be your goal. You sit in His presence and offer yourself up as a living sacrifice, and you let God talk to you. Let God minister to you, and you minister to God, making covenants with Him. You can make agreements with your Heavenly Father and voice your dedication to Him. Tell God how much you love Him. Spend time telling God who He is and thanking Him for what He has done for you.

You watch what happens when you make God the focus of your life. In the coming days, you will receive briefings from Heaven. You will receive revelations, spiritual dreams, and visions. You may receive open visions where everything disappears and you see what God wants to show you, and you will have angelic visitations. These things will happen in your time of holy altar ministry when you dedicate yourself to God. All of this initiates God's visitations, dreams, visions, and guidance. I have had the Word of the Lord come to me in my altar time with Him.

Choose an environment that will cause you to focus on God. I put on worship music. If I am going to be saying something to God or reading aloud, then I have on instrumental music, and it creates that atmosphere of Heaven. I acknowledge that I am making a covenant with God. I acknowledge that He came and bought me, and because God bought me, I am going to give Him my life. I lay myself on the altar, and I picture the Lord accepting this sacrifice. As the holy fire consumes me, it starts to burn out all the impurities, all the chaff, and everything that is hindering in my life.

The hindrances being burned out happens first spiritually, but then you start to see the manifestation in your life. You start to change in the way that you walk, in the way that you think, and the way that you act. It happens because the holy fire is getting rid of anything that is not of God that is in you. You need to yield to this altar time, to this holy fire, and let God consume you as a living sacrifice.

Present yourself to God every day and remember that God wants you to designate a place and a time for your altar. Then God wants you to lay yourself on that altar and acknowledge the things that He has done, the things that He is doing, and the things that He is going to do. You say, "Lord, not my will, but Yours be done." Allow the Lord to speak to you, be quiet before Him, and allow Him to speak to you and encourage you in all your ways. There is a process, and this process starts with just ten minutes a day. If you do this, you are going to start to hear the voice of the Lord, and you are going to see favor come into your life.

Genesis 13:2 says that Abraham *"was very rich in livestock, in silver, and in gold."* What happened was wealth started to come into his life so that he prospered in everything he did. Then it happened with Isaac and with Jacob, too. Even when Jacob was disobedient, the blessing was still on him. It all started with an altar in Bethel, where God met with Abraham, and so God meets with us today.

Your ministry starts at the altar, and it starts in this time where you meet with God, and you receive instruction. Do not worry if you don't receive anything right away. You offer yourself up to God and wait on Him, and He is going to hear your prayers. God is going to see what you have offered to Him, and He never forgets it. God told each one of the patriarchs to return to the altar that they had made, where they had made a covenant with Him. When they returned to that altar, God would renew His promises with them. It took a long time for Abraham to receive all of God's promises, but he did receive them, and so will you.

Chapter 6

BROKENNESS AND HUMILITY

*Come to Me, all you who labor and are heavy
laden, and I will give you rest. Take My yoke upon
you and learn from Me, for I am gentle and lowly
in heart, and you will find rest for your souls.
For My yoke is easy and My burden is light.*
—MATTHEW 11:28-30

B ROKENNESS AND HUMILITY are unpopular subjects for a lot
of Christians. In our culture today, people are being told all
the time to be strong and pump themselves up emotionally
and mentally. However, God wants us to know about this power
word—brokenness and humility. In Matthew 11:28-30, you can
see the character of Jesus, how He is gentle, lowly, and humble in
heart. Coming to Jesus, you can find trust, and in that trust, you
will have rest. You are going to find rest in your soul when you
come to the Lord in brokenness and humility.

God has a yoke, and there is a time when a yoke is good. For
example, a yoke is good when it has to do with God's discipline.

Jesus tells us that we must take His yoke upon us, which is God's purpose for our lives, and learn from Him.

In the Old Testament, God called Moses from the midst of the cloud, and Moses went up into it. During that time, the yoke of the Lord was not popular with the children of Israel because they had experienced a yoke of slavery upon them. In this age, we all want to be free to do our own thing. We do not want to be bound by anything, but there is a godly yoke that we need.

Moses was set free from Egypt, and he went out of Egypt with his people. The children of Israel thought they were not going to be slaves anymore (see Exod. 14). However, God wanted them to have His instruction so that they would be protected by Him. God wanted them to follow His laws and rules, and walk with Him. The Israelites did not want that because they were very rebellious, and that was why God called them *stiff-necked* (see Exod. 32:9). Being stiff-necked comes from not yielding to the yoke, not yielding to the discipline of the Lord, and the children of Israel were an example of that.

The New Testament reminds us that because of the Israelites' disobedience and unbelief, they did not enter into the Promised Land, and they missed out.

> *Therefore, as the Holy Spirit says: "Today, if you will hear His voice, do not harden your hearts as in the rebellion, in the day of trial in the wilderness, where your fathers tested Me, tried Me, and saw My works forty years. Therefore I was angry with that generation," And said, "They always go astray in their heart,*

and they have not known My ways." So I swore in My wrath, "They shall not enter My rest."

—HEBREWS 3:7-11

Moses had to be yoked to God, and God told him to go up on the mountain, but the children of Israel did not want to go with him. Because they would not go, it ended up causing many problems. It took years and years for the children of Israel to go into the Promised Land. The entire first generation that came out of Egypt never got to enter in. A journey that should have only taken a few days to reach the Promised Land instead took years.

We need to take heed of what the book of Hebrews is telling us. We do not have to stay in Egypt through unbelief and disobedience. We can go into the Promised Land, and we can enter into the rest in the New Testament through Jesus Christ. Jesus has been designated as the new and living way into the Holy of Holies. We do not resist God.

James 4:6 tells us that God *"gives more grace"*; in fact, it tells us He *"gives grace to the humble,"* but He pushes back against the proud and resists them. That is why humility and brokenness are not popular subjects today, but we need to have both in our lives because God resists the proud, but He gives grace to the humble. I want God's grace in my life, don't you?

When Jesus spoke a word, the demons would leave. Yet, Jesus had full humility, full brokenness, and complete submission to Father God in His life. Why were His words so powerful? Jesus had learned to yield His Spirit to God, and because of that, when He spoke, it was with power. People were completely healed by His word. Jesus said that He cast out demons by the finger of God (see

Luke 11:20). The finger of God itself is more powerful than whatever is facing you, and the finger of God is going to take care of your needs. God's finger is enough.

Jesus was submissive to God and humble, but He still spoke with authority, and because Jesus was under authority, He walked in great authority. It was with authority that Jesus called the Pharisees, *"You brood of vipers,"* because He knew His Father, and Jesus was in submission to Him (Matt. 12:34). Jesus did not speak His own words, but He only spoke what the Father told Him to speak (see John 12:49). Jesus was submitted to God the Father, as we should also be submitted.

EMPOWERED BY HUMILITY

One of the secrets of the Kingdom is found in First Peter 5:6-7, where we read:

> *Therefore humble yourselves under the mighty hand of God, that He may exalt you in due time, casting all your care upon Him, for He cares for you.*

You need to humble yourself under the mighty hand of God. When you are under authority, God's hand is over you. When you submit yourself to God, then God is going to exalt you in due season. In God's timing, He is going to raise you up, and you will be promoted. However, the first thing you must do is humble yourself under His mighty hand.

The other thing you need to do is let go of your problems. Your promotion will happen when you cast all your cares upon God, *"for He cares for you"* (1 Pet. 5:7). You have to release them all to God. People today take so much pride in trying to do things themselves and being self-sufficient, but as a Christian, you cannot be self-sufficient. You have to be relying solely on your Father God, casting your cares upon Him, knowing that He cares for you. In essence, you are saying to the Father, "I need You, I cannot carry this alone. I cannot do this by myself."

You must remind yourself every day, through brokenness and humility, that without Him, *"you can do nothing,"* as Jesus is the vine and we are the branches (John 15:5). These two traits of brokenness and humility are a power word that is coming back into the Church and our vocabulary. This is a power word that satan fears. He fears people being broken and humble because he knows that it is through humility that God empowers His people. Humility and authority are related, and they are not contrary to each other. A person who understands authority submits to authority, and then they have great authority. If you want to walk in authority, you have to be submitted to God. God's authority will work through you when you are humble.

In every move of God that I have studied, I saw the characteristics of the people whom God had chosen to participate. The one characteristic of every person who was ever used of God was brokenness and humility. That included anyone who was participating in that move for their generation. I saw that each move of God had a characteristic of brokenness and humility. It was always part of the catalyst that brought forth the move because people were calling out to God. They were crying out to God, and they were humbling themselves by prayer and fasting. Every single time that God moved in a generation, these were the characteristics of His move.

One of my favorites says,

For thus says the High and Lofty One Who inhabits eternity, whose name is Holy: "I dwell in the high and holy place, with him who has a contrite and humble spirit, to revive the spirit of the humble, and to revive the heart of the contrite ones."

—ISAIAH 57:15

To me, it says it all. Here you have the Almighty God, who is the High and Lofty One. He is the Most High God, and there is no one above Him. He is great and mighty and powerful, and He inhabits eternity. He is in a timeless realm with no limitations whatsoever, and this is what He says. God not only dwells in the high and holy place, but He also dwells with the contrite person. He dwells with the person who is small and humble in spirit to revive the spirit of the humble. God, Himself, comes to live with those who are small and humble in spirit and revives their hearts.

If you are broken, if you are devastated right now, you are a prime candidate for God to come and live with you. God will come to encourage you, build you up, promote you, and revive your heart. God dwells with these kinds of people. God has a purpose and a plan for everything that happens. God does not do bad things to you, but He uses these times when you feel broken and humble. Such times become a perfect opportunity for God to come into your life and revive you.

There are three things that true humility and the fear of the Lord bring, and they are riches, honor, and long life (see Prov. 22:4 NLT). We all need to acknowledge that there are riches and honor, and there is a long life coming to us because this is what the Word of God says. However, we must look at how these are going to come, and the Lord gives us the answer. These three things come to you through true humility and the fear of the Lord. I know that you want these things, but they do not come automatically. You have to humble yourself, and you have to fear God.

HUMILITY OVER HUMILIATION

If you humble yourself, you are going to have honor, but if you do not, your pride will end in humiliation (see Prov. 29:23 NLT). Nobody likes to be humiliated. God says that if you humble yourself, then you are going to get honor, and you will not be judged. I would rather humble myself and let God honor me and promote me than try to do it on my own.

Even in your relationships, God is telling you to be dressed in humility and relate to one another that way because God opposes those who are proud.

> *In the same way, you who are younger must accept the authority of the elders. And all of you, dress yourselves in humility as you relate to one another, for "God opposes the proud but gives grace to the humble."*
> —1 PETER 5:5 NLT

Relationally, we have to be humble and treat others as better than ourselves (see Phil. 2:3).

ESCAPING THE WORLD'S CORRUPTION

When God made humanity, He made us in His image (see Gen. 1:27). With the fall of man, there is now a curse operating, and only through Jesus Christ are we redeemed spiritually. From the moment that we accept Jesus as Lord, our spirits are born again. Our souls—our minds, wills, and emotions—must be transformed by the renewing of our minds through the Word of God (see Rom. 12:2). Since we are in the fallen state in our flesh and our minds, we often cannot comprehend what God has done for us, and that creates discrepancies. There are discrepancies between what we feel in our spirits *should* be happening and what is *actually* happening. What is established as truth and what should be happening to us do not measure up, and this creates the discrepancy that we can sense in our spirits.

When we are born again, we know what should be happening, but it is not happening because we are living in a fallen world. It is only through brokenness and humility that we can escape the corruption that is in the world caused by lust (2 Pet. 1:4). The spirit and the flesh war against each other, and they are enemies (see Rom. 8:5-11). There is a war going on all the time, and even in our minds, we oppose ourselves. Because of this, brokenness and humility must come back into the Church and our Christian vocabulary.

To escape the corruption that is in the world caused by lust, we have to be partakers of the divine nature available through the promises of God. We must implement the promises of God that have been given to us into our lives. When we accept them humbly and accept the engrafted Word into us, then we will prosper in every area (see James 1:21-25).

Humble yourself before God and ask Him for help, and then accept His help. In that brokenness and in that humility, you will receive from God, and you can escape the curse that is in the world. You can escape the corruption that is in the world caused by lust through humility and brokenness because you accept the engrafted Word that has been spoken into yourself.

You will continually struggle unless you take the yoke of God upon you and accept discipline. If you do not accept the Word of God into you and become humble and broken before Him, you will wear yourself out with your struggle. Then you will not see the results that you should, and you will be discouraged. These kinds of things must go from a Christian's life.

We must humble ourselves and not think of ourselves more highly than we should. When we consider others more than ourselves, and we serve others, then God comes in, and He provides for us in every area of our lives. Sometimes, we hold onto things that we are supposed to give away, and the reason we are supposed to give is that God wants to give us everything. He wants to redo everything completely, and He is looking to see if we will be humble and obedient to listen to Him and give.

God is looking to see if we will give like the woman with the two mites (see Luke 21:1-4). The widow gave everything that she had, and she did not do it out of obligation, but because she loved God. Jesus said that the woman was going to receive her reward. The widow had given more than anyone else because she had given all that she had, and that only happened in humility and in brokenness. If you are doing this for any other reason, it will not be effective, and you have not come to the end of yourself.

Jesus gave me a teaching, and He told me to tell people that they need to come to the end of themselves and do it quickly. You need to draw a line in your life, and that line indicates where you end and God begins. What is going to occur after you come to the end of yourself is that your next step becomes a supernatural event. I saw that people are delaying this death to self, and because they are delaying, the supernatural events in their lives are not taking place.

Many people ask me to help them to move into the supernatural. I tell them that God is supernatural, and everything about Him is supernatural. However, we live down here in this natural world. Many people cannot escape the corruption that is in the world through lust because they have not humbled themselves. They have not let God discipline them by putting the yoke of God on them as Jesus said and walking with Him.

DIVIDING FLESH AND SPIRIT

I do not want you to have to go through this process any longer than you should. You must get to the end of yourself as quickly as possible, and the Word of God will do that for you. The Word of God is the sword of the Spirit, and the Spirit of God is going to rightly divide between your soul and spirit (see Heb. 4:12). Whatever is of you is going to be on one side, and whatever is of God is going to be on the other side. Until that sword comes and separates, there is no way you are going to know the difference. It is only the Spirit of God and the Word of God that can divide your soul from your spirit.

As I've said a few times before, your soul is your mind, will, and emotions. Your spirit is the God part of you that God breathed into you when He made you a living spirit. God breathed and made you a living soul as well, but your spirit is the part that becomes born again, and that is the *real* you. You are in a body, and you have a spirit and a soul. There are three parts to you. I call your body your *earth suit.* Your soul ties your spirit to your body so that you can enjoy what is happening in your spirit.

Man fell in the garden. When you were born, you were born into this fallen world, and there you learned things that were not right to God. Your soul has responded to what it has been told, influenced, and taught. When you become born again, your spirit has to become the dominant factor in your life, or your emotions and your mind will rule you. Brokenness and humility are your escape mechanisms. They will get you out from under the control of your flesh, and the control of your mind, will, and emotions. Brokenness will cause you to humble yourself and start to yield to the Spirit of God.

I know that you want to humble yourself and yield to the Spirit. There is something that you can do to help yourself, and it is fasting (see Matt. 6:16-18). Fasting works because your body needs food to survive, and in your mind, you think that if you do not have food to eat, you will not survive. When you fast, the first thing to realize is that you are not going to die. You can fast for days without ever affecting your body except maybe losing a little weight. It is not until you get past forty days that your body deteriorates.

When you fast, what you are doing is shutting down the voice of your body and your mind, and then all that is left is your spirit. When you fast, your spirit comes to the forefront, and then you can hear from God more clearly. You are not trying to move God to do something by fasting, but what you are doing is getting yourself to a place where you can receive from God. You want to hear from God and become more effective. Fasting is more about getting you in a place where you can encounter God and get things done, things that would not be done if you had not silenced the voice of your body.

Fasting puts you in a place where your body is under submission and you learn to focus on the will of God. When you fast, you should always have the Word of God in your mind and have your flesh under submission. You are doing that by not eating. Your spirit will come to the fore because you have placed yourself in a position where you can hear from God. God will answer you because you are listening and are ready to receive from Him.

I have found that when you have this brokenness and humility, you come to the end of yourself. Then, all of a sudden, the supernatural is right there, and from then on, you are very thankful. You become very thankful because you become mindful of what God has done for you. You realize that in your powerlessness, God comes in and makes you powerful. He causes you to triumph over your enemies. It is a process of you being broken and being humbled, and then being thankful.

When you are thankful, it causes you to start to walk in a new power, and satan *does not* want this to happen. Satan was lifted up in pride, and he was blinded. Because of that pride, he fell. *"Pride goes before destruction, and a haughty spirit before a fall"* (Prov. 16:18). The enemy does not want us to talk about brokenness and humility, and this is a power word that is being taken out of our vocabulary by satan. We must focus on laying our lives down and saying, "Father, not my will, but Yours be done" (see Luke 22:42). Being in submission brings God's power.

There is promotion coming when you humble yourself under the mighty hand of God. He is going to promote you in due season, and He is going to lift you up. God is on your side, and He wants you to be submissive to Him. God wants you to depend upon Him for everything. He is your God, and He loves you. God puts you through the fire because He wants you to be pure gold. God wants you to be able to walk in authority on this earth. He wants you to display and manifest the glory of God in these last days. Satan fears the power word of brokenness and humility, and brokenness and humility should be evident in the lives of every Christian.

Chapter 7

THE CRUCIFIED LIFE

*I have been crucified with Christ; it is no longer I
who live, but Christ lives in me; and the life which
I now live in the flesh I live by faith in the Son of
God, who loved me and gave Himself for me.*
—GALATIANS 2:20

O NE OF THE things that we should talk more about is the crucified life because there is power in the cross. The power of
God that caused Jesus to be crucified is the same power that
rose Jesus from the dead (see Rom. 6:10-11). Jesus set His face like
flint and went to the cross, and He did it for you. When I was with
Jesus in Heaven, He told me that He thought about me when He
was hanging on that cross. Jesus told me that everyone's book was
written before He even came to the earth.

You need to know that Jesus had *you* in mind when He was
crucified. I know that is hard to understand, but you have to know
how very much God loves you. The Father, the Son, and the Holy

Spirit had a board meeting, and They decided that Jesus would come and be crucified before They even created man.

Another one of these powerful words is the crucified life, and you might ask, "What does that mean to me as a Christian? I am already born again and Spirit-filled. I believe the Word of God, and I see God moving in my life with miracles. What is it about the crucified life that I need to know?" If you do not yield to the crucified life, and if you do not walk in the Spirit, putting to death your flesh, satan knows that he has got you. The enemy of your soul knows that he can trip you up if you walk in the flesh.

If you yield to the flesh, and it is predominant in your life, then the works of your flesh are at enmity with God.

> *For those who live according to the flesh set their minds on the things of the flesh, but those who live according to the Spirit, the things of the Spirit. For to be carnally minded is death, but to spiritually minded I life and peace. Because the carnal mind is enmity against God; for it is not subject to the law of God, nor indeed can be. So then, those who are in the flesh cannot please God.*
> —ROMANS 8:5-8

The flesh *wars* against the Spirit. If you yield to the flesh, you are working against the Spirit of God, according to the apostle Paul. It is very important for a Christian to crucify the flesh daily because it is right there where a war is taking place. Have you ever noticed how the media appeals to your flesh? The media tries to entice your mind and emotions, but very little appeals to your spirit. In this world, the devil does not want you to feed your spirit.

As you know, there are three parts to you. You have a spirit, a soul, and a body, and God made these three parts of you to work together in unity. Because man fell in the garden, we now live in a fallen state, and to enter the Kingdom of God, Jesus said our spirit needs to be born again.

> *Jesus answered and said to him, "Most assuredly, I say to you, unless one is born again, he cannot see the kingdom of God."*
>
> —JOHN 3:3

You can understand that if your spirit is born again and made new, then what about your mind, your will, and your emotions? And what about your flesh?

> *Therefore, if anyone is in Christ, he is a new creation; old things have passed away; behold, all things have become new.*
>
> —2 CORINTHIANS 5:17

The truth is that the day after you became born again, you were not changed in your mind, and you were not changed in your body. That day, you were changed in your spirit. The day after you were born again, you still thought the same way that you did before you were born again. Your body still wanted to do the same things it had done before you were born again. Why? It was because there was a separation between your spirit, soul, and body, and they were no longer unified.

THESE ARE SONS OF GOD

The Spirit of God has reconciled us inside of our hearts, and now we have this ministry of reconciliation.

> *Now all things are of God, who has reconciled us to Himself through Jesus Christ, and has given us the ministry of reconciliation, that is, that God was in Christ reconciling the world to Himself, not, imputing their trespasses to them, and has committed to us the word of reconciliation. Now then, we are ambassadors for Christ, as though God were pleading through us: we implore you on Christ's behalf, be reconciled to God. For He made Him who knew no sin to be sin for us, that we might become the righteousness of God in Him.*
> —2 CORINTHIANS 5:18-21

However, before we can walk with God effectively as Christians, we have to do something about our flesh and our minds. Paul taught a lot about this in Scripture. When you were born again, a supernatural event took place. The supernatural event was of the spirit realm, and not of the flesh or mind. *"God is Spirit, and those who worship Him must worship in Spirit and truth"* (John 4:24).

Paul said, *"But I discipline my body and bring it into subjection, lest, when I have preached to others, I myself should become disqualified"* (1 Cor. 9:27). The apostle Paul said this, and he was a super apostle who visited Heaven and met Jesus. Paul said that he had to discipline his body daily, and if he did not, then after he preached Christ, he could become disqualified. That was why Paul wrote Romans 8.

Paul said that he had to yield to the Spirit and walk in the Spirit. He also said that those who are led by the Spirit are sons of God.

> *For if you live according to the flesh you will die; but if by the Spirit you put to death the deeds of the body, you will live. For as many as are led by the Spirit of God, these are sons of God.*
> —ROMANS 8:13-14

You are a son or a daughter of God because you allow the Holy Spirit to take you into the perfect will of God. The supernatural is all about manifestation, but it is also about something that is going on in your spirit by the power of God that has to come out.

The Spirit of God wants to take over and control your flesh. The Spirit also wants to come up into your mind and transform it and renew it by the Word of God. Paul said this about your mind, *"You need to be transformed by the renewing of your mind"* (Rom. 12:2), and this is done by the Word of God. Paul was essentially saying that your soul is not saved. Your spirit is already saved, but your soul needs to be renewed, and you need to renew it by the Word of God.

When you are saved, your mind, will, and emotions are not going to start doing what God wants them to do. You have to renew your mind and discipline your will and emotions. You must start to think differently. When you start to connect with the Spirit of God, you are able to tell your body, "No, we are not going to do that." Then as you continue to discipline it, your body will start to listen to your spirit. Then your mind, will, and emotions will start to be renewed and begin to side with your spirit. When that happens, the Spirit of God will have free reign in your life, and you will become a powerhouse for God.

Every day when you wake up, the devil will fear you because you are living the crucified life. You are rendering your flesh crucified. As you continue to make the Holy Spirit the predominant power in your life, you will no longer allow your flesh to rule you anymore. Your mind will stay focused on the things of God because you are looking at the Word of God. It is then that you will become unified within yourself.

Paul mentioned that there are people who oppose themselves within themselves.

> *In meekness instructing those that oppose themselves; if God peradventure will give them repentance to the acknowledging of the truth; and that they may recover themselves out of the snare of the devil, who are taken captive by him at his will.*
> —2 Timothy 2:25-26 KJV

You could have a war going on inside you, and you could be fighting yourself. Many people realize that there are things that are going on inside their thought lives, emotions, and wills that need to bend toward their spirits. The answer is to live the crucified life.

Ruling and Reigning over Our Flesh

In the garden, Adam and Eve had a relationship with God, and He loved them. They did not have any resistance to Him, and God would show up and walk with them there in the garden. When Adam and Eve fell, and they were taken out of the garden.

Everything turned against them, and they had to work by the sweat of their brow (see Gen. 3:19). Curses came into their lives, and they did not have the access to God that they used to. When Jesus came, He restored man all the way back to Adam before the fall and brought man back into fellowship with God. God wants to walk with you and talk to you just like He did with Adam and Eve.

When you accept Jesus as Lord, God sees you as sinless. You know in your heart that God is pleased with you, but in your mind, you fear, you doubt, and you struggle with things. That was what Paul meant when he spoke about people who oppose themselves within themselves. Paul saw that there is a war going on within us. The crucified life is how you win this war.

Paul saw this war going on inside us, and he talked about it in Romans 7. When Paul wanted to do something right, he could not always do the things he wanted to do. Paul said that sin was right there to oppose him. He ended up doing the wrong thing when in his heart, he only wanted to please God (see Rom. 7:14-25). We can all identify with this struggle within us, but Paul knew we needed to graduate, and so he wrote Romans 8. There, Paul shows us that we can live victoriously through the crucified life. I urge you to read Romans 7-8.

You can sometimes feel defeated, and you cannot seem to get a handle on your life and your flesh. Remember that Jesus was sent to walk out this life for us as a perfect example. If you look at the life of Jesus, He walked as a son of man. Many people will say Jesus was God. Yes, Jesus was God, but when He came in the flesh, He came as the Son of Man. Jesus only did what the Father showed Him to do, and He only spoke what He heard the Father say because Jesus was in total submission to the Father. There is a walk in the Spirit if you are willing to be disciplined, and through that, you can walk in power. If that is what you want, you can have that but you are going to have to live the crucified life.

In this Scripture, there is the key. *"For if you live according to the flesh you will die; but if by the Spirit you put to death the deeds of the body, you will live"* (Rom. 8:13). You need to speak from your spirit and tell your body, "No." As a Christian, you live from your spirit, and you rule over your body. You do not let your body tell you what it wants. Every day you tell your flesh, "This is what we are going to do." If your body does not want to do it, you make it do it. God is not going to make your flesh obey Him because it is *you* who needs to rule over your flesh.

When I was born again, I thought that I was not going to have any more trouble with my flesh, and things within me would fall into line. When I was in Heaven, I saw that we need to rule over our flesh and make it listen, because it doesn't want to listen. Your flesh wants to do the same things that it did before you were a Christian. If your mind does not side with your spirit, then it is going to side with your body. Then you are going to have two against one. Your spirit is full of God, and yet you are struggling with your mind and body because you have been waiting for God to do something with your flesh. However, God is not going to do anything more with your flesh. God is waiting for you to rule and reign over them from your spirit.

The Spirit of God is enlightening you and showing you that you are anointed and have power. The Holy Spirit is anointing you to walk in the Spirit, and that is His job, and you should be aware of His presence. The Holy Spirit will come alongside you and take hold of you in your weakness and cause you to triumph (see Rom. 8:26). This will cause your flesh to have to listen to you now. Unless you say *no* to your flesh, it is going to take you where you do not want to go. I have heard many people say, "I don't know how I got here." I know how you got there, one step at a time. You let your mind convince you of something that was not true, and you let your body walk you out of God's will. As Christians, we are not to be body-ruled. We are to be spirit-ruled.

> *Then He said to them all, "If anyone desires to come after Me, let him deny himself, and take up his cross daily, and follow Me."*
> —LUKE 9:23

Jesus said this *before* He died on the cross. This is not a popular message, but it is so vital, and satan knows that. When I was in Heaven, I looked back, and I saw that satan was trying to extract this whole idea of the crucified life out of Christian terminology. I saw that he was taking this out to where it is not even popular to preach or teach on it anymore. The only way that satan can win is when he gets your flesh to rule you, and if he can do that, he has got you. If you are spirit-ruled, if you are led by the Spirit of God, then you are a son of God, and satan cannot do anything about that.

Jesus said that if you really want to follow after Him, then you are going to have to deny yourself. Were you told this when you were born again? I wasn't, and it was a shock to find out that my life was not my own anymore and that now I was going to have to walk by faith (see Gal. 2:20). I was going to have to turn away from what I wanted, and no one had ever told me that. Jesus said that you are going to have to take up your cross daily. That means that *every day,* you are going to have to tell your body that it is dead to sin. Now, I think it is funny how I thought that God would take care of my flesh and that He would make it listen, but God does not. God gave us His Spirit, and we are supposed to yield to the Spirit of God—*"to put on the Lord Jesus Christ, and make no provision for the flesh, to fulfill its lusts"* (Rom. 13:14).

Here is another Scripture verse you do not hear very often. Paul is saying that you are supposed to be putting on the Lord Jesus Christ like He is a coat that you wear. Then Paul tells us to make no provision for the flesh to fulfill its lusts. You must deny your flesh access to your will. Living the crucified life is just saying *no* to the flesh.

ENTRANCE TO THE SUPERNATURAL

I have been crucified with Christ; it is no longer I who live, but Christ lives in me; and the life which I now live in the flesh I live by faith in the Son of God, who loved me and gave Himself for me.

—GALATIANS 2:20

Paul had an understanding of this concept because he was caught up into Heaven, and he understood the crucified life. He said, *"For me to live is Christ and to die is gain"* (Phil. 1:21). People every day are missing an opportunity to have a supernatural event. When they are feeling weak, they do not take that next step into the supernatural.

To have a supernatural encounter every day, you must not yield to the flesh or your own understanding, but instead, you must yield to the Spirit. You stand back, you wait, and you do not respond right away. You wait for God to speak to you, and you will hear the Spirit say, "Walk this way and do that." The Holy Spirit always provides a way of escape for you (see 1 Cor. 10:13). When you live like this, supernatural events are going to start happening in your life. The crucified life is a power word the devil fears because it is coming back to the Church, and it is the entrance into the supernatural.

Think back over the last 24 hours of how your flesh has tried to get you out of the Spirit. Your flesh wants to do what it wants to do. When you are not strong enough to tell it what to do, your will bends toward your flesh. What if you built yourself up in the Word of God? What if you begin increasing in the knowledge and understanding of God, and the Holy Spirit starts to come upon you so powerfully that you feel like Samson? Suddenly, you are ruled by the Spirit of God, and you have command about you. Then you can easily tell your flesh *no*.

I have found that when you get hungry, especially when you are fasting, all you have to do is speak to your flesh. Say, "We are not going to eat today, and if I hear another word from you, we are not going to eat tomorrow either." All of a sudden, your hunger will go away, and it is amazing. You will see that your body has had a voice all this time. I found that if I treat my flesh like a disobedient pet, and I am strong and firm with it, it starts to fall into line.

It is the same with my mind. I speak to it and say, "We are not going to do that," or "We are not going there." Sometimes, those negative thought processes continue, and you feel like you are being steered off course. All you have to say is, "I am going to read my Bible for an hour," and suddenly, all the bad thoughts will stop. It is the same way if you cannot sleep, just say, "I guess I'll just get up and pray and read my Bible." You will not believe how sleepy you will get. It is then that you will start to see the spiritual war that is going on within you.

HOOKED IN THE FLESH

Paul talks about the works of the flesh, and he lists all of their manifestations.

> *Now the works of the flesh are manifest, which are these; adultery, fornication, uncleanness, lasciviousness, idolatry, witchcraft, hatred, variance, emulations, wrath, strife, seditions, heresies, envyings, murders, drunkenness, revellings, and such like: of the which I tell you before, as I have also told you in time past, that they which do such things shall not inherit the kingdom of God.*
> —GALATIANS 5:19-21 KJV

One of them is witchcraft, and I thought that witchcraft was spiritual warfare, but Paul lists it as a work of the flesh. That is because satan desires to manifest through a person, and the only way he can do that is to get someone hooked in the flesh. He works on your mind until he gets a manifestation through your flesh.

Witchcraft, in its purest form, is when a demon is able to manifest through another person. First, satan overcomes their will, and then he manifests through them. The works of the flesh are evident, as Paul said, and these things are enemies of God. You never want to yield to these evil spirits, and part of that is not yielding to your flesh. If you tell the flesh *no*, then what you are really doing is spiritual warfare. When you do not allow the demonic to affect you to the point of manifesting, then that is true warfare.

> *For the weapons of our warfare are not carnal, but mighty in God for pulling down of strongholds casting down arguments and every high thing that exalts itself against the knowledge of God, bringing every thought into captivity to the obedience of Christ, and being ready to punish all disobedience when your obedience is fulfilled.*
>
> —2 Corinthians 10:4-6

Most people only quote the first part of this verse in Second Corinthians. However, it says that these weapons are mighty through God to the pulling down of strongholds *and* anything that exalts itself above the knowledge of God, *bringing every thought into captivity.* I thought we were talking about spiritual warfare here. As you can see by this verse, when a demon is seeking manifestation, he is going to start with your mind.

The enemy of your soul is going to suggest things to you in your mind. The whole idea is to get you to follow through in your body and manifest it in your flesh. If you do not allow that thought to take root and manifest, then that demon has lost. There is no manifestation, and this is what happens when you crucify the flesh. You must renew your mind by the Word of God, and you must discipline the flesh, crucify it, and keep it crucified.

> *But you, beloved, building yourselves up on your most holy faith, praying in the Holy Spirit, keep yourselves in*

the love of God, looking for the mercy of our Lord Jesus Christ unto eternal life.

—JUDE 1:20-21

You are going to build yourself up in your spirit while you are disciplining your flesh and renewing your mind. You are going to be a powerhouse. You are going to walk in the Spirit, and you do that by praying in the Holy Spirit, building yourself up on your most holy faith, and keeping yourself in the love of God. God is love, and in Him, there is no fear because love drives out fear. When you are made perfect in love by building yourself up on your most holy of faith, then you are driving out fear. Fear cannot come near you when you are walking in the Spirit. You pray in the Spirit, and you keep yourself in the love of God, building yourself up.

You must also meditate on the Word of God (see Josh. 1:8-10). In the Old Testament, Moses was told to tell the people to keep the Word of God always before them. You are to meditate on the law, day and night, so that you will stay in obedience and walk with God. Then God will be with you, and He will prosper you in everything you do. When you keep the Word of God and meditate on it day and night, it will cause you to do the right thing.

There is a weakness in every person, and I found it is rejection. There are a lot of people who have been so rejected that they cannot grasp that God actually accepts them. Fear is the number-one entrance for most demonic spirits, but the second one is rejection. Rejection is a device that the enemy uses against you. He causes you to get into this cycle where you feel that you are rejected. Certain similar things will continually happen no matter who the person is that you encounter, and you feel rejected. It is a demonic cycle, and you need to have that broken because you are not rejected. You have been accepted in the beloved (see Eph. 1:5-6).

Paul said that we have received the Spirit of adoption and that the Spirit of God inside of us is the Spirit of acceptance (see Rom. 8:15). That acceptance is constantly calling out to the Father and declaring that He is *your* Father. The Holy Spirit within you has not rejected you. You are not rejected, and you need to break that cycle in your life. You break those cycles when you crucify the flesh, and you live the crucified life and concentrate on the Scriptures. You will know the hope to which you have been called, the glorious inheritance in the saints (see Eph. 1:18). You will know that you have been accepted, that you are a child of God and beloved of God.

Chapter 8

THE WORD OF GOD

*So shall My Word be that goes forth from My mouth; it
shall not return to Me void, but it shall accomplish what I
please, and it shall prosper in the thing for which I sent it.*

—ISAIAH 55:11

Y OU WOULD NEVER think that the Word of God would start
to be extracted out of a Christian's life and vocabulary. I have
heard sermons that went on for an hour, and the speaker
never mentioned Jesus' name at all and did not even quote one
Scripture verse. The Lord had asked me to watch Christian televi-
sion, and I did that for two years. I began to mark down every time
the power words were used, and so far, there are 23 of them that
are being removed from our vocabulary.

It was amazing to me that these words are disappearing out
of people's messages, and these messages are from ministers of the
gospel! They are not using these power words anymore. The Lord
started to minister to me about how one day I would write this
book and would teach on this subject.

This power word is the Word of God, and it is very important. If you notice, not many people talk about the Word of the Lord, and they do not exercise their authority in quoting Scripture anymore. Some ministers seem like they just want to have a nice talk. Jesus did not have a nice talk about the Father; He had a strong word about Him. Jesus only spoke what His Father was speaking, and He was constantly telling the truth.

The Word of God is the foundation of everything that a Christian believes. You must include the Word of God in everything you do and say, and it should be on your lips all the time. Jesus Himself lived off every word that came from the mouth of God. Jesus set the example in the desert when He was tempted, and He told the devil, *"Man shall not live on bread alone, but on every word that comes out from the mouth of God"* (see Matt. 4:4). That applies to us, too. As Christians, we are supposed to live off the Bread from Heaven, and Jesus is the Bread, and He is the Word of God.

God sits on His throne, and I was there in Heaven and saw Him. The same spot where God spoke me into my mother's womb was the same spot where I reported back to God and gave an account for my life (see Rom. 14:12). That same spot where God thought of you and spoke you into existence is the same spot where you will stand before Him, and you will present yourself back to God. You will give an account of what you did with what He gave you, which is the Word of God. God's Word goes out and comes back around to Him, but it does not come back void.

So shall My word be that goes forth from My mouth;
it shall not return to Me void, but it shall accomplish

> *what I please, and it shall prosper in the thing for which I sent it.*
>
> —Isaiah 55:11

God's Word comes back accomplishing what He said, and God said, *"It shall prosper in the thing for which I sent it."*

As I was standing in Heaven with Jesus, He said, "Kevin, it is not just what God says; it is about His intent. God's purpose is far more than the volumes of books available to be written about what God's heart is on a matter." While Jesus was talking to me, behind me, the Holy Spirit was giving me seven different levels of understanding of the Scriptures, for everything that Jesus was saying. The entire Word of God has great depth so that's why it is very important for us to study to show ourselves approved (see 2 Tim. 2:15).

It seemed like I was with Jesus for a week, but it was only for forty-five minutes. Even now, over twenty-six years after my visit to Heaven, I still have things coming up in my spirit that are brand-new from that visitation. The revelation I received is never going to end. When the Holy Spirit gave me all those different levels of what Jesus was saying to me, I have experienced much deeper levels of revelation for everything ever since.

When God spoke the worlds into existence, we think God just spoke it, and it happened. God did do that, but contained in those words was God's plan for man for an extended period. When God spoke you into existence, there was a book written about you before you were born, and your whole life was entered into the record. God then assigned angels to you. Jesus even agreed to die for humankind before man was ever created. I saw that the

Holy Trinity had met, and They discussed that They were going to make man in the image of God. They decided to create someone to whom They could talk and someone who could talk to Them and have fellowship with Them.

For God to create man in His image, God would have to give man free will. God, the Father, knew that man would fall, so Jesus said, "I will go back and redeem them so let Us create them." They agreed to make man, knowing that man would fall. Just think about that for a moment. And then Jesus volunteered to come back, and He was the Lamb that was slain before the foundation of the world (see Rev. 13:8). When God spoke man into existence, He had already designed a way to redeem him, knowing that he would fall. It was all decided before God ever created man.

It is the same with your life. Everything was written down in order, a perfect life for you, and God's perfect will for you written in a book (see Ps. 139:16). Heavenly angels were assigned to you to help and assist you. You were breathed into your mother's womb, and that seed, that word of God, germinated and caused you to be formed in your mother's womb and later be born. The angels were assigned to you help you fulfill what God had written about you in Heaven. The psalmist tells us that God has already gone to your future and prepared a whole pathway to it, and He is standing there. Then God went around to your past, and He blocked the past from hurting you (see Ps. 139:5 TPT). God had already written everything down before you were even born. You have to realize that the Word of God is very powerful.

When God sat on His throne, and He created everything that you see, He framed it all by His words. God's intent was that everything He spoke would prosper and that it would succeed, and that is what God wants for you. You can understand how satan does not want people to know about the potency of God's Word and the potency of God's intent. It is not just God's Word. It is His intent, which has seven different levels to it.

Did you know that there are seven levels to every word and verse in the Bible? God has designed His Word to be so deep that it is mysterious, and only the Holy Spirit can unlock it. God did that on purpose because He wants you to seek Him, and He wants you to look for the treasure hidden in the Word of God. Did you know that you are also hidden in the Word of God?

FINDING YOURSELF IN THE WORD

Daniel was an Old Testament prophet, and he lived about four hundred years before Jesus. Daniel and his people were taken out of Jerusalem and were held captive in Babylon, which is modern-day Iraq. Daniel was sitting there captive, and he was reading a scroll that was written by the prophet Jeremiah. Jeremiah wrote the scroll 175 years before Daniel was in Babylon, and Jeremiah had already gone on to be with the Lord.

Daniel was reading the scroll, and he got to what is our Jeremiah 29, which talks about a people being held captive. He read about how they were held captive for seventy years, which was how long Daniel's people were captive. It said that one day they were going to call out to the Lord at the end of the seventy years of captivity, and the Lord was going to answer them. The Lord was going to take them back into their land because God had a good and expected end for them. God had plans to prosper them (see Jer. 29:11).

Suddenly, Daniel knew that God was talking about him and his people. Daniel started to do what the Word of God told him to do, and he started to seek God (see Dan. 9). Daniel started fasting and praying and confessing his sins, but nothing happened for twenty-one days. On the twenty-second day, at the evening offering, the angel Gabriel appeared.

Gabriel told Daniel that, the day Daniel had set his heart to seek the Lord, God had heard him and sent Gabriel. The entire time that Daniel prayed and fasted, the angels of God were warring in the heavens to get to him. Daniel got to see so many wonderful visions of the future, and he was even shown the end times, things that we have not even seen yet.

Daniel found himself in the Word and realized that it was all rigged. He saw that if he would just seek God, then God would answer. Daniel knew that God was going to bring them back to the land of Jerusalem. He saw in the Word of God that they were set free in their seventieth year of captivity, and he knew it was time for the Israelites to be delivered from their seventy years of captivity.

Daniel saw in the Word that it was already God's intent for them to be delivered, and Daniel knew that he was going to get his answer. That is how we have to be. We have to look into the Word of God, and we have to find ourselves there. We have to know that it is already written down, that we are delivered, and that God is always going to cause us to triumph in Christ Jesus.

GOD CALLS SAMUEL

Samuel, as a very young boy, was taken to the temple and left there by his mother, who promised Samuel to God as an offering. He was there to serve God. We read:

Now the boy Samuel was ministering to the Lord before Eli. And word from the Lord was rare in those days, visions were infrequent.

—1 SAMUEL 3:1 NASB

As this verse says, the Word of the Lord was rare in those days, and visions were infrequent. The boy Samuel ministered to the Lord before Eli, the high priest in the temple (see 1 Sam. 3). One night after Samuel had gone to bed, the Lord called Samuel's name, and Samuel thought Eli had called him, so Samuel asked Eli what he wanted. Eli told Samuel that he had not called Samuel. Samuel heard his name being called again and went to Eli again, thinking Eli had called him. Once more, Eli told Samuel that he had not called Samuel. After this happened once more, Eli realized that God was calling Samuel. Eli then told Samuel that the next time it happened, he was to say, "Speak, Lord, for your servant hears," and Samuel did as Eli told him. God started a relationship with Samuel that very night.

Even though the Word of God was rare in those days, it says, at the end of Samuel's life, not one word that Samuel had spoken fell to the ground. Samuel was the most accurate prophet who ever walked the earth, and he never missed it. The word of the Lord can come to you, and you can speak it and not miss it. Here you have Samuel as your example. He was a mighty prophet. However, Samuel was dedicated to God, he lived in the temple, and he was not part of the world. He had an environment that had to do with God's house, and because of that, God used him in a mighty way.

Are you ready to set yourself up to receive the Word of the Lord? Then you need to meditate on the Word of God every day.

You need to put God's Word foremost in your life, quoting the Word of God and eating it every day. I do not read whole chapters and whole books of the Bible. My goal is not quantity; it is quality, so I eat one slice of bread a day. I eat a couple of verses, and I meditate on them every day.

Samuel was separated from the world, and he became a very accurate prophet. Paul told Timothy,

> *You therefore must endure hardship as a good soldier of Jesus Christ. No one engaged in warfare entangles himself with the affairs of this life, that he may please him who enlisted him as a soldier.*
> —2 TIMOTHY 2:3-4

As a Christian, God has called you to wage war. Paul also told Timothy to wage war with the prophecies he had received, and to use them as weapons (see 1 Tim. 1:18).

The word of the Lord starts coming to you by your meditating on God's Word, and then God will send you a word from His throne. I have noticed that when I spend time in the Word of God now, God gives me words all the time. I do not even need to have a word from anybody else unless it is a confirmation because I get a word every day.

I place myself in a position just like Daniel reading Jeremiah, and just like Samuel being set apart in the temple, being separate from the world. I position myself like Timothy when Paul said that, as a soldier of Jesus Christ, we are not to be involved with the world because we are soldiers engaging in warfare. These examples show you that it is about your environment and allowing the Word of God to be the sole influence in your life.

You can still go to work, and I did for thirty years, but I would take Scriptures with me, and I would put them up at work. I would look at them, and I would rehearse one each day and let it become part of me until it would ignite inside me, and then it would become a spiritual experience. If you want a spiritual experience, an encounter with God, it is as easy as eating the Word of God. You meditate on it until the Holy Spirit ignites it inside you, and then it becomes part of you.

Jesus knew that we were to live off of every Word that came from God.

> *But Jesus told him, "No! The Scriptures say, 'People do not live by bread alone, but by every word that comes from the mouth of God.'"*
> —Matthew 4:4 NLT

In Heaven, I saw that if you will feed yourself on the Word of God, your way will be lit up. Your way will prosper in everything that you do. The Word of God lights up your path, and I literally saw a path being lit up from our spirits because our spirits are like a furnace. I saw that the Spirit of God is a fire inside us, and it needs fuel, and when we feed ourselves with the Word of God, we light up and just ignite.

If you want to walk in your destiny, you need to feed your spirit with the Word of God, and you need to allow the Holy Spirit to light you up and start to cause a burning fire inside you. God wants you to prosper, but the only way that He can get you to that place is through your relationship with Him. You need to feed that relationship, and you have to control your environment.

What is it about us that we want to get involved with things that take us away from our purposes and our plans? The most successful businesspeople dedicate all their time and all their lives to pursue the business that they feel they should do. They isolate themselves from negative people and anyone who does not share the vision that they have. They only concentrate on and get people around them who are part of their plan or vision. The people who are very successful now will tell you that it cost them everything. You see their wealth, and you see their success, but what you do not know is that it cost them everything.

When I met Jesus, I realized that if I sold out to Him, it would cost me everything to follow Him. If I left family and houses and everything for Him in this life, I would be rewarded with family and houses and persecutions as well (see Luke 18:29). As the Jesus said, *"But seek first the kingdom of God and His righteousness, and all these things shall be added to you"* (Matt. 6:33). I have seen this verse fulfilled in my life, but when I first started seeking Him, it seemed as if I were experiencing loss because I had to let go of other pursuits and interests.

As with Samuel and all these men and women of God in the Bible, they all had to leave something. Abraham had to leave his own country and go to a place that he did not know. God did not even tell Abraham where he was going. God, in essence, said, "Start walking." When I got saved, the Lord started to tell me things to do, and I had to do them, and so it is with you.

The Lord is speaking to you right now and showing you that you might need to come out from among the world and isolate yourself a little bit more to where your environment is conducive to growth. You need to spend time meditating on the Word of God.

You need to spend time praying in the Spirit, igniting the fire that is within you. You need to fan the flame of the gift that was placed within you, just like Paul told Timothy (see 2 Tim. 1:6). Fan the flame and allow it to ignite because your gift will make room for you (see Prov. 18:16). Your gift inside of you is going to cause you to be promoted. You want to isolate yourself from the world and draw near to God.

You do not have to feed yourself with stuff that is going to be contrary to where you are going, and you only pursue those things that are your destiny. Jesus is standing on your destiny, and He is telling you, "Come to Me." He is already in your future because He has been to your future. He built your future for you, and now He is bidding you come to Him. You just have to walk to Him and pursue Him with all your heart. If you first seek the Kingdom of God and His righteousness, you are going to receive all these other things, and you will not have to worry about anything. The Word of God has to become foremost in your life. Satan does not want you to do that because he cannot win against the Word of God. However, the primary thing that satan cannot win against is God's intent for what He has spoken about you.

God is never going to change. He changes not, and His Word is established as a platform and a foundation in His throne. God rules by what He has already established and spoken. You can rest assured that God has already written this beautiful book about you, and you do not need to worry about your future. As Isaiah 40:8 tells us, *"The grass withers, the flower fades, but the word of our God stands forever."* You need to reaffirm your trust in Him and His Word. You can believe that there is a substance somewhere that is the end of your faith, and God is working it out in your life.

You eat the Word of God. You not only make the Word of God predominant in your life, but when you find God's words, you take them into yourself, and you eat them. Jeremiah said,

> *Your words were found, and I ate them,*
> *And Your word was to me the joy and rejoicing of my*
> *heart; for I am called by Your name, O Lord God of*
> *hosts.*

—JEREMIAH 15:16

Do not let the Word of God slip from you. Always keep it before you. Keep it on your lips because, when God spoke, He was calling things that were not as though they were, and it is the same with you (see Rom. 4:17). You pray in the Spirit, and you speak forth out of your mouth. It might be something that does not exist to you, but in Heaven, it does. God's will is coming forth, and it is coming forth out of the belly because when you pray in the Spirit, you are praying to God, and you are praying forth mysteries.

Chapter 9

THE NEW COVENANT

And for this reason He is the Mediator of the new covenant, by means of death, for the redemption of the transgressions under the first covenant, that those who are called may receive the promise of the eternal inheritance.
—HEBREWS 9:15

THE NEW COVENANT is the covenant that God gave us through Jesus Christ, and satan does not want us to rely on this covenant. We have a very powerful relationship with God in the new covenant because Jesus Christ made a new and living way into the Holy of Holies. We now have access to the Holy of Holies, and we can freely enter in (see Heb. 10:19).

The new covenant that was given to us will never go out of date. The same God who made the old covenant is the same God who made the new covenant, and He has not switched thrones. He is still on the same throne. Here in Hebrews 9:15, through Jesus' death, we have a new covenant, and that covenant has better promises and benefits that are even greater than the old covenant.

This word *covenant* is something that satan does not want us to use, and he does not want to hear that word even being mentioned. The new covenant is a very important power word, and I invoke the covenant every day. There are times where our faith will fail, but the covenant that God makes with us will never fail, and we need to rely on that covenant.

What is a covenant? It is an agreement between two people or a group of people. One of the parties in a covenant can benefit by being the one who "covenants up," meaning you get into covenant with someone who has greater benefits than you. In this case, we have better benefits because we covenant with God, and we get everything that He has, and He gets everything that we have. I think we get the better end of the deal because God owns everything.

In the past, people would covenant with other people because it was advantageous for both parties. Each party would get what the other party had, and it was an agreement where both parties benefited. In this case, we benefit in an even greater way because we want to rely on the covenant. We want to realize where we end, where our limitations are, and then we want to invoke the covenant. The covenant is what God, through Jesus Christ, has done for us.

Jesus talked about the fact that the Old Testament law will never be abolished, and it will not pass away.

Do not think that I came to destroy the Law or the Prophets. I did not come to destroy but to fulfill. For assuredly, I say to you, till heaven and earth pass away, one jot or one tittle will by no means pass from the law till all is fulfilled.

—MATTHEW 5:17-18

Jesus came to fulfill the law, not to abolish it. Even the Old Testament is fulfilled through Jesus Christ. Think about Deuteronomy 28 for a moment. It talks about how God is going to prosper the people who obey Him and walk with Him and fear Him, and all the blessings that will come upon such a people. In Deuteronomy 30:19, God advises us to choose life, and then all of these benefits are ours, and this is under the old covenant. There are many more instances of benefits. However, in the New Testament, there are far greater benefits, and Jesus came to give us an even better covenant.

THE HEART OF MAN

Moses went up on the mountain, and God talked to him. He told Moses that He was going to give the people guidelines, laws that they were going to need to obey. God did this because, up until that point, as recorded through the first several chapters of Genesis, the people were continually in rebellion and disobedience. When man is left to himself, the thoughts and intents of his heart turn to evil (see Gen. 6:5-7).

During the time of Noah, the Lord saw that the wickedness of man was so great and so evil that God was sorry that He had made man. God decided to destroy man from the face of the earth by a flood, but Noah found grace in God's eyes, and he and his family were saved (see Gen. 6:6-8).

A few chapters later, we read about the Tower of Babel and how God had to come down and separate the people by their language and continent (see Gen. 11:1-9). God separated and scattered everyone because they were doing such evil. Throughout the book of Genesis, we see that God had to correct things continually because, when left to himself, man will destroy himself and destroy creation.

Abraham was called out by God from Ur of the Chaldees, which today is the area of southern Iraq, and he was brought to a Promised Land (see Gen. 12). God called out a man and formed a whole nation out of him. All this happened because Abraham met with God and cut a covenant with Him, and then God made a promise to Abraham (see Gen. 15:8-21). To this day, we have Abraham as our father because of a covenant that God made with him long, long ago.

Joseph was being held captive in Egypt (see Gen. 39). After Joseph died, the Israelites were kept in slavery in Egypt for four hundred years until Moses took the people out and received the law on the mountain. God gave Moses the Ten Commandments to give to the people. Jesus said that these commandments could be summed up with two commands, which is to love the Lord your God with all your heart and love your neighbor as yourself. If you love God with all your heart, and you love your neighbor as yourself, you can fulfill those Ten Commandments according to Jesus (see Matt. 22:35-40). Jesus came to fulfill the law of the Ten Commandments.

When the Pharisees confronted Jesus, they had made those ten laws into over six hundred laws. That is what man did with Ten Commandments, and that is religion. Jesus was confronting the

Pharisees and said that they were putting too many burdens on the people. He had come to take the burdens off people and set them free, *"Therefore if the Son makes you free, you shall be free indeed"* (John 8:36).

In Second Corinthians 3:6, Paul told the Corinthians,

> *Who also made us sufficient as ministers of the new covenant, not of the letter but of the Spirit; for the letter kills, but the Spirit gives life.*

Jesus came to set us free and to fulfill the law by the Spirit. The law of the Spirit causes us to fulfill the law. So, if you love God with all your heart, you are not going to sin, and if you love your neighbor as yourself, you are not going to sin against your neighbor. God resolved this through Jesus Christ and by loving God and loving your neighbor as yourself. Consequently, your relationship with God and your relationship with others are what's important.

A Promise of Help

The covenant that God cut with us through Jesus Christ is so powerful that the enemy cannot penetrate it. According to a covenant, if your enemy comes against you to make war, then the person, tribe, or whoever it is that you made a covenant with has to come and help you. They are your allies, and it is like the agreements that our country has today with other countries. If a country gets attacked by those with whom we are allied and with those with whom we have a covenant, then we are obligated to come in and help them in time of war. If satan comes after you, he is coming after God because God is in covenant with you, and you have to start thinking like this. That is why satan does not like this word *covenant*, and he is trying to extract it from our vocabulary and our thinking.

God, who is rich in mercy, is bringing back the meaning of and the word *covenant* into your life and your daily vocabulary. Satan does not want you to invoke the blood covenant of Jesus. When I am dealing with devils and they start speaking out of people, they do not want me to mention the blood, and they do not want me to mention the name of Jesus. The reason is that when we invoke the name or the blood, we are talking about the covenant. Then what we have done is brought God into the picture. Those demons are no match for God because He is going to defeat them, and God is not going to let them touch us.

When I invoke the blood and I invoke the name of Jesus, the demons start screaming, and they have to listen to me. You can cast out many devils by using the name of Jesus and His blood. By mentioning the blood, you are invoking the covenant, because the blood is the enemy's enemy. What you are saying to the demons is that God is coming after them. When you encounter demons, they do not see you; they are seeing who is with you. It is very important to understand this because there is not a lot of talk about the covenant anymore.

God wants to give us His Kingdom, and we are going to inherit the entire Kingdom. Jesus said,

> *Do not fear, little flock, for it is your Father's good pleasure to give you the kingdom.*
> —LUKE 12:32

The Father *desires* to give you the Kingdom, so do not be afraid. We are heirs of God Himself and co-heirs with Jesus. We will inherit all that He is and has (see Rom. 8:17 TPT). We are joint-heirs with Jesus, and we should consider this every time satan attacks us. I have reminded satan about this to the point where he does not even bother with me anymore because I invoke the covenant. Satan knows I understand that if he attacks me, he is attacking God, and he is going to have to deal with God.

It is the same thing with tithing. People do not believe in tithing because they say that it is Old Testament. Only God said that if you tithe, He *"will rebuke the devourer for your sakes"* (Mal. 3:11). God will open up the Heavens for you to where you will not have enough room to store what He is about to pour out on you (see Mal. 3:10). In the covenant, when God rebukes the devourer, the devourer is never going to come near you.

It is important to consider tithing because it is part of a covenant, and it is *you* invoking the covenant, and it is *not* the law. Abraham tithed before the law because he gave a tithe to Melchizedek before Moses was even born. So tithing is not an old covenant law because Abraham tithed without ever being told that it was a law (see Gen. 14:20).

Jeremiah prophesied that there was going to be a new covenant coming.

> *Behold, the days are coming, says the Lord, when I will make a new covenant with the house of Israel and with the house of Judah.*
> —JEREMIAH 31:31

In fulfillment of Jeremiah's prophecy, Jesus took the cup after supper and said, *"This cup is the new covenant in My blood, which is shed for you"* (Luke 22:20). We can see the fulfillment of what was prophesied. Jesus did this at the Last Supper, before He went to the cross.

> *In the same manner He also took the cup after supper, saying, "This cup is the new covenant in My blood. This do, as often as you drink it, in remembrance of Me."*
> —1 CORINTHIANS 11:25

The apostle Paul also took a cup after supper and quoted Jesus in First Corinthians 11:25—*"This cup is the new covenant in My blood. This do, as often as you drink it, in remembrance of Me."* We often quote this at communion, but taking communion is not just a ritual. It is something that Jesus told us to do, and He instituted it. The reason Jesus instituted communion was so that you and I would remember what He did for us—that it would always be forefront in our minds. This stops satan from coming in and messing with you and me. When you take communion, you must recognize the importance of the blood and the body of Jesus that was shed for you. You are acknowledging and invoking the covenant. You are also honoring God and what He did through Jesus Christ. When you do that, it is so sacred that satan cannot get through, because he cannot get past the blood.

AFFIRMING THE COVENANT

One day Jesus looked at the crowd, and He said to them, *"You seek me, not because you saw the signs, but because you ate of the loaves and were filled"* (John 6:26). The crowds were merely spectators and were following Jesus for the wrong reasons. Jesus was all about relationship and fellowship, and He was about covenant, too. Those people were like people today who come, spectate, and do not participate in worship gatherings. They're just like how the Israelites spectated in the desert when they watched Moses go up into the mountain of God, but they did not go up with him (see Exod. 20:18-19). They stood there and watched, but they did not participate. *"Moses knew God's ways, but the children of Israel only saw His acts"* (see Ps. 103:7).

Jesus, that day, turned to the crowd of spectators and announced,

> *Unless you eat the flesh of the Son of Man and drink His blood, you have no life in you. Whoever eats My flesh and drinks My blood has eternal life, and I will raise him up on the last day.*
> —JOHN 6:53-55

It says that everyone left Him that day except His disciples (see John 6:66). Everybody walked away because they could not handle what He was saying and showing them regarding the covenant He was making with His people.

You are going to have to partake of Jesus because He is the Bread that came down from Heaven (see John 6:51). We are supposed to eat of Him, and if you do not do this, you cannot have any part in Him. Do you understand that? Many left Jesus that day, and He turned to His disciples when those multitudes left Him and asked, *"Are you going to leave me too?"* They had left everything to follow Jesus and Simon Peter answered, *"Lord, to whom shall we go? You have the words of eternal life"* (see John 6:68).

When with your mouth you affirm your relationship with God by saying that you are committed, that you love Him, and that you will follow Him, you are affirming the covenant. That is what Jesus wanted His disciples to do that night at the table, and that shows how powerful covenant is. Paul talked about communion as being something very sacred (see 1 Cor. 11:23-34). In Heaven, Jesus told me, at that time, people were following Him for the wrong reason. The reason that Jesus spoke about the communion table to the people was to show them that it was going to take a big commitment to follow Him. Yet, many of them could not handle drinking His blood and eating His flesh.

At the Last Supper, when Jesus enacted the first communion at the table, Jesus told me that up until that point, Judas could have repented (see Luke 22:20-22). It was not until Jesus passed Judas the bread, and he ate of it, that immediately satan entered him. Jesus said because Judas did not discern His body and did not consider the other disciples, he ate unworthily, and satan entered him. Then Jesus said to Judas, *"What you do, do quickly"* (John 13:27). Jesus knew there was no repentance because Judas had partaken of the table of the Lord and had not discerned the Lord's body.

Paul told the Corinthians that when they were getting together for the Lord's supper, they were not waiting for everyone to come to eat together as they should (see 1 Cor. 11:20-34). They were treating the Lord's supper in an unworthy manner, as something that was not sacred. Paul said, *"For this reason many are weak and sick among you, and many sleep"* (1 Cor. 11:30). Paul told them that many of them die early because they did not discern the Lord's body.

God wants you to have a relationship with Him, where you take into yourself the Word, which is the Bread from Heaven. God wants you to remember Jesus when you drink of the cup that represents Jesus' blood because Jesus is now your life. You are partaking of Jesus' death, and you are partaking of His life. You are having communion with Him, and you have a covenant relationship with Him.

Your covenant relationship with Christ is so important that God spoke it into existence. God said Jesus was the Lamb that was slain from the foundation of the world (see Rev. 13:8). God told Jesus that He would die, and when that happened, it was a fulfillment of Father God's heart for buying back His family—humanity. When you take communion, you are acknowledging that you have essentially given yourself over to God and that your life is not your own anymore (see Gal. 2:20). And you find yourself only doing what God desires for you to do.

Covenant is a powerful word! Satan fights it so much. God has established His covenant, and it is irrevocable.

> *I have made a covenant with My chosen, I have sworn to My servant David: "Your seed I will establish forever, and build up your throne to all generations." Selah.*
> —PSALM 89:3-4

Even when you want to give up, God will stand there and let you throw a tantrum. He will even let you say that you are going to give up. Then God says, "Whenever you are done, let's go. You have got to get going because you have things to do," and God does not even acknowledge that you quit. It does not affect Him because you have made a covenant with God who is never going to fail, and He is never going to fail you. It is because of that covenant that God is going to stand there, and He is going to stay in there with you even when you feel like you cannot go on.

The covenant is so strong, and it is stronger than you are, so even if you give up, the Lord is still going to stand there. He is going to wait until you realize that He is not quitting you. The Lord is never going to quit on you because He loves you, and He is taking hold of you and not letting you go. That is why satan hates the covenant because God's children are so loved by their Heavenly Father. His sheep are so loved that Jesus would be sent out to leave the ninety-nine sheep to get that one stray sheep. The Lord wants you to invoke the covenant every day and acknowledge Him in all your ways. The Lord is going to lead you into a bright path, and you are going to have a bright future. You are going to finish fine, and you do not have to worry about a thing.

Chapter 10

KINGDOM DOMINION

*So God created man in His own image; in the image of
God He created him; male and female He created them.
Then God blessed them, and God said to them, "Be
fruitful and multiply; fill the earth and subdue it; have
dominion over the fish of the sea, over the birds of the air,
and over every living thing that moves on the earth."*

—GENESIS 1:27

KINGDOM DOMINION IS something that we do not hear a
lot about, and it is another one of those words that satan
fears. Did you know that Jesus spoke about the Kingdom
more than anything else? After Jesus rose from the dead, He had
forty days of ministry. In the book of Acts, it talks about how Jesus
went around teaching for forty days about the Kingdom of God
(see Acts 1:1-3). If you had forty extra days to minister, what subject would you choose? Jesus told me that He chose the Kingdom,
and because of that, Jesus told me that you should focus on the
Kingdom of God more than anything else, and that is what I
am doing.

This power word, *Kingdom dominion*, is not just about Kingdom authority. What would be the difference between having authority and dominion? There is a king, and he has a kingdom, so he rules with authority over a kingdom. Then there is the word *domain*, and it means "a territory." The dominion that you have is in your domain, your territory.

We are ambassadors of Christ, and we have been sent with the same authority that Jesus has. When Jesus sent the seventy disciples out, they were given authority over evil spirits and authority to heal the sick (see Luke 10:1-12). The twelve disciples were sent, and they demonstrated the same ministry that Jesus had (see Mark 6:7-13). Dominion, however, is when you establish and you obtain territory. In a kingdom, you have borders, but in a domain, where you have dominion, that's much stronger.

I realized something when I was with Jesus. He had dominion about Him, and it was more than just authority. When I was around Jesus, I understood that we had backed off using some of these terms. We say that we have authority in Jesus' name, and we drive out demons, but what I saw with Jesus was that He wanted to obtain property. Jesus wanted to own everything, and He needed to do that through the Church, through His Body.

When Jesus died and ascended on high, He gave us authority over serpents and scorpions (see Luke 10:19), but Jesus also told me that He had restored the dominion He had given Adam back to the Body of Christ. God gave dominion over everything to Adam—over the birds, the fish, everything that was on the earth. When God gave dominion, whatever was God's was now under man. It is different than only having authority. Adam essentially owned everything, and everything that Adam said and did was so.

Dominion is different than just driving out devils. It is about obtaining territory—establishing, advancing, and taking ground back from the enemy. You are obtaining real estate for God, and that is dominion. Dominion is not just about authority, and it is one of those words that is slipping away from us. When I was with Jesus, I saw that we were intended to be advancing and establishing continually, and never having to take back land that we had already obtained. It requires a cutting-edge walk with God, where we advance and establish, and we never have to take back that land again.

Most of us have experienced advance, we have experienced the authority, but many have gotten hit hard by the enemy because of it. Once you came at the devil and addressed him, you got hit twice as hard, and you lost ground. The devil tries to convince you that it is better just to leave him alone, and then he will leave you alone, but that is not the case. The devil is never going to leave you alone, and he could care less about your feelings or your future. The devil is a murderer, and he steals, kills, and destroys, and he does not care about you. That is the reason you must have dominion about you and not just authority.

You have to take the land and never give it back to the devil, and once you get this tenacity inside you, you will realize what I am talking about and how important it is. Jesus did not come back, suffer and die, and ascend on high for you to cast out devils. He did this so that you can go into your workplace, into your government, into your school, and everywhere you go, and all of that would belong to you. He wants you to have such an influence that people will start to fall in line with your dominion and your domain, and it will be far beyond your having authority.

The Lord has always instructed me to find out where the stronghold is and take it out. I take out the enemy's communications and take out his front line. I do this by praying in the Spirit, and I start to take on the environment of Heaven. Then when I walk into a situation, it paralyzes the enemy. Those demons cannot do a thing because their communication with each other has stopped. I have seen this happen many times.

I have walked into places where evil things were going on, and all the people turned around and stared at me, and I was silent. I just walked in there, but they were paralyzed and could not operate. The people were so irritated that I was there that they asked me to leave, even though I hadn't said a word to anyone. I merely showed up, but that evidences more than just authority. I believe that is dominion because, with dominion, the devil cannot operate when you are around.

ESTABLISHING GOD'S KINGDOM

Did you know that your job is not your provision? It's not; it's your mission. You are being sent into a place to take it over spiritually. You are sent there, so your job is not your provision. Many people will say, "Well, I do need that paycheck." You do not understand dominion. Dominion is your going in and establishing God's Kingdom in that area. God will then provide for you in many ways, and not just through your job.

I worked for a company for thirty years, but I have all kinds of other income coming in through other supernatural avenues. My job was my mission field, and I saw such fruit in my job through the ministry to people right there in the marketplace, right there in my job. I had people who came to me, and I did not have to go to another country, and I did not have to have an established ministry. I was sent by God to the people I came in contact with while on the job. I was sent there to make a difference, and every day I would pray in the Spirit. What I was doing was taking property, and the people would get around me, and they would start to break and cry.

I noticed that whenever I met someone new at work, for two days straight, they would resist me, and then they would start to confront me. I would pray, and those devils would lose the stronghold on that person because I kept loving them no matter what. Suddenly, I could see in their eyes that the devils were gone, and then I would say, "You need to give your life to Jesus. Let me pray for you right now." I would even have words of knowledge for them, and they were not even saved.

Can you imagine that the Spirit of God wants us to use the gifts of the Spirit on the people of the world? Jesus did just that for the woman at the well (see John 4:7-25). Jesus had a word of knowledge for this Samaritan woman, and she perceived that He was a prophet, but she still did not discern who Jesus was. Jesus was witnessing to this woman, and He explained that if she had known who she was talking to, she would have asked for water from Him, and she would never thirst again. That is what you must do in the marketplace, and when you step out, God will allow you to minister to people by His Spirit.

When I was in Heaven, and I was sent back, I was shown the first twelve to fifteen people who I was sent back for, and I knew each one of them by face. It took me twenty years to meet all of them. I remember one girl whom I met because I had seen her in a line-up in Heaven before I was sent back. Eventually, I met all of these people in succession. When I sat with her and started talking to her, I realized she was one of those people from the line in Heaven. When I began to talk with her, she started to weep, and she gave her life to the Lord right there.

I was sent back from the dead for a person who was not even saved yet. When I ministered to her, she was telling all the crew members, "I'm a Christian now because of this man, and there's no way he could have known what he told me." I did not know how I knew because I was only told by the Lord that I would meet these people, and I was to minister to them, and Jesus would reroute their lives.

Taking Back God's Property

Kingdom dominion has to do with you taking back what was once God's. Satan thinks that he has this world wrapped up for his own, and he is the god of this world, but God wants it back. God is going to get it back because He has given the keys of the Kingdom to the Body of Christ, the Church, and the gates of hell are not going to *"prevail against it."*

> *And I also say to you that you are Peter, and on this rock I will build My church, and the gates of Hades shall not prevail against it. And I will give you the keys of the kingdom of heaven, and whatever you bind on earth will be bound in heaven, and whatever you loose on earth will be loosed in heaven.*
>
> —Matthew 16:18-19

We are the Body of Christ, we are the Church of the living God, and we have been sent into this world to not just witness, but we are sent to take it back.

We are to have dominion and take back property for God, and that means souls. God says that if we ask of Him, He will give us the nations as our inheritance.

> *Ask of Me, and I will give You the nations for Your inheritance, and the ends of the earth for Your possession.*
>
> —PSALM 2:8

We are worried about asking for too much, and God wants to give us nations. People, the souls of men, are the most valuable thing on this earth. God wants us to go into the marketplaces and start to see our jobs as our mission field. We have been sent by God to take back what satan stole, and that is God's family.

In Heaven, Jesus told me that every person who has ever lived on this earth has a book written about them in Heaven (see Ps. 139:16 TPT). Jesus told me that it is written as though they are coming there, only many do not come. Jesus said. "We write their books before they are born as though they are coming to Heaven. Angels are assigned to every human being on the earth, whether they are saved or not saved." I was sitting there thinking, *I never knew this.*

Jesus said, "Their angels keep bringing people around to a decision to give their life to God. If they do not, then their angels start the cycle over again, and they will send people to help them."

The angels are instructed to bring people to a decision so that their books can start to be lived out and activated in their lives. It was amazing to me. Jesus told me that no human being was ever destined to go to hell, ever! He said hell was made for the devil and his angels, but not for man (see Matt. 25:41). I saw all of these books up there that tell beautiful stories of people's destinies.

Jesus told me that some of these books have not even seen their first page fulfilled because the people have been so resistant. They have not accepted God as their Creator, and they have not acknowledged Jesus Christ. Some of them do not even know anything about Jesus Christ. God's angels are instructed to help position people in a place where a believer can come in and tell them about Jesus.

It is all part of God's dominion, and the angels are helping to take back God's family. When we pray, we should be asking God for the nations and asking to be sent. You do not have to be sent to another country, just sent to a marketplace where you can witness to people. You can be a witness and tell people about Jesus Christ wherever you go.

I saw that the Kingdom of God was advancing at an alarming rate. No matter where I went, even if I walked down the aisles of the plane serving people, they would start shaking or crying, or they would start laughing, and they were not even saved. I would ask them, "What is going on with you? Why are you laughing?"

They would say, "I don't know. Every time you walk by, something hits us, and we start laughing."

One lady was crying, and I asked her, "Why are you crying?"

She said, "I don't know. There is something on you, and every time you walk down the aisle, it comes over me."

I said, "Well, you know, I died." Now I have a tray of drinks in my hands, and I am telling people that I died, and I saw Jesus. They always asked me what Jesus looked like, and I would tell them, and then I would say, "You know, there's a wonderful book written about each one of you in Heaven."

People do not know about their books written in Heaven, and I was sent back to tell people about them. They would start crying and ask me to tell them more. Before I knew it, I would have a whole section of the airplane asking me questions like it was a Q & A session. I was supposed to be doing my job, but the point is that God wants to take back what is His, and He is going to do it through you. Kingdom dominion has to be part of our vocabulary. Satan does not want you to go this extra step and acquire property from him and take it back for God.

Here is a verse that contains your assignment.

> *If anyone speaks, let him speak as the oracles of God. If anyone ministers, let him do it as with the ability which God supplies, that in all things God may be glorified through Jesus Christ, to whom belong the glory and the dominion forever and ever. Amen.*
> —1 PETER 4:11

If you minister, you do it with the ability that God supplies. If you speak, you speak as though you are speaking the very words or oracles of God. That means you do not have to go out and witness, you are a witness wherever you go because God is with you. When God starts to take back His property through you, that is dominion, and that is why you have the job you have.

Did you know that everything that you are going through right now at your job is because you are on satan's property? And satan does not want you there. What is going on at your job is spiritual warfare, because it is the property of God being taken back from the devil, and the devil wants to silence you. He does not want you at your job because you are going to manifest the glory of God.

When you go out of your house and go to work or anywhere else, even shopping, the devil does not want you in there. He doesn't want you in the store. He does not want you at work, and he certainly does not want you talking to anybody about the Lord. You are going to experience rejection, and you are going to have a fight on your hands when you go places because satan knows that you have come to take back God's property.

PUSHING BACK DARKNESS

I encounter warfare at work all the time because these demons that are in people know they are about to lose that person if I talk to them. The devil will try to fight you with rejection because he knows that he is about to lose the person that he has to the Kingdom of God. If you tell them about Jesus, there is nothing satan can do, and he will have to leave. Everywhere you go, you encounter people, but you are also encountering the devils that *have* those people, and you are pushing back the kingdom of darkness everywhere you go.

That is why Peter says, when you talk, you should be talking as though yours is the very voice of God. When you minister, you should be doing it only from the ability that God supplies through the Spirit. We should be using the gifts of the Spirit, like the one that Jesus used with the woman at the well, which was the word of knowledge. Jesus told her things that there was no way He could have known, like how many ex-husbands she had and her current situation, apart from the gift of knowledge.

Through the gift of knowledge, the Samaritan woman realized that Jesus was a prophet. However, Jesus was even more than that, and He kept pushing her further and further toward the truth about herself and then her need. Jesus was emphasizing that He could supply the perfect scenario for her life if she would just rely solely on Him, but she did not discern Jesus as the Messiah.

When you get into a situation, remember that the devils know that you are sent to take back something for God. Remember that when you speak, you speak from your spirit because the devils cannot withstand when God speaks through you, and they cannot stop it. Place yourself in a situation where God can use you, and you can take back God's property. Remember that wherever the Spirit of the Lord is, there is freedom (see 2 Cor. 3:17). It is this freedom that is going to knock the devil right between the eyes, and it is going to push him out. You are going to start to feel that people will be set free just by you standing there and talking to them.

DISARMING THE DEVIL

There is a simplicity to the Kingdom of God, as the simplicity of a child. Jesus said,

> *Assuredly, I say to you, whoever does not receive the kingdom of God as a little child will by no means enter it.*
> —LUKE 18:17

You have to receive the Kingdom, the dominion, and the domain of God as a child. Jesus also said, *"Therefore be as shrewd as snakes and as innocent as doves"* (Matt. 10:16 NIV). I asked Jesus about this verse because I thought that it did not make a lot of sense to me in light of Luke 18:17. Jesus explained it to me this way, "Kevin, a dove trusts because it is innocent, and so you stay as innocent as a child." Then Jesus said, "A snake always rises up to protect himself, but he does not strike right away." If you notice when you come upon a snake, a snake will try to get away, but then at a certain point, he will come up to defend himself. What the Lord is saying is always be ready, ready to be in defense of what God is doing in a situation.

Anytime that I am attacked verbally, I wait to see what God wants me to do in that situation. Sometimes, a devil may be talking through a person and cause them to get angry. God can use you to disarm a person by soft words of love or being compassionate toward them, and it will disarm the devil. Do you understand how a serpent is shrewd? He is always in a position to defend himself, but he doesn't strike right away, and even a rattlesnake will warn you before he strikes. That is how you are to be in the Kingdom.

You are going to disarm the devil by love. However, you must always be ready, just like a serpent is shrewd and always ready to protect himself. You are not a doormat, you are bold, and you walk in love. You do not allow people to take advantage of you. You always have a word and are ready for God to speak through you.

In certain situations, especially when I was in authority at my job, I would have to say things and do things that I did not want to do, but I had to because I was in charge. I would try to talk to people and reason with them, and sometimes they would start to get belligerent or rebellious with me. Then I would say, "What has gotten into you that you are acting like this. You know, I have nothing against you, but this is your job, and it is what you were told to do." All of a sudden, you could see that they were asking themselves, *What is wrong with me?* I started to disarm them and talk them out of what was happening to them because they had been taken over by the devil.

There may come a time when you will feel persecuted because you are going into the devil's kingdom, being sent in, and you will be mistreated. However, you are to rejoice when this happens.

> *Rejoice and be exceedingly glad, for great is your reward in heaven, for so they persecuted the prophets who were before you.*
> —MATTHEW 5:12

I have been attacked for being a Christian because I stood up for what was right, and the Lord told me, "Great is your reward because you have been persecuted for My sake." There have been many times when I have come home from work and wondered, *What just happened?*

The Lord has said to me in response, "It is just warfare, and you are going to receive a reward for that."

Your reward is great because you are going in and taking back what God has destined for you to take back for Him. Jesus said,

> *And everyone who has left houses or brothers or sisters or father or mother or wife or children or lands, for My name's sake, shall receive a hundredfold, and inherit eternal life.*
> —MATTHEW 19:29

Even if you feel like you have lost everything and have left everything, this verse promises you that you will receive a hundredfold in this life and eternal life as well. Be encouraged to walk in Kingdom dominion.

Chapter 11

THE BLOOD OF JESUS

*Therefore, brethren, having boldness to
enter the Holiest by the blood of Jesus.*
—HEBREWS 10:19

D O YOU INVOKE the blood of Jesus into your life every day?
That is one thing that satan hopes you never do because it
paralyzes him. When God does something, He does it for the
benefit of man. He loves humanity, and He created man, and we
are the desire of His heart.

When God planned redemption, He planned it for you and me
so that we can live and walk in victory in this life. We are down
here on this earth, and God could have planned that we were taken
out of this world as soon as we were born again. It could have been
that when we became born again, suddenly, we would go straight
to Heaven, but that was not God's plan. God's plan is for us to stay
here because He wants to be glorified through us. He wants to
show the enemy how powerful He is through our lives. We need

to implement into our lives what God has done for us for the world to see.

Everything that God does is for humanity. God has no needs in Himself, but He does desire fellowship with us, and He has restored that fellowship through Jesus Christ.

The *blood of Jesus* is a very powerful word, and if you have noticed, the blood of Jesus is not mentioned much anymore. The crucifixion, the blood of Jesus, and all that happened with Jesus are not very popular, and they have even become offensive to people.

People will go and see violent movies, and that's acceptable to them, but they do not want to go to church and hear about Jesus' blood and hear about the crucifixion. A lot of the religious churches will not present Jesus as the crucified Savior, and they will not even talk about the blood of Jesus. I saw in Heaven that this was a ploy of the enemy to take power out of our vocabulary by taking the name of Jesus out and taking the blood of Jesus out.

The blood is a very powerful word, and here in Leviticus, it tells us that life is in the blood.

> *For the life of the flesh is in the blood, and I have given it to you upon the altar to make atonement for your souls; for it is the blood that makes atonement for the soul.*
>
> —LEVITICUS 17:11

What is it about the blood? The blood has a voice. When Cain killed Abel, God asked Cain where Abel was, and he told God that he did not know (see Gen. 4:8-13). Then God said, *"The voice of your brother's blood cries out to Me from the ground"* (Gen. 4:10).

The voice of the blood of Abel was calling out to God because the blood has a voice.

Jesus died, and His blood speaks. When Jesus' blood is offered at the mercy seat in Heaven, the Father looks down and sees that blood, and He looks past what we have done. If we acknowledge God's Son in our lives, God looks past our condition, and our sins are completely cleansed. This is very powerful.

The enemy does not want us to invoke the blood of Jesus because there is a blood covenant. If you encounter someone who has demons, begin talking about the blood of Jesus, and you will see how important the blood is. I have had demons, one by one, as they came out of someone, begging me not to mention the blood because it had defeated them, and they knew it. It is very important that you use the blood of Jesus every day in your vocabulary and your life.

THE BLOODLINE

My wife and I plead the blood of Jesus over us all the time, especially when we get into a car or on an airplane. Any time where we are handing ourselves over to someone else's care, we plead the blood. The reason we do that is Jesus' blood is a line that satan cannot cross.

The demons will try to infiltrate your situation, and they will even try to infiltrate you. These demons are constantly trying to get into your soul or your *mind, will,* and *emotions*. When you are born again, you are a new creature in Christ. Your spirit man becomes new, and you are filled with the Spirit of God, but your mind, will, and emotions are a different part of you; as we've discovered, they are the soulish part of you.

The enemy of your soul, satan, will try to infiltrate your mind by suggesting things to you to see if you will consider thinking about them. He tries to convince you by constantly bombarding you with thoughts and feelings, causing your perceptions to shift into an altered reality. To get a much-needed dose of reality, we need the Holy Spirit to come upon us in our lives. We need the Word of God, but we also need the blood of Jesus to protect us. If you want to discourage demons from entering into any part of your life, just keep pleading the blood of Jesus over yourself because they cannot cross the bloodline.

I know a pastor who was told by the Lord to have the elders pray over each wall in the sanctuary of the church and plead the blood of Jesus on the walls. The pastor and the elders did as the Holy Spirit requested, but the pastor did not understand at the time why God had them do this. A few weeks later, he was preaching, and there were a couple of witches who had come into the service, and they were seated toward the back of the sanctuary. After the service, they left. The pastor did not know that they were witches at the time.

At the next service, a warlock who was the head of the witches' coven and the head priest for that satanic cult came and sat in the service. He was there because the witches who went before him had not been able to do anything to disrupt the service. The demons had told the warlock that they were unable to penetrate and told him that they could not get into the building because of Jesus' blood on the walls. The warlock came to the church to get inside the building to operate those evil spirits from within, but God had another plan.

Before the end of the service, the warlock went up to the altar and was delivered of all the demons in him and got saved. After he was saved, he got up before the pastor and the congregation. He gave this testimony, "I have been trying to penetrate this church, and the demons would come back and say, 'We can't get in there because he pled the blood of Jesus on the walls.'"

You can see that the blood of Jesus is very, very effective, and demons understand the blood because the life is in the blood.

Jesus' blood was untainted. It was perfect. There was no genetic flaw in His body or His blood. If you look at the lineage of Jesus, He was perfect in His generations, and that is why all those lineages are in the Bible—to testify of Jesus' perfection.

The seed of the serpent tried to infiltrate human blood and genetics to alter the perfect Lamb that was to come from a woman's womb. That is why we see all of Mary's lineage, which shows that Mary was a human being, and she was not part of a hybrid race.

God had to destroy the earth through the flood because the serpent's seed was getting in and creating a hybrid race. That would have made a human being only part human, which would mean that it would be a blemished lamb that was born in Mary's womb. The hybrid race on the earth was trying to infiltrate the genetic line of the human race.

God knew that satan was trying to do this so that when Jesus died on the cross, He would not have been fully human and would not have been the perfect sacrifice. Satan was ready to go to God and say, "I got you. Jesus is imperfectly human because I infiltrated the bloodline." It did not work because God kept that lineage completely free of any reptilian or Nephilim or any kind of hybrid race that was trying to infiltrate.

That is why it was required to have a spotless lamb for the sacrifice in the Old Testament. It was a type and shadow of Jesus being the perfect Lamb without spot or blemish. That meant that Jesus' bloodline was perfect, and He was a perfect human being. This was so important because lucifer tried to infiltrate the human race, and he lost; Jesus triumphed over him in the cross.

> *And He has taken it out of the way, having nailed it to the cross. Having disarmed principalities and powers, He made a public spectacle of them, triumphing over them in it.*
>
> —Colossians 2:14b-15

Jesus came as a perfect human being, and He died, and it was a perfect sacrifice, and because of that, we can now invoke the blood of Jesus. Besides the name of Jesus, the blood of Jesus is one of the strongest weapons we have against the enemy.

Jesus has already declared that the devil is defeated. Not only did Jesus triumph over satan on the cross, but then Jesus said that *we* are more than conquerors through Him who loved us (see Rom. 8:37).

On the cross, Jesus defeated the devil, and then He handed the enforcement of the devil's defeat over to us, and now we inherited it so that nothing can separate us from God.

> *For I am persuaded that neither death nor life, nor angels nor principalities nor powers, nor things present*

nor things to come, nor height nor depth, nor any other created thing, shall be able to separate us from the love of God which is in Christ Jesus our Lord.

—ROMANS 8:38-39

Jesus Christ has been crucified, and His blood has been shed. Now we have the perfect scenario where, through the blood, we can continue to enforce this defeat of satan.

THE BLOOD'S AUTHORITY

Are you tired of being beaten up? If you are tired and done with fighting the devil, then God says you are ready. You are ready to go on to your next phase. It is time to turn the tables on the enemy in your life. It is time to make the enemy of your soul the victim. It is time to make him pay, scream, and feel pain. The demons felt this way when they encountered Jesus.

Jesus would get out of a boat, and demons would start screaming at Him, and they would say, *"Have you come here to torment us before the time?"* (Matt. 8:29). The demons begged Jesus, saying, *"If You cast us out, permit us to go into the herd of swine"* (Matt. 8:31). The demons did not want to be sent out of the area, and they wanted to negotiate with Jesus. They knew that they were going to have to leave, and they were tormented and terrified of Jesus. Why? Because Jesus was sent to defeat them, and He was the Son of God.

Jesus said that He came as the Son of Man and that He was transferring His works and His ministry to us. In John 14:12 Jesus says, *"Most assuredly, I say to you, he who believes in Me, the works that I do he will do also; and greater works than these he will do."* So, now *you* are going to cast out devils. *You* are going to heal the sick.

You are going to raise the dead. Some people argue about doing the works of Jesus, and they say that it is not for today, but Jesus already said that we can do His works and greater works than He did. We have not even gotten to the greater works, and we are arguing about the works.

Through the blood of Jesus, we have received authority, and we have received leverage in the Spirit to do these works because of the blood. Not only were we made perfect through the blood of Jesus, but we were also made righteous and holy, and we are set apart by the blood. Furthermore, the blood of Jesus is part of warfare in obtaining territory and property for God.

> *Behold, I give you the authority to trample on serpents*
> *and scorpions, and over all the power of the enemy, and*
> *nothing shall by any means hurt you.*
> —LUKE 10:19

There are demonic spirits that are hovering over cities, and they rule over those cities. Disembodied spirits are walking around us as devils that are bound to earth. They are trying to manipulate people to do their will. There is a ruling class of spirits that are in the heavenly realms above cities. These spirits are the serpents and scorpions that Jesus talked about in Luke 10:19.

Jesus said He has given us the authority to trample on these earthbound spirits of serpents and scorpions. We are to cast them out, and we are to drive them out because Jesus came to destroy those works and has given us the authority to accomplish it. There are other levels of spirits besides these that Paul lists in Ephesians 6:10-19. Some of these spirits have to be taken care of through the corporate body, and some of these only God can take care of for us.

Our focus and authority are on the earthbound devils that are serpents and scorpions, and they crawl along the ground. Jesus said you are to trample on them, and you will have authority over them to drive them out. When Jesus would show up, demons recognized Him as the Son of God, and they begged Him not to do the things that He could do to them. For us now, through the blood of Jesus, we can call upon the blood and the blood covenant, and these demons must listen to us just as though we were Jesus because His blood has defeated them.

You must remember that satan is limited against you, and you must submit to God and resist the devil. *"And he will flee from you,"* James 4:7 tells us. The word *resist* used here is the same word in Greek that means to *push back*. If a police officer is trying to detain you, and he is arresting you, and you push back, and you fight him, then you will get another charge against you for resisting arrest. That is the same word used here; you are to *push* satan back. If you resist the devil and push him back, he is going to flee from you, but you have to be submitted to God. Why? It is because God is your authority, and when you are submitted to authority, you also walk in authority.

STANDING UP AGAINST THE DEVIL

I am a representative of Jesus Christ on this earth, and so are you. If you are submitted to God, the devil knows it. Then when you resist him and you push him back, he flees. Remember, the word *resist* here does not mean standing there with your arms folded, waiting for God to do something. It means to push back! The Lord told me, "Kevin, when the devil hits you, you hit him back twice, so hard and so fast that he does not even know what happened."

I found out that you can, very quickly, make satan and his demons victims. If you get hit by the devil, immediately hit him back twice as hard. One way to do that is to sow something to God. If you have to help someone else, or go to your church and vacuum the carpet, do something to get back at the devil right away. Start praying in tongues and quoting the Word of God; hit him back really hard and tell the devil he is going to pay now.

If you keep doing this, after a while, the devils begin to know who you are. They know that you are going to hit back twice as hard, and they will start to back off. You never have to back off from the devil because you will have him afraid of you by hitting him back twice. The devil's eyes will be as big as saucers, and he will be so scared because he is not used to having Christians doing that. He is not used to people pushing him back. Now when he hits me, I say, "That's all you got? You have got to be kidding me." I mock the devil.

Some people say, "I wouldn't do that because, you know, he's just going to come after you more." No, the blood of Jesus is effective, the name of Jesus is effective, and the Lord is standing with you! The Lord is always with you, and if you acknowledge Him in all your ways, He is going to direct your paths (see Prov. 3:6).

The devil is the victim here, not you, and you have to establish your authority. The blood of Jesus has cleansed you from all your sin, and you are established in the Kingdom through the covenant (see 1 John 1:7). You have the authority to hit the devil back hard.

The devil overplays his hand all the time. What happens is that after he has hit you so much, you start to get pushed into the glory because you begin to cry out to God. You become like King David, who always knew where to go when he got into trouble. He would run to God and chase after Him. King David would go into the tabernacle, worship, cry out to God, and repent of his sins. King Saul did not know to repent, and he even went to a witch to inquire about his future. King David would have never done something like that. King David always went to God; he ran to God, and that is what you must do.

Spiritual warfare is not what you might think. It's not wrestling with demons. You are not going to go and have a wrestling match with a devil because it is not going to last that long. If you establish your authority by knowing that you have a blood covenant, then the devil will leave you alone because he gets beat up every time you mention the blood.

Once I was casting demons out of someone, and there were eight of them inside the man. The first seven were screaming at the top of their lungs because I started to mention the blood of Jesus, and they said, "Don't talk about the blood." They told me that the blood was very powerful and it defeated them, and I said, "Well, thanks for letting me know." I started to talk about the blood more, and I got a friend who was there to start preaching about the blood. All of the demons were screaming out of this guy because they were paralyzed and being tormented by the blood. Then suddenly, they all left because Jesus' blood had defeated them.

Once you hear the gospel, you get this feeling that you are not a victim anymore. When you hear the true Word of God, you realize that Jesus defeated satan, and He transferred that authority to you. You begin to understand that it is time to arrest the devil. We do not wrestle against flesh and blood, but against these evil spirits. What if you established your authority and the demons started to know that you know what you are doing? They would not mess with you anymore because they would get beat up.

You should have heard the screams the different times that I have cast out devils, and how they were tormented. They did not want to have to deal with me. Why? Because they knew that I had merged with God's heart, and I knew my authority. I knew the power of the blood of Jesus.

Ephesians 6:12 tells us,

> *For we do not wrestle against flesh and blood, but against principalities, against powers, against the rulers of the darkness of this age, against spiritual hosts of wickedness in the heavenly places.*

There are so many different levels of these rebellious spirits, and there are different types. Some of them are very powerful, and the whole church has to come against them. You need the Body of Christ to pray together because you have to come against a whole city or country. These are things that are left for the angels to war against, and the Body of Christ needs to pray and intercede. The lower class, earthbound spirits, the ones that possess human beings, are the ones that Jesus gave us authority over. All of the other levels are for corporate prayer, for intercessors to pray and for the angels of God to war against them. Do not engage with certain classes of them.

You have the authority to cast out the earthbound ones, and then, corporately, you come against the ones that are over your city. Then you pray and intercede, and you let the angels war against those higher levels. I know it might be hard for some of you to accept, but Jesus gave us authority over serpents and scorpions, and the way that we deal with the devil is we cast him out. The devils that are in people, we cast them out, but the bigger ones we use the corporate setting, the church. The gates of hell cannot prevail against the Church (see Matt. 16:18).

When you are dealing with evil spirits, you must realize that people who are not saved, not born again in their spirit and not redeemed, have no power to resist the devil. Unsaved people cannot resist the devil. In fact, the apostle Paul said, when we were unsaved, we *"walked according to the course of this world, according to the prince of the power of the air"* (Eph. 2:2).

You could be standing there, and you could watch a demon go into a person just to get at you, and I see it all the time. I have watched demons come flying through airports and come into a person that is right ahead of me. They immediately look at me and walk right into me to knock me over. These people do not even know what they are doing because they are walking according to the course of this world and are not redeemed. The prince of the power of the air can enter any of those people at will. I am telling you that the blood is the only thing that you have to protect yourself when you encounter these things. The unsaved have no resistance to the prince of the power of the air because they don't have the blood of Jesus in their lives. They have no authority over the devil because they are the sons of disobedience, as Paul also said in Ephesians 2:2.

In First Peter 1:2, Peter said, *"The elect according to the foreknowledge of God the Father, in the sanctification of the Spirit, for obedience and sprinkling of the blood of Jesus Christ."* God had already told Jesus that He was going to redeem mankind. The Holy Trinity had made this plan for man before man was even created. Peter was talking about the elect and the fact that everyone was written down to be in the Lamb's Book of life. We were not written in when we were born again because we were already written in before we were created. Before we were born again, we were already ordained to be born again before the foundation of the world. You can be blotted out of the Book of Life, but you do not get your name written in the Lamb's Book of Life at the moment you are born again (see Ps. 69:28).

God had already ordained that all of mankind be saved and no one go to hell, yet we have people going to hell because of their free will. The blood of Jesus, His Son, cleanses us from all sin (see 1 John 1:7). That means that every human being has been bought, and there is no reason for anyone to go to hell. The blood of Jesus is so powerful that it bought every person back to God, the Father.

Chapter 12

RESURRECTION POWER

*But if the Spirit of Him who raised Jesus from
the dead dwells in you, He who raised Christ
from the dead will also give life to your mortal
bodies through His Spirit who dwells in you.*

—ROMANS 8:11

RESURRECTION IS ANOTHER word that is not being mentioned enough. Every person who is born again of the Spirit should be acknowledging the resurrection because the same power that rose Jesus from the dead is dwelling in them. Jesus told me that the Holy Spirit was waiting to resurrect Him, and Jesus started to choke up when He told me this. He said, "Kevin, I had to relinquish my communication with the Father, and the Holy Spirit did not go with Me to the belly of the earth." He said, "I had to go to the deepest part of hell where the vilest person would go, and I had to go down there to redeem that place" (see 1 Pet. 3:18-20).

Jesus said, "It did not just end at the cross." He said, "I spent hours down there in the belly of the earth, and I had no communication or presence at all with the Father." Jesus then said, "I stayed down there until the Father gave the command for Me to come out of the belly of the earth. The Holy Spirit was waiting for the Father to give the Word, and then I came forth in resurrection power." Jesus started to cry when He said, "Kevin, while I was down there, I had no feeling at all of the Father. I was completely abandoned to hell."

While Jesus was down in hell, He told me that He rehearsed Psalm 16 over and over again for those few days that He was there. He said, "The Spirit of God had David write that psalm for Me, and I rehearsed it in hell." Then Jesus quoted parts of Psalm 16, *"My body will not see destruction. You are going to show me the path of life and lead me out. I set the Lord always before Me, and because He is at my right hand, I shall not be shaken"* (see vv. 8-11).

Jesus said that when the Father gave the command, and He rose from the dead, an enormous surge of the power of God came down there to that holding area in hell. He said that lucifer was down there, and demons were standing around. Jesus said that lucifer said to Him, "You should have taken the deal that I gave you in the desert. You could have had everything, and now You've blown it, and I've got You."

Jesus said everything was against Him down there, and He was abandoned, but it says in Psalm 16:10, *"For You will not leave my soul"* in hell. That is what Jesus rehearsed. All that He had was the Word of God. He said, "Kevin, when you are in your deepest, hardest times, rehearse the Word of God and reach down deep within you because I have paved a way. I cleared that area so that every person can have a place where they can abide in God. In the deepest, darkest pit they might find themselves in, My resurrection power can come."

Whatever you are going through right now, Jesus has already gone to that place, and He has already suffered for you in that place. He has felt abandoned, and He has been rejected. Jesus has had satan tell Him, "You should have served me because You could have had all these kingdoms, and now You are here, and You blew it." You might feel like you are in a pit right now, you have blown it, and there is no way out.

Jesus told me to tell this to everyone. He said, "I went to the deepest, darkest vilest place in hell, and I redeemed it back, and I blew that place wide open." He told me that it ignited down there, and the demons are still talking today about what happened there because they thought they had Him. Then Jesus took captivity captive, and He led a whole bunch of people out with Him (see Eph. 4:8-9).

When Jesus went to Abraham's bosom (see Luke 16:22-23), He preached redemption to those spirits of every person of faith from the Old Testament. Then Jesus brought them out with Him, and they ascended on high to Heaven (see Eph. 4:10). Everything that Jesus did was all done in the unseen world. The apostle Paul was caught up by God, and he wrote about what he saw from behind the veil, for he had seen all of these things.

I am not as great as the apostle Paul, but I saw that what we have here is resurrection power, and it is vibrating inside us. We do not tap into this power enough, but it says, *"The Spirit of Him who raised Jesus from the dead dwells in you, He who raised Christ from the dead will also give life to your mortal bodies"* (Rom. 8:11).

There is a power that will even bleed over into our bodies if we tap into it.

THE LAW OF THE SPIRIT OF LIFE[1]

There was a man named John G. Lake who received a revelation about Romans 8:2—*"For the law of the Spirit of life in Christ Jesus has made me free from the law of sin and death."* In fact, he saw that the law of the Spirit of life in Christ Jesus was working in his body during the plague in Africa.

John G. Lake had become a missionary and had decided to go to where the plague had broken out. So, he went down into Africa in 1908, and he started laying hands on people. The plague was especially virulent there, and if it got on you, you would come down with the plague. Wherever John went, he would lay hands on people, and he would never catch the disease.

The doctors and the scientists of that day could not understand how this man of God never came down with the plague. The scientists reasoned that if they could make a serum from John's blood, then they could develop a cure. John told them, no, it wasn't something that could be found in medicine. He said that it was the law of the Spirit of life that was operating in him, and that was what was killing the disease.

John told the doctors to put the plague germ onto his hand, and they did, and then they put his hand under a microscope. As soon as the disease touched his hand, it died because he had a revelation of the Spirit of life that rose Jesus from the dead, and that dwelled in his body.

After five years in Africa, John G. Lake returned to Spokane, Washington, and he established healing rooms there. The rule was that people could come for thirty days only and no longer than that. Sick people would check in, but no one ever stayed for more than fifteen days because everyone was healed. So many people were healed in that city that they had to close down two of the three hospitals, and it became the healthiest city in the United States. The mayor of the town gave John the key to the city—all because he had a revelation of the knowledge of this verse.

What have we not discerned about the resurrection power?

There is power in our spirit that comes out of our mouth, and our words are ignited with power. Proverbs 18:21 affirms that *"death and life are in the power of the tongue."* Not only do you have the power of God in your spirit that comes out into your body, but then your words can be ignited with the power of God as well. When I was on the other side, I saw that demons tremble when people who know they are walking in the power of the resurrection walk into a room and those demons are in there. When they speak, it vibrates, and their voice is paralyzing to devils.

Your words have power, and there is power in your tongue, so you need to speak from your spirit because it will paralyze devils. As you are walking in this resurrection life, you need to be mindful of this all the time. I have seen one person raised from the dead, and I did not even know that I was going to raise him from the dead.

I was praying over him because he had died on a flight that I was working on, and he had no pulse and no respiration at all. I could not pronounce this man dead because I am not a medical doctor. I asked his wife if she was a Christian and if she was a believer, and she said she was. When she said that, it permitted me to pray over the man who, at this point, had been dead for several minutes. He had fallen asleep on the plane and died, and he had turned gray and cold. I put my hand on him, and instead of just praying over him, out of my mouth came, "Come back in the name of Jesus!" He suddenly came back, and He got up and sat back in his chair. When we landed, instead of being carried out on a stretcher, he got up and walked off the plane.

I had to think about this because what was inside me wanted to come out. That resurrection power that dwelled in me and that is always available through the Holy Spirit, was there and willing because of my words. The power came because I said, "Come back in the name of Jesus." We cannot be afraid to tap into the resurrection power.

Jesus said you can raise the dead, heal the sick, and cast out devils, all in the same sentence (see Matt. 10:7-8). So, what is harder? Is it harder to cast out a devil than it is to heal the sick? Everyone is afraid to raise the dead, but Jesus said there was no difference. Jesus said that you are going to do all these things, *"And these signs will follow those who believe"* (see Mark 16:17-18). We have to *choose* to believe in the resurrection power.

In Heaven, I was shown my resurrection body, the one that I am going to get back on the day of the resurrection. There is going to be a day after Jesus has returned that we will be given our resurrection bodies (see Phil. 3:20-21). These will be our new bodies, our heavenly bodies that will rule and reign with Jesus in the next age, and there is going to be a thousand-year reign with Him (see Rev. 20:6).

I was outside of my body in the operating room as I died on the operating table during surgery. As I stood there looking down at my body, Jesus showed me my body being transformed on the table while I was dead. I saw myself transfigured right before my eyes into my heavenly body. I was standing next to Jesus, and I had on a robe of righteousness, and I was in my spirit. As I watched my physical body being transfigured on the table, I suddenly realized that this was how you get your body back.

Do not ask me how God does it, because it does not matter. Even if your body is in the grave, you will still come out. You will get your body back, but it will be glorified, resurrected, and very powerful. I have to tell you that I had to look away because I was perfect, and I saw that God had made man perfect. I know what Adam and Eve looked like because I saw the image of God in myself.

Inside of your body right now is the real you, and it is your spirit man, your heart. It is the new creation that is in Christ Jesus that will never pass away. Old things are gone, and God has made you new on the inside (see 2 Cor. 5:17). If you saw what you looked like, you would never doubt another day, and you would not be fearful ever again because God has made you beautiful through the resurrection.

CONFORMED TO CHRIST

The apostle Paul wrote to the Philippians about wanting to know Jesus, the power of Jesus' resurrection, and also the sufferings of His death.

> *That I may know Him and the power of His resurrection, and the fellowship of His sufferings, being conformed to His death.*
> —PHILIPPIANS 3:10

You can see that the crucified life is the first thing you do. Jesus said to me, "Tell My people that they are always praying for resurrection power because they want to experience My power, but none of them want to die to self. The crucified life has to come back before you can have resurrection."

Be mindful that we also suffer with Jesus, being conformed to His death. Jesus said that because people hated Him, they are going to hate you also (see John 15:18-25). You are going to be persecuted for being a Christian. The devil thinks you are trespassing because you are on the earth, and he wants to rid the earth of Christians. We are down here, irritating him all the time, which is kind of fun because we can go out and just irritate those devils.

You can go out for a cup of coffee and irritate devils all day. It is kind of exciting after you finally see that you are walking in resurrection power, and it is no match for satan. In your life, you are going to suffer, and because of that, great is your reward. You will receive a reward for that in Heaven, and you are going to encounter resurrection. Remember that you have been bought with a price, God owns you now, and your body is not your own. Your body is a temple of the Holy Spirit (see 1 Cor. 6:19), and inside you is resurrection power.

Even though you will die physically, you never cease to exist, and you will live forever. When you are born again, and you believe in Jesus Christ, then you have eternal life, and you will never cease to exist.

Jesus said to her, "I am the resurrection and the life. He who believes in Me, though he may die, he shall live."
—John 11:25

Your physical death is actually a promotion. When I died, I did not even know how I died, and I was never told until I came back, and I found out what happened to me. Jesus just told me that I had died, but I had not felt any pain, and I was being celebrated. I was being promoted because I had died, and I was going on to eternal life. Then Jesus informed me that I was coming back. I came back with this knowledge that we need to be mindful and use the word *resurrection* often because it immobilizes satan, and he cannot compete against resurrection power.

THE POWER OF THE COMING AGE

Romans 11:15 is powerful, and it shares the concept talked about in Romans 8:19, that creation eagerly waits for the revealing of the sons of God. It all has to do with the revelation of what is going to happen with Israel and with the Gentiles who are coming in now.

> *For if their temporary rejection released the reconciling power of grace into the world, what will happen when Israel is reinstated and reconciled to God? It will unleash resurrection power throughout the whole earth!*
> —ROMANS 11:15 TPT

There is going to come a time when attention will be back on Israel again. According to this verse, when Israel is reinstated and reconciled to God, it will unleash resurrection power throughout the whole earth. At the end of the age, the sons of God are going to be revealed, and then we are going to go into the next millennial reign of Jesus Christ.

We who believe live today because Jesus raised us from the dead, and there is resurrection power in us in the born-again experience.

For we've been buried with him into his death. Our "baptism into death" also means we were raised with him when we believed in God's resurrection power, the power that raised him from death's realm.

—Colossians 2:12 TPT

I had an angelic visitation, and they took me back in time before the flood. I got to see Enoch take his last step from this physical realm into the spiritual realm. I saw the Spirit of God wrap around him, and God's resurrection power take him to Heaven bodily, and Enoch still has his earthly body up there in Heaven.

The angel said to me, "You have asked for this revelation. The power of the coming age is resurrection." Then the angel took me to a time after the flood, and he showed me Elijah being swept up into Heaven with this whirlwind of fire and chariot. Elijah was also wrapped up and taken by resurrection power up into Heaven in his body. The angel said to me, "This is resurrection power, and it is the power of the coming age."

Then the angel said to me, "You can participate in this because inside you is the resurrection power. Your mission is to go out and compel people to come in and tell them the price has been paid. You can raise people from the dead spiritually as well as physically by telling them that Jesus has paid the price."

When people are converted, they go from the old to the new, and they are born again. That is resurrection power because they are raised from the dead spiritually. I had never even thought about that until the angel told me. He said, "You are raising people from the dead every time that you witness to them and they accept the

Lord Jesus Christ. They are born again, and they are being raised into life eternal." You have that power by going out and telling people that Jesus Christ has died for them and that they do not have to pay for their own sins anymore. God has given us the ministry of reconciliation (see 2 Cor. 5:18-21).

FREED FROM FEAR

Do you believe that you are going to live forever? Did you know that the last enemy that we face is death? Physical death was not taken care of through the cross. Born-again Christians still die physically; you have not escaped that physical death. Paul said that we have the mind of Christ (see 1 Cor. 2:16). We are to have this same mind that is in Jesus, and we are not to be afraid of death. If you can get rid of the fear of death, then what happens is that you can live your life in power down here because you are not limited and are not afraid.

Many people are fearful because they are afraid of the unknown, and some are afraid of failure. There are many different fears. God, through His resurrection power, showed you that you cannot fail, that you are never going to cease to exist. You are going to be transferred from this realm to the heavenly Kingdom. If you can catch this, you can live your life in such freedom. You will no longer be afraid to die because death does not have any power over you.

I am telling you this because I died, and I came back, and I see that this fear of death is what satan uses to keep people in a small cage. As a believer, you have resurrection power, you have a bright future, and you are never going to be defeated. You are a Christian, and you are going to live forever. You need to be released from the fear of death because, if you get released of that, then that resurrection power is going to start to work in your life in a greater way. Many people are kept in a small place because they do not discern what God has done through the resurrection.

Jesus conquered death, hell, and the grave, and resurrection power did not stop when Jesus came out of the grave. Jesus then ascended on high and is seated at the right hand of God, and He took us with Him. Scripture says that we are seated with Him in the heavenly realms (see Eph. 2:6). Paul said, *"If then you were raised with Christ, seek those things which are above, where Christ is, sitting at the right hand of God"* (Col. 3:1). We are not supposed to focus on the earthly things, but on things above where Christ is, and that is the place of authority.

The book of Revelation says, *"To him who overcomes I will grant to sit with Me on My throne"* (3:21). When I was in Heaven, Jesus allowed me to sit on a throne beside Him in the heavenly realms. He told me that this was bought for me and that I have authority because of what He bought for me through the resurrection, and He seated me with Him.

What I saw from sitting on that throne was the future. I saw all of the saints who have ever existed and ever will exist, and they were all worshiping the Lamb. They were worshiping Jesus, who was right beside me. As far as I could see, I saw myriads of angels and myriads of saints. I looked at the faces of millions of people. I could see on their faces that they realized they had made it, and they all were relieved because of this resurrection power. They realized they had gone to the throne room of God and their life had meant something.

They were worshiping Him at the end of the age, singing a song that I was not allowed to bring back with me. It was the song of the redeemed that we are all going to know and sing at His throne, and the angels will join in and sing. I saw white-robed saints as far as I could see, and they had accomplished the heart of God and lived their lives out faithfully, and now they were in Heaven.

Jesus said to me, "You come here in prayer, and you sit with Me in this heavenly place of authority. You will get your answer because, at the throne, there are no questions; there are only answers." He said, "Come here and sit often and get your answers and take them back to the earth with you."

YOU CANNOT LOSE!

Your life is at the right hand of God right now, and you cannot lose. Whatever you are fighting in your life, satan cannot win because that situation is not as high as where the throne is. The highest point in the universe is at the right hand of God. You need to allow God to implement His healing and resurrection power in your body and your soul. You need to be transformed and allow your mind to side with God and with the Word of God. You have been ignited with the same power that raised Jesus from the dead. You are seated with Him in the heavenly realms, far above all rule and authority, and everything is under your feet.

NOTE

1. Parts of this section taken from John G. Lake, "The Law of Life and Death," from the writings of John G. Lake, accessed September 21, 2020, https://healingrooms.com/index.php ?src=johnglake&document=143.

Chapter 13

THE BELIEVER'S DESTINY

*Having determined our destiny ahead of time, he called
us to himself and transferred his perfect righteousness
to everyone he called. And those who possess his
perfect righteousness he co-glorified with his Son!*
—ROMANS 8:30 TPT

D ESTINY IS ONE of the power words that is not used much
anymore. If it is used, it is in the sense that it is something
mystical, but destiny is not just romantic or mystical. Destiny
is a destination that God has determined for you. He had already
put you on the map before you were even born, and you had a location where you were going to be born. You have a location where
you are going to end up at the end of your life.

Spiritually, your destiny was with Jesus Christ before He was
even slain because Jesus was slain from the foundation of the world
(see Rev. 13:8). That means that all the books of all the people who
were ever going to live on the earth were already written in Heaven.
Your destiny was with God way before you were even born and way

before Jesus Christ even came to the earth. God existed, and He had a plan for your life (see Eph. 1:4-12).

Jesus wants you to learn from Him, and when He walked this earth, He was showing people how to walk in their destiny. He said,

> *Take My yoke upon you and learn from Me, for I am gentle and lowly in heart, and you will find rest for your souls. For My yoke is easy and My burden is light.*
> —MATTHEW 11:29-30

I know that you want to work for God, but it is not just about working for God. It is walking with God, and there is a difference because there is no labor involved. Jesus said here in this verse, if you take His yoke upon you, you will learn of Him. He said His work is easy, and His burden is light.

If it is getting too difficult for you, that means that you are in warfare. You have to distinguish between warfare and what God has for you because the devil is going to try to complicate things. You will get into situations where you are in the perfect will of God, but then, suddenly, satan will come against you, and it will feel like work. You are being opposed by the enemy, and he is standing against your destiny.

God does not want you to opt out of your destiny because you have trouble. Jesus said we are going to have trouble in this world. Then He said, *"But be of good cheer, I have overcome the world"* (John 16:33). Jesus conquered the earth, and He has already walked it out for you. When satan came to Jesus to tempt Him, Jesus quoted the Word of God to him (see Matt. 4:1-11). Jesus was making sure that satan understood that Jesus' destiny for Himself and man was already written down. You must do the same thing with satan. Jesus said, *"My sheep hear My voice, and I know them, and they follow Me"* (John 10:27). He also said, *"Yet they will by no means follow a stranger"* (John 10:5).

BE LED BY DESTINY

If you are being led by the Lord, it is going to be a walk, and if you are being driven, then it is satan because satan drives people. He will try to get you into fear, and then you will be driven by fear. You can be driven by all kinds of different emotions, but God leads us by His Spirit. Being led by God into your destiny is something like sailing a sailboat. You put your sails up, and God blows into your sails, and you just move along by the Spirit, by the breath of God.

If you are being driven, it is a forceful thing, and it is warfare. Satan is going to want to drive you, push you, and pressure you, but God does not do that. God gently leads you by His Spirit.

When you are ministering to people, you have to remember that satan wants to confuse people into thinking that God is telling them to do things and pushing them into something that is not what God has for them. You have to focus people on their destiny and get them off things like fear. Get them away from where they are being controlled and manipulated because it is satan, the spirit of this world, who does all those things.

The governments of the world can become controlling and manipulative and bring fear because satan gets in there, and he wants to control the people. God said, *"Where the Spirit of the Lord is, there is freedom"* (2 Cor. 3:17). Jesus said, *"If the Son makes you free, you shall be free indeed"* (John 8:36).

When Adam and Eve came on the earth, their destinies would need the Deliverer to come. Jesus had already planned to do that long before in the heart of God. Now that salvation has been taken care of, people have to acknowledge and accept Jesus Christ as their personal Savior to be able to participate in the Kingdom of God. You must know Jesus as your personal Savior to participate in your God-given destiny written in Heaven, and that puts you on track with God. Jesus bought humanity back to the Father.

Jesus spoke of our destiny, and He spoke it out before we were even born.

> *You saw who you created me to be before I became me!*
> *Before I'd ever seen the light of day, the number of days*
> *you planned for me were already recorded in your book.*
> —Psalm 139:16 TPT

When Jesus created the worlds, He already knew all of our names, and He knew the books that were written about us because God can do that. God knows way ahead of time, and time is not something that hinders Him in any way because God is not bound by time or distance. A believer's destiny was written long before they were ever born. If you are an unbeliever, or if you encounter an unbeliever, you and they still have a book written about them. They are not engaging in that book because they have not acknowledged Jesus Christ as their Deliverer and their Savior.

Once God has revealed His salvation message to you, then you come to a place where you must make a decision. That decision is, "Do I accept Jesus Christ as my personal Savior? Do I accept God's destiny for my life?" When you accept Jesus, He comes in, and then He sends in the Holy Spirit, and your spirit becomes born again (see 2 Cor. 1:22 AMP). You are made new inside, and that born-again spirit ignites you. You connect to your book of destiny that was already written in Heaven.

YOUR FRIEND, THE HOLY SPIRIT

God has written all these wonderful things in His library in Heaven, and I saw all the people's books there. God's angels have access to these books that are written about people. I saw that everyone has an angel, even unsaved people have angels because God wants everyone on the earth to come into Him. God wants everyone to accept the salvation message and then come into the family of God. The books written in Heaven are starting to be revealed to people all over the earth right now.

People come into the family of God, and their books are opened, and they can see what God has for them. Everyone wants to know God's will for their lives, and many people ask me about this. Once you accept Jesus, the Holy Spirit is your Guide, and He comes alongside you and counsels you. The Holy Spirit is your Advocate and your Standby, and He is the one who is going to implement your book in your life, so you have to be friends with the Person of the Holy Spirit.

When I saw that the Holy Spirit was a person, then I realized I was not treating Him as such. Before I had this experience of going to Heaven, I did not know that the Holy Spirit was a real person just like Jesus and that He wants to help us. Angels come, and they want to help you, and they want to implement our books. The Holy Spirit is like that but even greater because He is part of the Holy Trinity. He is one of the Persons of the Godhead who is inside you and wants to comfort you, and He wants to reveal the will of the Father to you. It is very important to grasp this.

Job acknowledged that God controls our destinies, and He wants to lead and guide us into them. Job said, *"So he will do to me whatever he has planned. He controls my destiny"* (Job 23:14 NLT). The psalmist said it this way, *"You guide me with your counsel, leading me to a glorious destiny"* (Ps. 73:24 NLT). You should acknowledge this every day and be like Job, saying, "God, whatever You have planned, You control my destiny, lead me, and guide me." And like the psalmist say, "You guide me with Your counsel." I want the whole counsel of God. You have to have ears that hear and eyes that see, and the Spirit of God gives you those through Jesus Christ.

You have the Holy Spirit inside you, and He has anointed you, and the Father and the Son are going to come and live with you (see John 14:23 TPT). The reason that you have not realized this in your life, and there is such a discrepancy, is that you have not been led by the Holy Spirit. You have been driven by the world. Jesus wants to lead you as the Good Shepherd, and that is what He said He was. When you feel pressured and overwhelmed, and you want to give up, that is how you know you are feeling satan's influence. He is the one who drives you and pushes you.

When someone tells you that they have been trying, trying, and trying so hard, then you have to determine if that person is being driven by an evil spirit or if they are being led by the Spirit of God. Their frustration usually comes from the fact that an evil spirit is trying to take the place of the Holy Spirit. You must be able to discern between the Holy Spirit and an evil spirit.

When there is pressure to perform, then you need to stop and sit down and ask yourself, "What is pushing me? What is controlling me? What is speaking to me?" It takes discernment to ask yourself these questions. If you feel like you are under pressure to perform, then you need to sit down and relax and let God start to speak to you and love on you. I see this all the time. People in their desire to be led by the Spirit and their desire to please God move into doing works in order to receive from God what He has freely given to them, and they start to be driven.

When I met Jesus in person, I did please Him, but not because I was a good boy or a good person, but because of what Jesus did for me on the cross when He completely eradicated sin. Jesus wiped it out, and He took care of our position with the Father. In the eyes of God, you are pleasing to Him through Jesus' blood. When you think about destiny, you have to understand that Jesus was slain from the foundation of the world to take care of your sin problem, so you are pleasing to the Father.

Satan fears the word *destiny* just as much as any of the other power words. He fears the fact that Christians all over the world are going to begin to realize they have a destiny with God, and then the doors of opportunity will be open to them. You are going to feel the power of the Holy Spirit begin to open up doors in the Spirit, and you are going to have an open Heaven over you. As the truth enters into you and your eyes are opened, you are going to be set free to walk with God as a friend of God, and you will no longer be driven, but led.

DESTINY IS A DESTINATION

This word *destiny*, if you think about it, has to do with your destination. God has already determined where you are going to end up in your life. I have already been to everyone's future when I was taken to the end of this age, where everyone was gathered in Heaven in the throne room. We all make it, and we are worshiping Jesus Christ, the Lamb slain before the foundation of the world. When I came back from Heaven, this moment was what I took back with me.

People have to engage God and obey His Word, obey His voice, and walk with Him in the fear of the Lord. They have to grasp the fact that they are going to make it, but they must walk sober-mindedly here on the earth (see Titus 2:6). When Jesus was on the earth, He submitted to the Father and only did what His Father was doing and what His Father told Him to do. That is the way that it must be with us. We must humble ourselves under the mighty hand of God, and He will lift us up in due time (see 1 Pet. 5:6).

The Holy Spirit has given gifts to each one of us as the Spirit wills, and it is to build up the Body of Christ in unity.

> *For the equipping of the saints for the work of ministry, for the edifying of the body of Christ, till we all come to the unity of the faith and of the knowledge of the Son of God, to a perfect man, to the measure of the stature of the fullness of Christ.*
> —EPHESIANS 4:12-13

Your destiny also has to do with the gifts of the Holy Spirit, because the Holy Spirit wants you to fulfill your mission on the earth, and that helps others fulfill their mission on the earth.

God is fulfilling your destiny, and He is talking to you, walking with you, building you up, and causing you to triumph over your enemies. At the same time, there is a domino effect happening because the Spirit of God is also unifying the Body of Christ, and you are an important integral part of that. Your destiny involves many other people. When you are successful, when God heals you, prospers you, and gives you revelation, it is not just for you; it is meant to influence everyone around you.

As you walk with God and begin to receive open heavens in your own life as God imparts to you, it causes a rumble in the Spirit, and it begins to push away the spirits of darkness. As you start to walk in that freedom, your friends and everyone around you start to walk in that freedom, too, and it catches on. This is what ministry is. A ministry is not a profession; it is the Holy Spirit working through our lives, bringing us into our destinies so that others around us can begin to live their destinies as well.

Jesus said,

> *Enter by the narrow gate; for wide is the gate and broad is the way that leads to destruction, and there are many who go in by it. Because narrow is the gate and difficult is the way which leads to life, and there are few who find it.*
> —MATTHEW 7:13-14

When He spoke this, many people were wondering what Jesus was saying. In the world, there is a way that everyone seems to go, and it is a wide way, but it leads to destruction. However, there is a narrow gate, which Paul talked about in Second Corinthians 6:14-18. As it says in verse 17, *"Come out from among them and be separate, saith the Lord."* If you want to be separate and holy before the Lord, you must choose the narrow way. Not a lot of people are going to follow you in that narrow way, and that is why you need the Body of Christ. That is why you need to gather together and unite with other Christians who believe the way that you do.

Jesus explained that the gate is very narrow, and it is a difficult way that leads to life. You might be lonely at times because you walk in the narrow way. When I started walking with the Lord, and He was leading me, He put me in a place where there was nothing that could be on either side of me. I was completely stripped of all the things that I would want in this world. You might be going through that right now, but it is part of the process of your destiny. You have to be stripped of everything that is not necessary so that you can walk through that narrow way.

Once you get through the narrow way, and you have walked your life in obedience to Christ, then the Spirit of God will start to allow you to experience those things again, and you will get them back. At the time, it seemed as though I was giving more than I was receiving, but God remembered all those things. After I went through this narrow way, and I had this process of purging, it caused me to get through there and develop character, knowing that I can encounter anything and still survive it. That is what God wants for you.

CHARACTER OVER COMFORT

God does not always cater to your comfort because there are times that He wants to develop your character. It can feel like you are giving up everything, but be encouraged because God has a destiny for you. God has you in that narrow way so that your character can control the evil influences that come against you. You have to learn to filter through and control all of the thoughts that come to you as well as through other people.

People are going to say things and do things that are not correct, and you are going to have to say, "No, this is not the way that the Lord has for me. He has a narrow way for me." I have had to say *no* to my friends many times to stay on the narrow way. I could not explain to them why I could not join them; I only knew that I could not. I spent my time with the Lord in study and prayer, and now when I look back, I am so glad that I did. The Lord has blessed me in so many ways because I chose to study and to stay alone with the Lord, and I now see that I am walking in God's destiny and perfect will for my life.

Much of what you go through as a child of God is training, and you may think that all this bad stuff is happening to you. At a certain point, as you continue with the Lord, the devil runs out of ammunition. The devil has nothing left to throw at you, and you realize that your character was being built all along. Never be discouraged by hardship because God is teaching you how to walk through the difficulty; your destiny involves setting other people free. You will have a command about you and tenacity about you that God has developed in your character. You will be able to say no to ungodliness and worldly passions, and you can live an upright life in Christ Jesus.

The way that you live your life will cause others to be drawn to you, and you will find that there is strength in your walk with God. Others will be encouraged by being friends with you because you have set the pace. I want to be a trendsetter, a history maker, and I want to see people set free. If you want to live like this, you must be set free yourself, and God is going to come in and break things wide open for you. The breakthrough comes through these hard times and these narrow ways that God says are part of your destiny.

MULTIPLE DIMENSIONS OF PRAYER

Right now, the Holy Spirit wants to pray through you. He wants to speak out through your lips, praying in the Spirit. Praying in tongues allows the Holy Spirit to speak out your destiny through you constantly. When I was in Heaven, I saw that when the Holy Spirit is allowed to pray through a person, the person is then praying the perfect will of God that is not even known to them. I saw that the mind is not able to comprehend what the Spirit is saying, but you are still praying it out. It is as though the Holy Spirit is proclaiming your future before it even happens.

I had people tell me what I was saying when I was praying in the Spirit because they knew the language that I was speaking, even when I did not know it. The apostle Paul said, *"If I pray in a tongue, my spirit prays, but my mind is unfruitful"* (1 Cor. 14:14 NIV). Your mind does not comprehend or understand what the Spirit is saying because you are praying out mysteries by the Spirit (see 1 Cor. 14:2). Yet, you are praying out the perfect will of God.

Romans 8:27 (TPT) reads,

> *God, the searcher of the heart, knows fully our longings, yet he also understands the desires of the Spirit, because the Holy Spirit passionately pleads before God for us, his*

holy ones, in perfect harmony with God's plan and our destiny.

This verse is talking about the Spirit coming in and passionately praying out the perfect will of God for our destinies. You need to yield to the Holy Spirit and pray in the Spirit as much as possible. Paul said, *"I speak in tongues more than all of you"* (1 Cor. 14:18 NIV). I would say that the most important ingredient to my own successful prayer life would be the fact that I always pray in the Spirit, for hours a day, even under my breath. I am always praying in the Spirit, and I believe it is very necessary to pray in tongues all the time.

Did you know that you can pray in the Spirit without moving your lips? A lot of people ask me that if they pray in tongues silently, does it still count? Your spirit is always praying, and it is always talking. Even when I am speaking, or I am teaching, or I am writing by the Spirit, I can hear my spirit praying in tongues as well. I know that does not sound possible, but in my spirit, I am also praying in tongues. You are so much more than you think you are within, and spiritually we are beyond our understanding. There will be many times that the only way you are going to overcome in this life is by praying in the Spirit and doing spiritual things. Your spirit is alive and has many dimensions to it, and the Spirit wants to pray through you in another dimension that is beyond the physical realm.

The verse below describes a visitation, and in this visitation, the person receiving guidance was told,

Get up and stand to your feet, for I have appeared to you to reveal your destiny and to commission you as my

assistant. You will be a witness to what you have seen
and to the things I will reveal whenever I appear to you.
—Acts 26:16 TPT

Whether it was an angel or Jesus Christ Himself who spoke, something like this can happen to you at any moment as you walk with God. We do not seek angelic visitations or seek after visitations of the Lord, but they do happen. I do have angelic visitations, and I have had visitations of Jesus, but I never seek those things.

Paul and all of the apostles discerned that their destinies were to preach the gospel, and they went around the world to preach and proclaim the good news of the gospel.

But whether I live or die is not important, for I don't
esteem my life as indispensable. It's more important
for me to fulfill my destiny and to finish the ministry
my Lord Jesus has assigned to me, which is to faithfully
preach the wonderful news of God's grace.
—Acts 20:24 TPT

Just as God fulfilled their destinies, God is going to help you to fulfill your destiny, and He is only going to do that by you yielding to the Holy Spirit.

Chapter 14

HOLY FIRE

Those who repent I baptize with water, but there is coming a Man after me who is more powerful than I am. In fact, I'm not even worthy enough to pick up his sandals. He will submerge you into union with the Spirit of Holiness and with a raging fire!
—MATTHEW 3:11 TPT

THE DEVIL HATES the word *holy fire* more than any other word because he used to walk on those stones of fire on the holy mountain of God (see Ezek. 28:14). I saw those beautiful fiery sapphire stones when I was in Heaven, and they are full of the white flame of the fire of the Holy Spirit.

The devil hates the fact that he was thrown out of Heaven. Jesus said, *"I saw Satan fall like lightning from heaven"* (Luke 10:18). Have you ever seen a lightning bolt come down? It is so fast that you can hardly see it, but before you know it, it is over. That is how hard satan hit this earth when he was thrown out of Heaven, and he remembers that day because it was so bad. Holy fire is one of those words that satan does not want any Christian to talk about, especially in church, because it is so powerful.

In Matthew 3:11, John the Baptist announced to the crowd that when Jesus comes, He is going to baptize them with the Holy Spirit and with fire. There are two different things that you can be baptized with: the Holy Spirit and fire. We know that when the Holy Spirit came to the 120 believers meeting on the day of Pentecost, fire appeared on everyone's head (see Acts 2:1-4). The Holy Spirit's introduction manifested flames of fire, and this was the day when the Church was formed.

In the throne room of God, there is fire coming from the altar, and the seraphim, the great angels of God with six wings, are over the throne of God. The seraphim are circling God from above, saying, "Holy, Holy, Holy," and they are engulfed in flames (see Isa. 6:3; Rev. 4:8). The seraphim are physically over God, and the cherubim are on either side of God's throne (see Isa. 37:16). The cherubim have immense wings, and they cover God because His glory is so strong that God has to have a covering over Him.

The prophet Isaiah saw the throne room of God, and in Isaiah 6, he described the train of God's robe filling the temple. Isaiah saw the cherubim and the seraphim, and heard the thundering of God. Isaiah was a major prophet in the Old Testament, but when he saw all these things happening in the throne room of God, he became undone.

Isaiah said, *Woe to me for I am undone! Because I am a man of unclean lips, and I dwell in the midst of a people of unclean lips* (6:5-8). Then one of the seraphim flew to him with a live coal from the altar fire and touched it to his lips. The coal took away Isaiah's iniquity, cleansed him, and wiped away his sin. Suddenly, Isaiah said, *"Lord, here am I send me!"* God did send Isaiah to his people, but that encounter that he had, was all about holy fire (see Isa. 6).

Many people ask me how they can encounter holy fire. I tell them that they have to encounter the Spirit of God, who is from the other realm. Jesus told Nicodemus that you hear when the wind comes, but you cannot see where the wind comes from or where it goes (see John 3:8). You cannot see the wind, and that is the way of the Spirit of God. Jesus was saying to Nicodemus that you do not see the Spirit of God, but you see the manifestation of the Spirit of God. Just like you can see the trees when the wind blows, we do not see the wind, but we see the effects of the wind.

FIRE FROM THE OTHER REALM

To encounter holy fire, you have to have something introduced from the other realm into your life. The first thing that must happen is you must be born again. You are introduced to the Holy Spirit through the born-again experience when your spirit becomes alive unto God. You encounter the Holy Spirit, and He renews your spirit, and it is called being *born again* because your spirit becomes a new creature in Christ. You become a new species, one that has never existed before. *"All the old things have passed away; behold, everything has become new"* (2 Cor. 5:17). Now your spirit is born again.

After you are born again, the next thing to encounter is holy fire; you are to be baptized in the Holy Spirit. The Holy Spirit came on the day of Pentecost, and one of the manifestations was fire; there were flames of fire on people's heads. God does not talk to you through your body or your mind. Jesus said, *"God is a Spirit, and those who worship Him must worship Him in Spirit and truth"*

(John 4:24). God is going to speak to you through your spirit. Once you are born again, the Holy Spirit is going to blow on you, and the spiritual part of you, your spirit, is going to pick up what God is saying. What He says is not going to come in through your head, and it is not going to come into your body; it comes into your spirit.

A lot of people make the mistake of thinking that God can speak to them through their bodies. That is why there are people who mistakenly believe that God teaches them things by giving them sicknesses. Other people think that the thoughts in their head are God speaking to them. God is not a body or a mind, God is a Spirit, and He speaks to you Spirit to spirit.

Jesus said, *"That which is born of the flesh is flesh, and that which is born of the Spirit is spirit"* (John 3:6). He also said, *"The spirit indeed is willing, but the flesh is weak"* (Mark 14:38). You are willing in your spirit, but your flesh might not be so willing, and your mind might not comprehend what is happening. If you want to encounter holy fire, you have to yield to the fire, and that means you have to yield to the Holy Spirit. The Holy Spirit is your friend, and that means fire is your friend, but it is the fire from the altar of God.

Every day I ask God to take a coal from the altar and put it on my lips and inside me. I want to have a coal from the altar of God, from the other realm in my spirit. You are just visiting this earthly realm. It is not your home. It clearly says in Scripture that we are aliens in this world. We are foreigners and not of this world, and we will never fit in (see 1 Chron. 29:15).

You now have the born-again experience and the baptism of the Holy Spirit. However, John the Baptist said that Jesus was going to baptize you with fire as well. We are not led by the signs and wonders that happen around us; we are led by the Spirit of God. *"For as many as are led by the Spirit of God, these are sons of God"* (Rom. 8:14). This verse does *not* say those led by prophets are sons of God or those led by signs and wonders are sons of God. No, it says those who *are led by the Spirit of God* are sons of God. It is the Spirit of God who introduces you to holy fire; you must become friends with the Holy Spirit.

The carnal mind and the flesh are enemies of God, and if you yield to the flesh, you cannot please God.

> *Because the carnal mind is enmity against God; for it is not subject to the law of God, nor indeed can be. So then, those who are in the flesh cannot please God.*
> —ROMANS 8:7-8

If you want to please God, you must yield to the Holy Spirit. You must accept this fact to be able to encounter the spiritual things of God. If you are led by the Spirit of God, you are a son of God. If you are going to be yielding to the Spirit, then your flesh is going to war against you because the flesh is an enemy of God. Your flesh does not want to do what God wants you to do. Your flesh only wants to do what *it* wants to do, and that is why you have to crucify the flesh and walk with God in humility.

FIRE THAT BRINGS HEALING

The psalmist wrote:

> *You've gone into my future to prepare the way, and in kindness you follow behind me to spare me from the*

harm of my past, with your hand of love upon my life,
You impart a blessing to me.

—PSALM 139:5 TPT

God has already set your path, and you are going to walk on this path with Him. God wants you to know that He goes behind you and sets a guard behind you to protect you from the hurts of your past. One of the things that holy fire will do is it will expose your hurts and expose the vulnerable points that you have. If God is there behind you, protecting you from the hurts of your past, you can be healed.

God is standing in your future, waiting for you to come to Him, but He is also behind you, guarding you against all the previous hurts and all the mistakes you have made. God wants to heal you and reconcile you to Himself in those areas. There is a process of receiving the holy fire that will expose these very sensitive areas where you are hurt. Demons know that you have wounds, and they want to keep those wounds open so that they can continue to inflict pain by harassing you.

To be completely engulfed with the holy fire, you are going to have to allow God as a centurion to come behind you and guard you against the hurts of your past. The holy fire needs to be able to burn out all of the infections of the past, and anything that is hurting you needs to be healed as you are in the protection of God's love.

Some believers are not able to overcome to be able to encounter the holy fire in its completeness. That is because they do not acknowledge God is the guardian behind them watching to make sure that there is no inflicted hurt from anything they have done in their past.

You need to be healed of your past, and you need to know that God has forgiven you. Once the holy fire comes in and cleanses those areas of your past, there is no longer an access point for satan to get in. Once you are healed, satan will come at you, but you will be able to laugh at him because you know that you have been forgiven, and the wound has closed up. Satan can no longer inflict pain on you in those areas because they do not exist anymore.

Jesus said this, *"The evil one is coming, but he has nothing in Me"* (John 14:30). Essentially Jesus was saying, "There is nothing within My flesh that satan can hook me with, and there is no place for him to attach himself to My flesh." Jesus had allowed the Holy Spirit to seal His life up completely and seal His flesh up to where He was walking in the Spirit all the time. Jesus' life was our example. He showed us how to allow the Spirit to seal up His life. Holy fire will expose all of the places within us that are access points being used by evil spirits.

The apostle Paul wrote, *"Do not quench the Spirit"* (1 Thess. 5:19). You can quench the Holy Spirit's work by not allowing Him to set you free in an area, to deliver you, to heal you, or to lead you into all truth. If you resist the Holy Spirit, you are not allowing Him to take you where you need to go. If you are encountering some sort of resistance within yourself, you may be feeling the hurt and the pain of rejection or fear, but remember these things are access points for demons in your life. You have to let the Holy Spirit take you there and heal you. If you do not want to go there, then you are not going to get delivered until you resolve to relinquish your will to God through the holy fire. You will begin to realize that you no longer have to quench the Spirit of God, and you no longer have to grieve Him.

When you resist God, you are resisting the holy fire. If you want to participate in the holy fire in your life, you have to yield and let the fire have its way. The Holy Spirit is going to say, "I need access into this place in your life." You may be so hurt that you are in a survival mode, but in Heaven, there are no survivors, and there are no victims. When I was in Heaven, I saw that a believer is supposed to allow the fire of the Holy Spirit to come in and burn up everything that is not of God in their life.

I saw that not everything in a believer's character was of God. Some of the ways that they were as a person was because of the demonic influence that was handed down through their generations. This demonic influence had caused them to be a certain way, but that does not make it right. There are certain character traits that people permit. We may excuse these and say, "That's just the way they are." No, that is not the way they are. That is a demonic influence that is enforcing a curse through their generations. A generational curse can propagate a certain characteristic that is handed down in their family.

If you think that you act like your father or your grandfather, make sure that it is a godly trait (see Gal. 5:22-23). Is it a fruit of the Spirit, or is it a manifestation of the flesh? If that family trait is born of the Spirit, then it is good. However, certain character traits are not born of the Spirit, and you need to discern if a demon has been assigned to your family line. God has destined you to break that trait so that it is never handed down any further, and you can break that chain in your life right now. If you identify that this trait is not a fruit of the Spirit, then it has to be a demon because a demon will propagate the fruit of the flesh.

The fruit of the Spirit is born from Heaven, and that is what you are. You are born from Heaven, and as a Christian, you only manifest the fruit of the Spirit. If you manifest anything else, then you have to realize that it is not natural as a Christian. What would be natural as a Christian would be to let the Holy Spirit reign in your life, but because you are in this fallen world, you encounter demonic forces all the time.

OUR GOD IS A CONSUMING FIRE

Remember that Jesus said, *"The ruler of this world is coming, and he has nothing in Me"* (John 14:30). This is where people get stuck because there is no way for the enemy to get in there and influence you through your flesh if he cannot hook you. You are encountering holy fire because the Spirit of God is fire, and He is inside you. The problem is you are not yielding to the Spirit because you are yielding to the flesh, and you are not allowing a spiritual process to happen that is natural for a Christian.

You are a Christian, and you are born again of the Holy Spirit, and you have the Holy Spirit inside you, and He is full of fire. You have your Heavenly Father, who is a consuming fire (see Heb. 12:29). You have the baptizer of the Spirit of fire, which is Jesus, and you have the Holy Spirit who is the fire. You also have angels of God around you that are spoken of in the Bible as being flames of fire (see Ps. 104:4). You have a lot of fire around you. Remember also that the throne room is full of fire, and the altar of God is always lit up, and it is burning, and the immense seraphim angels are engulfed in fire. There is plenty of fire in your life, so the reason you are not encountering holy fire is that you are not yielding.

As soon as you yield to the Spirit of God, you are going to have the holy fire consume you, and you are going to start to see improvement in your life. Meditate on God's Word and let the Holy Spirit ignite that Word inside you, and let it begin to burn. As it burns and gets bigger, there are going to be certain issues in your life that are going to go away because they were never meant to be in your life. You will begin to see the things you cannot overcome, but the fire is going to burn that all up. You have to yield to the fact that the Spirit of God wants to take that all out. God's purpose and plan for your life are much greater than what you are encountering. The fire is your friend, and it is going to consume all those things that are not necessary.

Ezekiel 28:14 is about lucifer who walked in the midst of the stones of fire. Now we, as children of God, get to walk on those stones of fire. We get to be restored back to Adam and Eve and what they were before they fell. Satan does not get to walk on those holy, fiery stones anymore, because he has been judged, and he has been made a show of openly through the cross (see Col. 2:15).

Isaiah 10:17 tells about the holy fire of God coming upon Israel, but we as believers also have that holy fire coming upon us. The Holy One is a flame, and that Holy One is the Holy Spirit, and He is inside you, and He is going to devour the thorns and the briers in a single day. The prophecy in Isaiah 10 was talking about judgment against the Syrians. In our lives, the briers and thorns talked about in the Bible always represent the curse and the fall.

FIRE REVERSES THE CURSE

In the garden of Eden, before man fell, everything was perfect. Thorns and briers came when the world fell and became cursed. Roses did not even have thorns before the fall. Another thing that holy fire does is it reverses the curse. It causes those things that were part of this fallen world to be burned up and judged. God wants us to yield to the fire and judge ourselves. *"For if we would judge ourselves, we would not be judged"* (1 Cor. 11:31). Let the Holy Father come in and consume everything that is not of Him.

Satan understands holy fire more than any other being. He was made perfect, he was the epitome of perfection, and he had the seal of perfection (see Ezek. 28; Isa. 14). There was no one more perfect than satan of all the created beings, and he knew what holiness and holy fire were because he would walk on those fiery stones. When satan fell, he wanted to pull man down with him and take man away from God, and he knew exactly how to do that. When satan got in there and corrupted man, then man was rejected by God, and satan now continues to keep the whole world away from God through corruption.

Holy fire would cleanse people if they accepted Jesus Christ as their Savior, receive the Holy Spirit, and begin to walk in holy fire. They would be cleansed and walk with God and be ignited with God for the rest of their lives, and this is what satan fights. The message is, now that you are a Christian, you should not stop there. You have to continue with being transformed by the renewing of your mind. You have to allow the Holy Spirit to lead you into all truth about holy fire. This holy fire from the altar will completely shift your whole environment, and it will shift everyone else around you. Once you encounter holy fire, it starts to burn outward.

Your destiny is to walk on the holy sapphire stones in Heaven. You can do that right now by saying, "Lord, my life is not my own anymore. I want to walk in holiness, and I want to walk in Your holy fire." The Lord is going to give you that. I picture myself in the Spirit walking on those stones of fire every day. You can picture it in your mind and see that you are walking with God and that there is fire all around you. It will not happen overnight because it is something that is developed. Be encouraged because you will start to see God's holy fire around you as you continue to be led by the Holy Spirit of God.

Chapter 15

DIVINE PROSPERITY

For I am planting seeds of peace and prosperity among you. The grapevines will be heavy with fruit. The earth will produce its crops, and the heavens will release the dew. Once more I will cause the remnant in Judah and Israel to inherit these blessings.
—ZECHARIAH 8:12 NLT

IVINE PROSPERITY HAS to do with godly prosperity from Heaven. The is no poverty in Heaven; there are only riches and abundance above and beyond what we could ask or think. Nothing is lacking in Heaven. When I was there, I saw that everything had been provided for us through Jesus Christ. Down here in this earthly realm of the flesh, it is a fight because satan is the god of this world, and he is biased against Christians because he was thrown from Heaven. He is out, and you are in as a child of God.

There is a divine prosperity that comes from Heaven and translates into this world, being manifested through the saints. God in Heaven is going to favor His people, but on this earth, satan is going to favor *his* people. When Jesus addressed the Pharisees, He told them that their father, the devil, was a liar from the beginning and that they were just like him (see John 8:44). Jesus attributed the characteristics of satan to the characteristics of the religious people of His day, who were the Pharisees and the Sadducees.

As it was in Jesus' day, so it is with us today regarding prosperity. Satan wants the Church to believe that poverty is a holy institution, and it is set in the Church to cause people to believe that they can be holy if they are poor. The problem with this is it does not say that in the Bible. Satan wants to deceive Christians into thinking that if they are poor, they are going to have more favor in God's eyes, but it is not true. Israel was always blessed and prosperous in the Old Testament. Jesus came and died to give us the new covenant and, with it, greater promises. It is a greater covenant, and it is established through the blood of Jesus.

God is against poverty, and He said it in the Old Testament, and He is still the same God today. Satan has deceived the Church into believing that it is better to be poor because then you can be godlier. That thinking is contradictory toward what God has already revealed in His Word.

> *Except when there may be no poor among you; for the Lord will greatly bless you in the land which the Lord your God is giving you to possess as an inheritance.*
> —DEUTERONOMY 15:4

God greatly blessed the children of Israel, so that there would be no poor among them. If God has blessed us through Christ

Jesus, then poverty should be eradicated, and it should be taken out. That is the divine prosperity that comes from Heaven.

Paul said this to the Corinthians,

> *Let giving flow from your heart, not from a sense of religious duty. Let it spring up freely from the joy of giving—all because God loves hilarious generosity!*
> —2 Corinthians 9:7 TPT

Even in the New Testament, God does not do away with giving, and He does not do away with receiving. In Philippians 4:17, Paul tells us that what we do will be laid up to our account, which means that God is keeping track of everything that we give. God, your Father, wants to provide for you in every way; however, the god of this world is against any Christian having money. Jesus said, *"What man is there among you who, if his son asks for bread, will give him a stone?"* (Matt. 7:9). No, the Father desires to give you the Kingdom (see Luke 12:32). There a division within the Body of Christ as it relates to prosperity.

The Spirit Leads You into Prosperity

When I was in Heaven, I saw that God wanted to lead us into prosperity, and He wanted to lead us into truth. Jesus Himself told me, *"The Spirit of God leads you into all truth"* (see John 16:13). Jesus knew that I was a tither and that I also gave beyond the tithe. I was always giving, sowing seed, and helping the poor. I was doing all these things, yet He said, "I want to show you something different and greater that is not being addressed."

Jesus said to me, "One of the things that is not being taught and that you need to tell people is that the Spirit of God will lead them into prosperity." I could see that the Body of Christ is being deceived when they believe that God does not want them to prosper. When I came back, I saw that satan has us so divided and that he has gotten into the minds of some believers. These believers think that they do not have to prosper, and that being poor gives them more favor with God, which is a total lie. I saw that the Spirit of God wants to lead us into prosperity.

This power word, *prosperity*, has to do with God, and it has always had to do with God. It was always God who prospered His people because He is prosperous. God gave His Son to die on a cross, and because of that, He caused us to triumph over our enemies, who are led by satan. As our enemy, satan does not want any Christian to have money. Why? It is because money has to do with dominion.

> *For the Lord your God will bless you just as He promised you; you shall lend to many nations, but you shall not borrow; you shall reign over many nations, but they shall not reign over you.*
>
> —DEUTERONOMY 15:6

Understand that we are in the new covenant with better promises. Satan does not want a Christian to prosper because then he has no control over them financially. If you were completely out of debt, you would be out from under the control of the agencies that lent to you. You would be completely debt-free, and you would not need to answer to anyone. That was God's purpose and plan from the beginning.

You can see why satan is trying to influence Christians into thinking that they can borrow money all the time. But there is fallout when Christians do this: *"The rich rules over the poor, and the borrower is servant to the lender"* (Prov. 22:7).

In the Old Testament, God established His covenant with Israel, saying that they would lend to many nations, but they would *not* have to borrow. Israel was to be the head and not the tail (see Deut. 28:13). In the New Testament, God wants you to know that He wants you to be in control. He does not want satan having control over you, and so that you're not under his control financially, God wants you to get out of debt.

WALKING IN PROSPERITY

Divine prosperity is more than having money. It is walking in the blessings and the favor of God. When you walk in prosperity, what is going out of your accounts is just as important as what is coming in. God wants you to control what is going out of your accounts as well. If God favors you, then you will not have the expenses that are going out that you used to, and that is part of prosperity, too.

What if you did not get sick anymore? You would not need to pay a doctor, and you would not need to buy medicine. God can influence your life to where you do not have the expenses going out. If God healed you, that would save so much money every month because you would no longer have the expense of being sick. Satan does not want people to think that God wants them well.

Satan wants to keep control of you, of your body, and your mind. Yet the whole time, your spirit is free inside you because the Spirit of the Lord is in there. You must listen to what the Spirit of God is saying. Jesus told me, "I want to lead you into prosperity.

I want to lead you out of poverty and into prosperity." It is God's plan for our lives.

Psalm 25:13 tells us that *"he himself shall dwell in prosperity, and his descendants shall inherit the earth."* The psalmist is talking about what God wants to do for His people. God's people who adhere to His instructions will dwell in prosperity, and his descendants shall inherit the earth. That is God's plan for our lives—we are to inherit the earth. The meek shall inherit the earth.

> *Oh, taste and see that the Lord is good; blessed*
> *is the man who trusts in Him!*
> —PSALM 34:8

You can see that God's plan for your life is to bring you into the goodness and the favor of God. God is good, and when He introduces Himself to you, you have a revelation of His goodness. When you have that revelation of God's goodness, then the power of the Holy Spirit causes favor to come. When that favor comes, poverty has to go because God's favor drives out poverty. Suddenly, you are blessed, and you find that no matter what happens in your life, you always end up ahead. That is God's blessing on your life.

A curse is something where, no matter what you do, you always are behind. No matter what you do, something bad always happens, and that has to be reversed in your life. God wants you to have a revelation of His divine prosperity.

Having a revelation of God's goodness causes you to turn and face God.

Or do you despise the riches of His goodness, forbearance, and longsuffering, not knowing that the goodness of God leads you to repentance?
—Romans 2:4

Looking at God face to face turns you toward Him, which is repentance. Repentance is needed when something pulls your focus away from God and you are staring at it. Jesus told me that people need to repent daily. The world is trying to draw our attention away from God, and people need to give their attention back to Him. We need to repent, to turn our faces, stare at the Lord Jesus Christ, and see Him in His glory. In prayer, you can picture the face of Jesus and look at Him, set your focus on Him and seek Him. *"But seek first the kingdom of God and His righteousness, and all these other things will be added unto you"* (Matt. 6:33). The goodness of God leads us to repentance.

Divine prosperity in your life has to do with the revelation that God is good, He is a good God, and He is not trying to take anything from you. Jesus said, *"The thief comes to steal, kill, and destroy. I have come to give you life and life more abundantly"* (John 10:10). There is an abundance of life coming to you because Jesus gives that to you, and He has identified the thief for us. When you have a curse in your life, that is not God because He does not take things from you. God is not stealing from you and not trying to kill you. It is satan who is doing that because he is the god of this world. Our God is good, and it is His goodness that leads you to repentance.

You can lead others into repentance by telling them how good God is. The revelation of your testimony causes them to see that God is good. They will want to be part of that blessing and will give their lives to Jesus because you have been a witness to them with your life. That is not going out and witnessing. After all, you are a witness because you have a testimony, and *"the testimony of Jesus is the spirit of prophecy"* (Rev. 19:10). Many people will come to the Lord because of the goodness of God being revealed in these last days. You can be a part of this by allowing God to be good to you.

God made us in His image, which means we are like Him. We were made in the likeness of God (see Gen. 1:26). Part of that likeness is the fact that because God is good, then we are good. The goodness of God that is in Heaven is transferred to us on this earth. When we encounter the goodness of God, we are going to prosper. It does not mean that things are going to be taken away from us and stolen, for we know that is of the devil.

God takes pleasure in prospering His people.

> Let them shout for joy and be glad, who favor my righteous cause; and let them say continually, "Let the Lord be magnified, Who has pleasure in the prosperity of His servant."
>
> —PSALM 35:27

Satan does not want you to have anything, but God wants to give you everything. God desires to give you the Kingdom. Jesus said, *"Do not fear, little flock, for it is your Father's good pleasure to give you the kingdom"* (Luke 12:32).

INTO THE FAMILY OF GOD

The rebellious person gets nothing but dry land. However, if you are rejected, if you are solitary, God brings you into a family.

God sets the solitary in families; He brings out those who are bound into prosperity; But the rebellious dwell in a dry land.
—PSALM 68:6

Then God takes those who are bound, and He brings them into prosperity. If you are bound by debt, if you are bound by a curse, Jesus Christ died on the cross to break that curse. Jesus Christ, through the Spirit of God, wants to lead you into prosperity. You are not bound anymore because He takes you and puts you into prosperity.

Deuteronomy 28 is very important, and you should read it through. It says that we must choose between obedience and disobedience. Either you are going to obey, or you are going to choose not to obey. God says to you to choose this day. Which you are going to do? What you will receive will be based on your choice.

If you obey, God says that He is going to lead you into prosperity. He is going to bless you and prosper you. God is asking you, "Do you want to prosper, or do you not want to prosper? Do you want to obey, or do you not want to obey?" If you obey, you are going to be the head, and you are going to lend to many nations, and you are not going to have to borrow from any of them. There are just two choices, and that is the simplicity of the gospel.

Jesus told us that if we believe in Him, we should also believe in the one who sent Him (see John 12:44). He said, "*If you abide in Me, and My words abide in you, you will ask what you desire, and it shall be done for you*" (John 15:7). It is still the same covenant in the New Testament. It is just based on better promises. God did not restrict us in our prayer life.

In John 15:1-8, Jesus talks about being in the vine and how we are connected to the vine through Jesus Christ. The life source from the vine comes up into the branches, and we are the branches, and we receive our life source from God. That is why Jesus said, "You need to abide in Me, and I abide in you." Then we can ask what we desire, and I ask for as much as I possibly can through the Word of God.

SUPPLYING YOUR NEEDS

I do not pray for specific things in my life as far as provision because I have the revelation that all my needs are met according to His riches in Christ Jesus (see Phil. 4:19). I ask for the nations for my inheritance. I ask for the eyes of my heart to be enlightened, and I pray for other people. I already know that if I am seeking the Kingdom and its righteousness, that all these other things are going to be added to me as well, and you need to get that revelation. You need to get to that place where you realize, if you seek the Kingdom, that prosperity will come to you and that everything about the Kingdom will come to you. You will have all the provision you need to accomplish what God has given you in your vision.

Whatever God has shown you, know that He is leading you in it, and He is going to supply those needs. God cannot be mocked, and a man will reap what he sows (see Gal. 6:7). If you are sowing toward righteousness, toward the Kingdom, then God cannot be mocked. He is going to bring everything you need according to His riches and glory in Christ Jesus. God wants you to prosper. Say, "Yes, Lord, I want to obey You, and I want to prosper. I am the head and not the tail. I am the lender, not the borrower, and I am blessed, not cursed."

Choose this day, Jesus Christ, and when you choose Him, realize that what you have chosen is an abundance from Heaven in every area of your life. Know that all your prayers are going to be answered because you are not going to pray amiss. You are only going to pray according to what the Spirit says to pray. You are not going to seek after riches because they are going to seek after you. You have to seek after God, and then that abundance will come. Jesus sent me back, and He showed me that the Spirit wants to lead us into prosperity.

The reason why we are limited down here is that we do not understand what the Kingdom of God represents. We do not understand the love of our Father God. God has expressed everything through Jesus Christ. When God gave us Jesus, He gave us everything because Jesus is the Advocate. Jesus is the one who is seated at the right hand of God, and He receives us because He bought us back. We have been bought with a price, which means that we have been adopted into the family of God. We are part of the family of God, and we receive the inheritance of God, our Father, and in Him, all our needs are going to be met. Everything that we need is going to be met.

If our needs are not being met, it is because this kingdom down here of satan is restricting and controlling you. That is why you need to address the devil, and you need to use these power words in your life. Your prosperity comes from Heaven, and it does not have to do with a dollar bill or a denomination of money. It has to do with favor. It has to do with God's plan for your life, providing for you based on what is written in your book in Heaven. It has nothing to do with satan because satan has nothing to do with God's system.

HE REBUKES THE DEVOURER

God tells you that you need to tithe. You need to give, and you need to engage God in His Kingdom because then satan has no power over you.

> *Bring all the tithes into the storehouse, that there may be food in My house, and try Me now in this," says the Lord of hosts, "If I will not open for you the windows of heaven and pour out for you such blessing that there will not be room enough to receive it. And I will rebuke the devourer for your sakes, so that he will not destroy the fruit of your ground, nor shall the vine fail to bear fruit for you in the field," says the Lord of hosts.*
> —MALACHI 3:10-11

These verses were written by the prophet Malachi because God wanted people to know that if they gave a portion of what was brought in, the complete other part of it would be set apart, and the devourer could not come in and take it. When you set apart a portion of what comes in, 10 percent, it keeps the rest holy, and satan cannot come in. God says He will rebuke the devourer for your sake. He will open the Heavens and pour out such a blessing on you that you won't even have enough storehouses to keep everything that He gives you. When you tithe, you are participating in God's Kingdom.

Satan does not want you to give the tithe. He does not want you to give at all, and he *does not* want you to prosper. Once you realize that, then you have to realize that a good Father, a good God, would want us to have everything that we would ever need. Jesus said that it is hard for a rich man to enter the Kingdom of Heaven (see Matt. 19:23). There is a pressure to rely on money and riches down here, and you cannot do that. You must seek the Kingdom.

God testified through the prophet Jeremiah,

> *Then it shall be to Me a name of joy, a praise, and an*
> *honor before all nations of the earth, who shall hear all*
> *the good that I do to them; they shall fear and tremble*
> *for all the goodness and all the prosperity that I provide*
> *for it.*
>
> —JEREMIAH 33:9

Through prosperity, God is going to display how good He is to His people. All the nations will see His goodness and see that the God of Israel is the one true God. People are going to tremble for all the goodness and prosperity that God will provide for them.

The prophet Joel prophesied that there is going to be a restoration of prosperity to Judah and Jerusalem (see Joel 3:1 NLT). This is important to note because this prophecy is going to be fulfilled in the days in which we live. Israel is prospering, even though it is such a small nation. God is prospering Israel because that is His land. How much more will God do for us through Jesus Christ, through the crucifixion, and that blood covenant that God has given us as Gentiles? Don't you think that covenant would be at least as good as the old covenant? If God is going to restore the riches and prosperity to Judah and Jerusalem, then what He has done through Jesus Christ is even greater.

I believe that we need to repent and realize that God is good and that He wants to give us the Kingdom. We need to prosper down here on this earth for people to come and have to borrow from us, which means dominion to establish the covenant. God told us we are going to be the head and not the tail. That means people are going to need what you have. There is going to be a demand placed on you because God is blessing you, and everyone is going to need what you have.

You need to look at what is happening in your life right now to see if you are experiencing need, lack, or poverty. If you are, that is evidence of satan stealing from you. Our Father God is good, and He has given us Jesus Christ. He has given us all things exceedingly above what we could ask or think that He has available for us. God is laying up to our account everything that we give to Him. Jesus told us that if we would leave everything for His sake, including houses and people and lands in this life, we will be rewarded those things back a hundredfold, and with it, persecutions (see Mark 10:29-30). Anything that you give up, God is going to give back to you.

Chapter 16

CHARACTER

*The Son radiates God's own glory and expresses the
very character of God, and he sustains everything by the
mighty power of his command. When he had cleansed
us from our sins, he sat down in the place of honor
at the right hand of the majestic God in heaven.*
—HEBREWS 1:3 NLT

GOD HAS CREATED us in His image, and He has instilled character into us. The Spirit of God wants us to have godly character. He wants us to be able to have a command about us and for us to be established on this earth in authority. Character is very important because unbelievers look at Christians to see if we are different. When they see that we are different, then they want to know *why* we are different. When we say *no* to ungodliness and worldly passions, and we walk and live an upright life in Christ Jesus, then we are set apart.

In the world, people cannot resist the evil one, and they serve satan, whether they like it or not. Paul said, *"Whose minds the god of this world has blinded"* (see 2 Cor. 4:4). They carry out satan's desires. When you are born again of the Spirit, you are set free, and you have authority in Jesus' name to break every power that has tried to affect your character in an ungodly way.

In Acts 19:14-16, there were seven sons of Sceva, who was the Jewish high priest, and they were trying to cast out a devil. They had seen Paul and heard about Jesus casting out devils, and so they tried to do this themselves. The evil spirit spoke to them and said, *"Jesus, I know, and Paul, I know, but who are you?"* The evil spirit did not know who the sons of Sceva were in the spirit because they were not established. They did not have the character of God because they were not born again. These young men were trying to exercise authority that they did not have. The demon leaped on them through that person and beat them up.

As Christians, we have authority. God has created us to be in His image, which means we have His character, but satan does not want us to have the character of God. He does not want you to understand who you are as a son or a daughter of God. In Heaven, everything is established by God's throne and His authority. God's personality—His character—is part of the glory that comes out from Him. There is a cloud that is full of colors and glory that radiates out from God, and it is His character, His personality.

If you encounter the glory of God, you encounter the Father in His fullest sense. Moses asked God to have that glory revealed to him, but God's glory was too much for Moses to take (see Exod. 33:18-23). God protected Moses by putting him in the cleft of a rock as His glory passed by him. God only let Moses view Him from behind because the glory of the face of God would have killed Moses.

Moses experienced God's personality as He walked by because God said that He would make all of His goodness pass before Moses. God's goodness was revealed, and it is part of His personality and His character. Jesus displayed the character of the Father because whatever Jesus did on the earth, He did because the Father told Him to do it. Jesus was acting out His Father's wishes, and He is the perfect example of the Father.

REPRESENTING THE FATHER

One day the disciples asked Jesus to show them the Father. Jesus replied and said, *"He who has seen Me has seen the Father"* (John 14:8-11). The acts that Jesus did and the words He spoke were from the Father and were not from Himself. In this life of Christ, the character that you have has got to represent the character of God.

Peter spoke about the fact that if we are partakers of the precious promises that God has given us, then we will be partakers of the divine nature (see 2 Pet. 1:4). Being a partaker of the divine nature causes us to escape the corruption that is in the world through lust. We have overcome all the things in this world, and our character will show that. When people see you, they will have to see Jesus in you, and that will cause you to minister and be a witness.

Jesus was the example of God the Father. He went around doing good and healing everyone who was oppressed by the devil, and God was with Him (see Acts 10:38). God was healing people, and so Jesus healed people. God was raising people from the dead, and so Jesus raised people from the dead. When Jesus preached the good news, it was because the Father wanted that to be done. The Father was revealed in Jesus Christ, and Jesus Christ is revealed in us.

When we pray in the Spirit, the Spirit is giving us words from the Father. He is praying out the perfect will of God through our lips, from out of our spirits, and that is part of our character too. Paul the apostle talks about this in Romans 8:27, *"Because He makes intercession for the saints according to the will of God."*

Your character is also a witness, and when people see you acting a certain way, they want to know why. They want to know why you will not do a certain thing or go to a certain place. Every day at work, I would sit there, and the power of God would hit, and people would ask me, "What do you do on your overnights?" "Why don't you come and drink with us?" "Why don't you come and eat with us?" "Why don't you hang out with us?"

I would say, "Well, I died on the operating table, and I was sent back. My life is not my own now. I have been bought with a price, and I have been sent back to do God's will."

They would say, "You died?"

I would say, "Yeah, I died on the operating table, and I saw the future, and I saw all these things, and I met Jesus. He had all these books written about me and other people, and so He sent me back."

They would start crying right there, and the whole atmosphere would switch, and I would start ministering to them. Not one person has ever rejected me when I have told them that God has a destiny for everyone and that He wants to develop us in our destinies. The power of God was always made manifest in that situation.

There are certain things that we do not do because they are detrimental to getting us to where we need to go. I have never met a person who did not want to know what the plan for their life was and what they should be doing to be successful. All people want to be successful and want to fulfill whatever it is they are meant to fulfill.

Certain things must be developed in your character so that you can say *no* to the things that are taking you off track with God. Everyone who is missing it with God has instilled within them the fact that they are fallen and off track. So, I do not have to tell them that they are going to hell because many of the people who are not born again already know it. Even if they say, "I don't believe in this," if you keep talking to them, you know that they know inside that they are not fulfilled. Most people to whom I speak want to know if there is a God. They want to know if God loves them, and they want to know if He has a plan for their lives.

You, as a Christian walking in God's character, will cause them to see that you are different, but they will want to know what it is that makes you different. How can you say *no* to these things when they cannot say *no* to them? A Christian should walk in victory and walk in dominance over the devil, and people are hungry for that. I am trying to show you that Jesus gives you the ability to overcome evil, to overcome sickness and poverty. I want you to see that you can know God's will for your life. Every Christian should know God's will because we are part of the family. The Father desires to give you everything that you need for this life in order to walk this life out.

Through His Holy Spirit, God wants to show you His plan for you. Character is developed when you trust in God. It is developed when you know that the devil is a liar and that God always tells you the truth, and most people want to know the truth. There has never been a time where someone had stood before God at the end of their life and told God that He was wrong. God is always going to be right, and people are always going to be wrong. People will find out at the end of their lives that Jesus Christ was the only answer to their problems down here, and that they needed Him as their Savior and Deliverer.

GENERATIONAL PLUMB LINE

A plumb line is a piece of string that has a weight suspended from it. When you hold it by the string, gravity pulls the weight down and straightens the string tightly, revealing true straightness. Besides showing you perfect uprightness, a plumb line will show you if something is crooked or not. Did you know that you are a plumb line?

During the prophet Amos' time, people were saying that the crooked ways were straight, and the straight ways were crooked.

> *And the Lord said to me, "Amos, what do you see?" And I said, "A plumb line." Then the Lord said: "Behold, I am setting a plumb line in the midst of My people Israel; I will not pass by them anymore."*
>
> *—AMOS 7:8*

When God sent a prophet into Israel and prophesied, it was the Word of the Lord, and it was giving the truth about their condition with God.

You can be a plumb line to a generation. You can be a plumb line in your family, at your work, and wherever you go. God wants to use you to show people what true uprightness is and that there is a true God, and that there is an absolute truth. You can show there is a way to walk with God in Christianity where you can walk straight, and you can walk correctly in this generation. However, there may be conflict for you. Some people will want you to get out of the way because your life will show true uprightness. If you are walking in the Spirit, you are going to be an enemy of satan. As God is leading people into truth by the Spirit, satan is leading people into deception and falsehood. There will be many people going to hell who did not need to. There is a narrow way that leads to life through Jesus Christ, and very few find it (Matt. 7:13-14).

You can help others by letting God develop your character. This process is done by allowing the Spirit of God to dictate and talk to you, and to lead you and guide you through those situations by which your character becomes developed. Once you know the truth and it sets you free, as you continue to walk in that truth, you will see freedom develop in your life. When that happens, you become a plumb line. You will represent the truth of Heaven wherever you go, and that is real ministry.

Ministry is the Spirit of God, which is the Spirit of truth, leading people into all truth, and He does that through you and all of us. We, as Christians and as family, need to represent what God is doing in the earth. It was like when the word of the Lord came to the prophets and they spoke because they were moved by the Holy Ghost. When they spoke, they became the plumb line that became the truth. When the nation of Israel heard the prophets speak, they knew that they had heard the truth.

When you endure hardship as a good soldier, it strengthens your character.

And endurance develops strength of character, and character strengthens our confident hope of salvation.
—Romans 5:4 NLT

Then your character strengthens your hope, which is a part of your salvation, and people see that. That development of character is like a sign that is lit up, and people see that you are different. Not different in the sense of being weird, you want to be different in the sense of being in right standing with God, where righteousness is contrasted against unrighteousness, where it's light versus darkness. There has to be that contrast between you and the world, and the Spirit of God can do that for you.

It can work the other way too because people with bad character can corrupt your good character if you let them (see 1 Cor. 15:33 NLT). If you are not influencing people around you, then they are going to influence you. You have to be careful about the dynamics of your relationships. Are you supposed to be involved with certain people? God, by His Spirit, knows that you have to be salt in this world, but if you lose your saltiness, then you do not have the purpose that God intended for you (see Matt. 5:13). You have to be careful that other people do not influence you to the place where you have corrupted your good character.

THE BELIEVER'S RESPONSE

Your character brings glory to God. People will not only see that you are supernaturally being led by God, but you are supernaturally transformed in your character.

> *May you always be filled with the fruit of your salvation—the righteous character produced in your life by Jesus Christ—for this will bring much glory and praise to God.*
> —PHILIPPIANS 1:11 NLT

Your character, how you act, is very important, and this includes how you respond when you are mistreated. When you are mistreated, you need to act appropriately because people expect you to respond in a certain way.

When someone wrongs you and you do not retaliate, they realize that you are better off than they are. That is why Jesus said, *"If someone slaps you on one cheek, offer the other cheek also"* (Luke 6:29 NLT). Essentially, Jesus was saying not to respond in the way that most people would because people will see the difference in you. I have told people that I love people even when they hit me because I want them to know the love of God. People have turned and given their lives to the Lord because they saw my response. As Jesus said, if you are mistreated, *"Great is your reward in Heaven"* (Matt. 5:12).

Paul commended Timothy as being one who had served him well. Timothy's character was upright when he worked with Paul.

> *But you know how Timothy has proved himself. Like a son with his father, he has served with me in preaching the Good News.*
> —Philippians 2:22 NLT

Timothy was recommended by Paul because his character was proven.

In this generation, good character can be very rare, because it is not emphasized anymore, and satan does not want people to be of good character. These things have to be developed in you by you meditating on the Word of God and being transformed by the renewing of your mind. You must also allow the power of the Spirit to ignite you every day and be led by the Spirit of God, not driven by evil spirits or by fear.

There is a spirit of fear, and you can be driven by it. You can be driven because you have to be in control all the time, but God wants you to relinquish that. God wants you to have character to where you are led by God because you trust Him. You do not do anything out of fear, but you do it out of power and love and a sound mind (see 2 Tim. 1:7)

The glory of God has been given to us! Jesus tells us that we share in the same glory that He and His Father shared and that we are one with the Father, as They are one.

> *And the glory which you gave Me I have given them, that they may be one just as We are one. I in them, and You in Me; that they may be made perfect in one, and that the world may know that You have sent Me, and have loved them as You have Loved Me.*
> —JOHN 17:22-23

Jesus said that the Father loves us just as much as He loves Jesus. If that is the truth, then our character should represent that we are loved by our Father. We are one with the Father, and our unity is part of the Holy Trinity. We are representing Heaven on this earth, so you can imagine satan does not want us to walk as Jesus did.

DEVELOPING CHARACTER

Jesus was one with the Father, and His character was that no matter what, He was going to do the will of His Father. When Peter told Jesus that He was not going to be crucified, Jesus rebuked satan, who was speaking through Peter. Jesus said, *"Get behind me, satan! You are an offense to Me, for you are not mindful of the things of God, but the things of men"* (Matt. 16:23). Jesus had set His face like flint toward Jerusalem because He knew that He was sent to die. Jesus knew that He was sent to be crucified on a cross, and He set Himself to accomplish that, and that was part of His character.

Peter was in leadership in the book of Acts as apostle and pastor when Ananias and Sapphira conspired to lie against the Holy Spirit (see Acts 5:1-11). This couple secretly kept back money from the sale of their property. When they came and presented themselves to Peter, God revealed to Peter what they had done, and Peter said,

> *Ananias, why did you let satan fill your heart and make you think you could lie to the Holy Spirit?... How could you plot such a thing in your heart? You haven't lied to the people, you've lied to God!*
> —ACTS 5:3-4 TPT

Both Ananias and Sapphira dropped dead one after the other.

Peter was set in the Church as part of the fivefold ministry, and because of that, the power of God manifested so mightily that Peter would walk down the street, and if his shadow touched a sick person, that person would be healed. That same power brought judgment as well when the Holy Spirit judged those two church members. The power of God could manifest through Peter so powerfully because his character had been fully developed.

If you remember, Peter was always arguing with Jesus, and he was the disciple who had denied Jesus three times. One day when Peter was fishing, Jesus came and appeared to him and told him to turn back and to feed the sheep of God. You can see that Peter's character was quite different by the time he wrote Second Peter and taught about being partakers of the divine nature and having the character of God in our lives.

A Foundation of Good Character

As you recall, there had been none greater than John the Baptist. Then Jesus said everyone after John, even the least in the Kingdom, is greater than John.

> *For I say to you, among those born of women there is not a greater prophet than John the Baptist; but he who is least in the kingdom of God is greater than he.*
> —Luke 7:28

Here we have the new covenant coming in, and all believers who believe from now on are greater than all those in the Old Testament. We now have this amazing walk and relationship with God in this new covenant. We have everything that has culminated up to this point. We have that power with us from the foundation of the prophets and the apostles. They have laid the foundation, and now at the end of the age, we are greater than all those people. Jesus said, "Now the least in the Kingdom is greater than John." We are here to wrap it up at the end of this age, and we need to talk about character. We need to allow the Holy Spirit to establish character in us because it is the witness of God.

Chapter 17

DIVINE HEALTH

*Beloved, I wish above all things that thou mayest
prosper and be in health, even as thy soul prospereth.*

—3 JOHN 1:2 KJV

T HERE WAS A great healing revival that happened in the
Church in the 1950s and 1960s, and many people were getting healed. However, there is something in the Bible that is
rarely talked about, and that is divine health. It has to do with not
getting sick in the first place. We need to learn how to stay well and
walk in divine health.

When Israel left Egypt, they did not have one feeble person
among them (see Ps. 105:37). God said to them, *"I will take sickness
away from the midst of you"* (Exod. 23:25). God has the ability to
sustain people to where they do not experience sickness. Even the
shoes that the Israelites had on their feet did not wear out while
they were in the desert, and that was a miracle!

There is a step up from receiving your healing, as we saw in the
healing movements of the past. There is coming a time where we

are going to emphasize God's divine health, like when Israel left Egypt, and there was not one sick among them.

In Third John 1:2, John expressed his desire when he said, *"I pray that you may prosper in all things and be in health, just as your soul prospers."* He wanted you to prosper in your *health* and in your soul, not just in your finances. He was talking about your body because your body is your health. Your soul is your mind, will, and emotions, and God wants you to prosper in your body as well.

The Church has emphasized healing for so long, and we have healing, but what about divine health? Satan does not want us to talk about the next step up, which is not getting sick at all. This power word, *divine health*, points to God's desire for us to live a long life, a prosperous life, and be in health. We cannot settle for just seventy or eighty years of life on the earth. We need to extend out our faith to believe God for a long and prosperous life in the world because we are witnesses in this world.

We witness in the Scriptures that Israel did not get sick. They were in the desert all those years, and God took sickness away from the midst of them. He sent His Word and healed them (see Ps. 107:20 KJV). You must believe that the power of God that raised Jesus from the dead is dwelling in you, and it is quickening your mortal body (see Rom. 8:11). That power is being transferred out from a spiritual element to a physical manifestation, and not just for healing, but for divine health. God can and will supernaturally sustain you.

When the Israelites did not get sick, the nations saw that, and when their shoes did not wear out while they were in the desert, that was a testimony. When you do not get sick, people start to inquire and want to know what your secret is. You tell them that

God sustains you, that you have divine health, and that is a testimony people want to hear.

At any time in a room full of people, most of the people in that room need a touch in their bodies for physical healing. What if God started to move by His Spirit to take us from getting hands laid on for healing to people not getting sick anymore? What if God started to move in the Spirit that way?

When I was brought back from the operating room when I died, I saw that God's plan for us was that we would never get sick. Sickness is something from the fall. In this fallen world, sickness is part of it because there are all kinds of diseases and bacteria in the world now. In this fallen world, we have snakes and spiders, and bugs that have poison in them. We now have all these hostile things in our environment, but God wants to sustain us. God wants us to get to the place where we are not just concentrating on getting healed. He wants us to concentrate on staying well, and that has to do with divine health.

EATING THE BREAD OF LIFE

When you eat God's Word, it is health to your body: *"For they are life unto those that find them, and health to all their flesh"* (Prov. 4:22). This verse is talking about the Word of God. Also, Jesus said, *"I am the living bread which came down from Heaven"* (John 6:51). And He said to satan, *"Man shall not live by bread alone, but by every Word that proceeds from the mouth of God"* (Matt. 4:4). Jesus walked as a human being on this earth, and He was never sick. Jesus went around doing good and healing everyone who was oppressed by the devil. Jesus was always correcting the sickness that was in people because it was not God's will for them to be sick. It is satan's will for people to be sick.

In your walk with God, take it to another level. Start to see that God wants you well all the time, not just to believe Him for healing when you get sick. What if you never got sick? What if you never had to take medicine again? God's perfect plan that I saw in Heaven was that man was never to experience what he is experiencing in this fallen world. There are all these discrepancies and all these disappointments and discouragements. There are so many things that God does not want to happen, but they do happen because satan is in this world, and he is messing around with God's system.

Sickness is not part of God's plan, and it never was, but in this world, we are going to encounter sickness. What if you started to develop in your walk with God, just like Enoch did? God won Enoch over because Enoch walked with God for 300 years. Enoch started walking with God at 65 years of age, and at 365 years of age, Enoch pleased God so much that God just took him (see Gen. 5:23-24). Enoch never experienced death (see Heb. 11:5). There is this ability for people to walk with God today.

Enoch was in the Old Testament, and he did not even have the New Testament. Think of the new covenant that we have today as Christians to encourage us and unite us together. Enoch was walking alone, and there were not a lot of people in his day walking with God. The world was just about to be judged, it was right before the flood, and evil was everywhere. Enoch was one of those prophets who walked the earth in unity with the Spirit of God and unity with God's plan.

The power that raised Jesus from the dead—the power that came into Him, into His body, and raised Him from the dead—is the same power that is in us. Paul said that *that* power will quicken or make alive our mortal bodies, and mortal means death. The mortal body that seems to die at a certain age can be quickened by the Spirit and can be revived. We understand that healing is a spiritual thing first, even though we need physical healing, healing is not from this world; it is from Heaven.

THE REALM OF MIRACLES

You have to receive your healing from the Spirit realm, and it is by faith that you receive. That means you trust that God exists and *"is a rewarder of those who diligently seek Him"* (Heb. 11:6). You see *"Him who is invisible"* (Heb. 11:26-27), and because of that you skip over the limitations of your mind and your body. You are only limited in your body and your thinking if you allow yourself to be. However, if you allow the Spirit of God to supersede these things, then you will not have any problem receiving from God.

When you are healed, or when you receive a miracle, it comes from the other realm, and it manifests in this realm, but your miracle starts in Heaven. Your provision for healing is in Heaven. God does not have any sickness in Heaven, so He cannot make anyone sick. God does not have sickness to give to anyone, and that is why Jesus went around healing every person who was oppressed of the devil. Jesus went around doing good, and He was always doing the will of the Father.

The power of the risen Savior that is inside you is resonating within you with the same power that raised Jesus from the dead. It is the same power that the Spirit of God manifested while He was brooding over the waters at creation, and that same creative power is dwelling in you. At any one moment, you can receive your healing because it is not from this realm; it is from the other realm. Divine health, however, means you get to the place where you do not need to ask for healing anymore.

You are walking in divine health, but there is even a step beyond that. There is divine life where the life of God is resonating so strong within you because you have yielded just like Enoch. God won Enoch over, and he walked with God, and then that transformation in Enoch turned into translation. It turned into crossing over, and his flesh walked over to the other realm, and Enoch is in Heaven today with his body, and so is Elijah, and so is Jesus.

Jesus was made flesh on this earth and lived among us. Now, He has a glorified body in Heaven, but the blood that was in Him was shed and put on the altar there at the mercy seat. When Jesus was resurrected before He ascended to Heaven, He preached for forty days on the Kingdom of God *in His physical body* (see Acts 1:3). There is divine life, and there is divine health. There are greater things involved than the Church is even preaching and teaching on right now.

DIVINE HEALTH BECOMING DIVINE LIFE

When I was in Heaven, I saw the end of the age when people were being healed by the masses in church services without hands being laid on them. I saw that people at the end of the age did not get sick anymore, and they began living longer. I saw at the end of the age that God was going to display His glory through His people and that there was not going to be any feeble or sick among them.

It will be just like at the time of the exodus of the Israelites from Egypt, and so it will be in this age.

Right before Jesus comes back, there will be a time where people begin to walk in divine health. Then they will walk in divine life, which is even above divine health, and then they will disappear like Enoch. The Church, the Body of Christ, will walk over and disappear, and that is what people refer to as the rapture. It has to do with going from needing healing to walking in divine health, to walking in divine life, and then we disappear. That is what I saw happening. I saw that in the end times, people would live to be 120 years old and that it would become common for Christians to live longer. I saw at the end that it would be when this power word—divine health—would come into play. We will begin walking in freedom in our bodies to where our bodies will be healed. There was no explanation for what I saw other than that God had done a miracle, and it is going to become commonplace.

Jesus instructed me not to be surprised when I see people living longer on the earth. Jesus said that He was going to stretch it out at the end so that He can bring glory to the Father through people who are on the earth. The Church, at the end, will receive so much impartation from Heaven that we will live longer. We will walk in health, and diseases and sicknesses will not touch us.

God said, *"So you shall serve the Lord your God, and He will bless your bread and your water. And I will take sickness away from the midst of you"* (Exod. 23:25). You cannot get clearer than this; God is not giving sickness. God takes sickness away, and what He is doing is taking away demonic influence. God is taking away what satan is doing. It is time to have your mind transformed and start to frame your world, not just believing for healing but believing for divine health.

As Israel continues to progress toward the end of this age, Israel will come to the forefront in technology, and they already have in many areas. God is going to bless them in the medical field. God is going to give the Israeli scientists, biologists, and chemists the ability to eradicate certain diseases as part of the blessing. God is going to use Israel, and even though Israel is not serving God as they should right now, God has proclaimed them as His people.

Jesus told me that when He was walking on the earth, everywhere He went, He had compassion on the people. The reason He had compassion was that He knew their sickness and their condition were not God's perfect will. That is what moved Jesus with compassion, and He healed the sick. Jesus corrected the wrong things that He knew His Father wanted to change. What if God not only wanted to heal you, but He wanted to keep you from getting sick again?

WHO TOLD YOU?

Years ago, no runner could break the four-minute mile. Then one person suddenly broke that record, and within a couple of weeks, there were three or four other people who continued to break the record. What happened? People had limited themselves based on the fact that there was no manifestation of someone breaking the record. As soon as one person broke the record, then others were given permission. These runners' minds were now framed with new information, and that information did not limit them anymore. They were now able to break that record. Now many people run under a four-minute mile.

People are restricted in their minds. If I feel restricted in any way or if I feel confined, I remember what the Lord instructed me when He asked me, "Who told you that you could not do that?" What God was saying was He never told me that I could not do that. So, where had I gotten that information?

> *My son, attend to my words; incline thine ear unto my sayings. Let them not depart from thine eyes; keep them in the midst of thine heart. For they are life unto those that find them, and health to all their flesh.*
> —PROVERBS 4:20-22

In these last days, God has given us His Word. *"He sent His Word and healed them"* (Ps. 107:20), and *"By His stripes, we are healed"* (Isa. 53:5). What if God wants to sustain our health through that same Word? What if we are eating the Word of God with such conviction that it becomes a medicine to our flesh?

> *For I will restore health unto thee, and I will heal thee of thy wounds, saith the Lord; because they called thee an Outcast, saying, This is Zion, whom no man seeketh after.*
> —JEREMIAH 30:17

God comes in, and He heals our wounds, but then what if we stay healthy? I have noticed this with myself as God starts to heal things in my body. I did let things happen in my life, and bad things do happen, but I do not know anyone who is perfectly well. However, God began to change my mind about what I see. Not only am I seeing my body healed, but I am also starting to have the faith to walk in divine health, and this is part of God's covenant. God loves you, and He does not want you to be sick anymore.

When the people of Israel came out of Egypt, they wandered in the desert for forty years. They were in a desert, a hostile environment with wild animals, and a lack of water and food. Yet God provided for them and sustained them by giving them the manna from Heaven and water that came out of a rock. God supernaturally sustained them for forty years.

The book of Hebrews instructs us that we are not to operate in unbelief and be stiff-necked or rebellious like the Israelites were (see 3:7-19). We are to enter into the rest of God, and we are to believe. The writer of Hebrews tells us not to be like those who fell in the desert—who, through their unbelief, did not enter in and experience the promises of God. God wants you to experience His promises. As the children of Israel were sustained supernaturally, it is what God wants to do for you. Your mindset now is to receive your healing and then realize that God has a plan for you to walk in divine health.

The prophet Elisha died of sickness (see 2 Kings 13:14-21), and they buried him in a cave. Years later, when Israel was at war, a soldier's body that had passed away was let down into that cave where Elisha was buried. When that dead body touched the bones of Elisha, the man was resurrected and came back out alive from the power that was still resting in Elisha's bones.

Think about this: Elisha died of a disease, but the power of God that was available was *inside* him. Elisha could have received the same healing as that soldier. The resurrection power for healing that soldier received by accidentally touching Elisha's bones years later was in Elisha. Do not find yourself in a situation where you do not discern that the power that raised Jesus from the dead is dwelling inside you. That power will quicken your mortal body and supernaturally sustain you in this life with divine health.

Chapter 18

ACCOUNTABILITY

So then each of us shall give account of himself to God.
—ROMANS 14:12

A CCOUNTABILITY IS ANOTHER one of those power words that satan fears, but it should be one that Christians involve themselves in often. Accountability is a very powerful word to meditate on because, as it says in Romans 14:12, each one of us will one day have to give an account of ourselves to God. Today you will hear a lot of teaching on what we would call *extreme grace.* Yes, God is extreme in His grace, but as Paul said, it should not give us a license to sin: *"But put on the Lord Jesus Christ, and make no provision for the flesh, to fulfill its lusts"* (Rom. 13:14).

At a time when we should be accountable, we instead find ourselves, at the end of this age, with an extreme view of believing that because grace will cover our sins, we are free to sin. People are being given permission to sin, and it is not right. God wants us to be accountable, and one day we are going to give an account for our lives.

When I died and I was in the presence of God, I gave an account for my life, and I was, at that time, pronounced faithful. I was told that I had done everything God had asked me to do and would receive my reward. However, I was sent back and asked if I could do something for "extra credit," as Jesus referred to it.

I saw this in Heaven in the presence of God, and one day you will, too. You will see your life pass before you. It will happen in a flash, and God will show you everything that you have done in faith and the flesh. It is to reward you for everything you did in faith in the Son of God. Whatever you were supposed to do in your life for God, whatever gifts God gave you to do it, and what you did with them, you will be given rewards.

I received rewards for what I had done based on what God had given me to do. Now, if I had done anything that was not of God, I did not get a reward for that, and it was burned up. I was held accountable, and everything is being kept track of in Heaven, and I received rewards. There were only rewards for what God had written down for me to do, and anything that I did in the flesh, I did not receive a reward for doing.

As I have said, in Heaven, there are books written about each one of us, and God's angels can look at them, and then they are sent down to Earth to help us. I saw all of those books in Heaven. The angels were only sent down to help us in the things that were written about us in Heaven, and they know what the books say. The angels are accountable to implement those things into our lives, and then we are accountable to yield to that help.

There are times in your life when angels are standing right beside you, and they have been sent to implement what is supposed to happen at that time. There are seasons and cycles that happen in our lives. Sometimes, when there is a change coming, we resist it because we are afraid, and we do not want to change. We can get comfortable in what we are doing because we like its predictability, but God might want you to move on to something greater, and you should not resist that.

Accountability comes in to play by not being resistant to change and not being resistant to the angels that have come beside you to implement God's perfect will for your life. Why would you want to resist what God has for you? The spirit is always willing to do the will of God, but *"the flesh is weak"* (Matt. 26:41). There is absolute truth in Heaven, and that absolute truth is written down. Each person is going to be accountable for what is written in their book and what they did with it.

GOD IS NOT LIMITING YOU

I saw when I died that I did not do all that God had intended me to do. I was faithful at what I did do, but there was so much more that I could have done. I had not made myself available, and I was not accountable to do the "greater works." I only did the works of Jesus that I knew He wanted me to do, and I had not done the greater works that He had for me. There would have been so much more available if I had dug in and been persistent, and if I had sought God and believed His Word. Faith was being instilled in me by reading the Word, and it was expanding me, and there was no limit to what I could have done in this life.

When I was sent back, I was sent back knowing that there were no limits to what I could do in this life on the earth. I was given another chance to do the greater works of Jesus, which meant that I have to allow the limitations to be taken off of my mind. Your mind has framed your world based on data that was given to it, but that data is false. People have influenced you. Things you have read, things you have seen, and what has happened to you has limited you, and you have limited God. You must realize that God is not limiting you.

When I was sent back, I saw that failure was not even an option, and that there was no way that the Holy Spirit was going to lead me into failure. I saw the angels that were sent to me, and there was no way that they were going to lead me into failure. I saw that my inability to grasp the goodness of God was keeping me out of God's best for my life.

Accountability is when you turn yourself over to God, and you say, "I am weak, Lord, and I do not understand everything, and I cannot do this." As you turn yourself over, you are asking God to come in and help you. Say to Him, "Lord, your hand wrote my name in the Lamb's Book of Life, and I am rejoicing that my name is written there" (see Luke 10:20). When you do that, you are asking God to favor you, and you are asking for help. You are being accountable by acknowledging that Jesus Christ is your deliverer and redeemer. You acknowledge that your name is written in the Lamb's Book of Life, and you are a child of God.

> *Jesus replied, "Loving me empowers you to obey my word. And my Father will love you so deeply that we will come to you and make you our dwelling place."*
> —JOHN 14:23 TPT

Once you turn yourself over to God, you have asked for help, and you love God, then loving God empowers you to obey His Word. Your relationship with God has influenced you to the place where you engage Him. That engagement causes the power of the resurrection of Jesus Christ to ignite inside of you and empowers you to obey. You have to manifest what you believe. *"I will show you my faith by my works"* (James 2:18b). You show your faith by what you do. The power of God manifests through your flesh because you believe so deeply that it causes you to obey.

When you obey, you are accountable because you have heard the Word, and then after hearing, you do the Word. The manifestation is your accountability, and that is where you receive your reward. That transaction must happen, going from faith in your heart to action in your flesh. You have to obey, but loving God empowers you to obey. The Church of the Lord Jesus Christ is accountable under God as well. Even in this age of grace, we still have to manifest the works of God. We must discipline our flesh and make it do what God wants it to do. You have to live out of your spirit through your flesh.

HIGHER REALMS OF AUTHORITY

My brethren, let not many of you become teachers, knowing that we shall receive a stricter judgment.
—JAMES 3:1

Teachers in the Body of Christ are more accountable than a regular Christian. Those who teach in a church will be held to greater accountability. Even in the New Testament, certain people will be held in greater accountability because they are in a higher realm of authority. You will have the power of the Holy Spirit manifesting through a person who is teaching, but they are also being held in greater accountability.

Why do the wicked renounce God? He has said in his heart, "You will not require an account."

—Psalm 10:13

The world does not fear God, but they are deceived. The world thinks that they are not going to have to give an account of their lives to God, but they are wrong. Do not let anyone in the world deceive you or influence you in any way to cause you to think that you are not going to be held accountable. As a believer, your good works show that you are accountable. You are taking the faith that is in your heart, the experience in the encounter of the Holy Spirit in your life, and you are allowing it to manifest. The manifestation comes through what you do and what you say.

You are held accountable for the very words that come out of your mouth. Everyone will give an *account* on the day of judgment for every empty word they have spoken, and that means everyone (see Matt. 12:36). If you have said anything idle or you were not speaking the truth, you will be accountable for that, according to Jesus.

For what the law could not do in that it was weak through the flesh, God did by sending His own Son in the likeness of sinful flesh, on account of sin: He condemned sin in the flesh.

—Romans 8:3

God made sin accountable in the flesh, and then He sent Jesus to judge that sin. Then Jesus provided deliverance from sin through His blood. When Jesus walked on the earth, He walked in a body which is referred to here as *sinful flesh*. Jesus broke the power of the flesh by walking in the power of God and then being sacrificed as a perfect lamb. That was a legal transaction, and it happened. We now have the ability to do the same through the Spirit of God, if we yield to the Spirit, but if we do not, then we will walk in the flesh. However, we will be held accountable for walking in the flesh.

> *I am the vine, you are the branches. He who abides in Me, and I in him, bears much fruit; for without Me you can do nothing.*
>
> —JOHN 15:5

If Jesus turned off the life flow of the vine, then the branches would suffer lack because Jesus is the source. He is the vine, and we are the branches. We are held accountable not to manifest in the flesh, but to manifest through the life source that comes from Father God. When Jesus provides for us in life, we live off of that, and that is how we walk in the Spirit.

Many people ask me, "How do you walk in the Spirit?" I ask, "Well, how do you walk in the flesh?" You walk in the flesh because you yield to the flesh. When you fulfill the desires of the flesh, then you are walking in the flesh, which is an enemy of God, and you cannot please God. It is the same with the Spirit. If you want to walk in the Spirit, you have to yield to the Spirit, which means you have to yield to the fruit of the Spirit, which is in Galatians (see 5:22-23). You have to say *no* to the flesh and not give the flesh any ability to manifest.

The Spirit of God is going to manifest all the fruit of the Spirit, and you are going to walk in love. You are going to walk in First Corinthians 13:1-13, where love is patient, and love is kind. You are going to yield to all those different life sources that come from the Spirit of God, and you are going to manifest those in your life. You are going to be held accountable for whether you have yielded to the Spirit or the flesh. When Jesus provides life through the vine, you receive it because you are one of the branches. When you yield to that life source, it produces life. If you yield to the flesh, it produces death (see Rom. 8:13-14).

WAITING ON THE LORD

In my prayer time, I check in with God because I want to see what He is up to, what He is saying to me, and what He is doing. I ask, "Lord, what are you doing now? What are you saying now?" In the morning, when I wake up, I ask Him, "Lord, what is your desire? What are you thinking? What is it that you want me to do today?" I am accountable to God, and I keep in contact with Him all the time by speaking to Him and asking Him for help.

When you are accountable to God like that, you must wait on Him and trust Him because God does not always answer right away. That is why you have to get into a place where you wait on God, and that is part of being accountable to Him, and this impacts your life in a great way. I wait in His presence for a long period, and sometimes I am not thinking about anything except His Word. I just let God's Word impact my life, and in that waiting time of meditation, I start to encounter the other realm. The presence of God begins to fill up in the place where I am waiting on Him. God's presence might happen in a couple of seconds, or it might take a while. It depends upon your spiritual atmosphere at the time. If you are in war, you are going to have to fight through the devils and break their power and call upon the angels to help you and stand with you.

Once you are established, you can be accountable by waiting on God and letting the Holy Spirit come as your counselor. The Holy Spirit will start to show you the things that are going on and the desires of the Father. There are times where I wait on God, and I still do not hear anything. I will go about my day and my schedule, and then as I am doing that, later in the day, suddenly, the Spirit will begin ministering to me.

The reason the Spirit suddenly comes is that I turned myself to God earlier in the day, and I said, "Lord, I want to know what you are doing." Then when I went out and continued about my day, the Spirit of God spoke His plans hours later. So, do not be discouraged if it does not happen right away. You need to wait on God, give Him time, and meditate on His Word.

REFUSE TO ENGAGE THE DEVIL

You may encounter the devil, an attack of the enemy, or encounter an evil presence around you. Remember that part of what you are doing in the Spirit is sizing up the devil, and you see what his intent is through the Spirit of God. You are discerning, and you are allowing God, through accountability, to begin coaching you on what the enemy is doing.

God can show you the battle strategies of the enemy. He can show you what the devil is doing, and your discernment can be developed, but this happens because you are accountable. You turn yourself over to God, and then you can size up the devil. You can look at him, and you can discern ahead of time before anything even happens. You will be able to discern and see his plans and strategies.

Paul said, *"For we are not ignorant of his devices"* (2 Cor. 2:11). You can encounter warfare, but you must let the Spirit of God show you what is truly going on. When you begin to receive that revelation, then you start to pray against the enemy according to the revelation you received. You break satan's power, you drive him out, and you continually force him out of everything. Wherever you go, you are driving satan out, and that is what Jesus did all the time, and He taught me to do this. Jesus said, "Build yourself up in your most holy faith, praying in the Holy Spirit. Meditate by waiting on God, turning yourself over to Him, and being accountable."

Next, as a good soldier, you engage in warfare, and what you do is you drive the enemy out. You do not have to discuss anything with him. I never talk to the devil except to address him and give him commands, because he does not understand anything else. The enemy wants to try to compromise with you, and he wants to talk to you and try to get you pulled away. Never do that with the devil, you just give him commands. You keep it short and tell the devil that he is a liar, tell him who he is, and tell him to go.

You drive the devil out, refusing to engage him in any other way except through the authority of the Spirit of God. You can drive out sickness, drive out fear, and drive out poverty that way, and you do everything that Jesus did. If the devil looks in your eyes, he will know you mean business, and that is what Jesus showed me.

Jesus said to me, "You can size the devil up, and the Spirit of God can show you what he is doing, but then you have to be bold. You have to know that when you are addressing the devil, he is aware that you know he has to go. You must see that satan does not want Christians to be fully established in their authority in Jesus Christ. You have to have a command about you, and it comes by you being accountable.

When you turn yourself over to God, you have to overcome, and you have to get to the place where you are not the victim anymore. It is time for you to victimize the devil. You continually drive him out and never let him rest and treat *him* as the victim. You have to have a Spirit of deliverance about you and be rough with the devil. You must realize that satan has to listen to you because he knows that he has to go.

You can uproot and drive out thousands and thousands of devils in a lifetime. You can drive devils out of your life and through your walk with Jesus Christ. Do you realize that all of those deliverances and all the times that the enemy was driven out, that God was keeping a record of those too? God gets excited by the fact that the enemy is being driven out, and that He is using you in that process.

CENTURION FAITH

Think about the idea of a commanding officer who is in charge of soldiers and gives commands to his soldiers under him. Then that commanding officer is also accountable to someone above him. It is the same way with us, we are accountable to our Commander, and because we are accountable, we walk in the authority of our Commander. We can then implement His command in our lives and through the lives of others.

Jesus marveled at the centurion's faith in Matthew 8:5-13 because that soldier understood authority and understood accountability. The centurion was in submission to his commanding officer, and because of that he had authority. The centurion also had soldiers submitted under him. Jesus said that the secret to having great faith is having centurion faith. That is the position where you understand accountability, you understand authority, and you have been given the name of Jesus. When you use the name of Jesus, then the devil is held accountable.

Every time that you drive a devil out of your life or someone else's life, it is written in Heaven. God keeps an accurate record of His enemies being driven out and territory that has been claimed back for the Kingdom. God is excited that His Kingdom is expanding daily through believers who are taking their authority in Christ and driving out the devil. It all starts with centurion faith, where you are in submission to authority, and through your submission, you are accountable. That accountability then makes the devil accountable, and he has to listen to you.

Did you know that there is a spirit of deliverance, that there is a command about you as a believer? In the book of Acts, the believers were being persecuted, and they were told to stop preaching in the name of Jesus. They got together, and they prayed, and they asked God for boldness. They said, *"Now, Lord, look on their threats, and grant to Your servants that with all boldness they may speak Your Word"* (Acts 4:29). By the power of the Holy Spirit, boldness came upon them, and they went back out. They were accountable because they prayed and asked God for help. Then they went out and spoke the Word of God with great authority and great boldness.

The Roman officers and the people spoke of Jesus with the Pharisees. They had heard the Pharisees teach the people, but they told the Pharisees that they had never heard a man speak with such authority as they did Jesus. They could see that the Pharisees did not have the authority that Jesus spoke from, and that was because Jesus was accountable to the Father; He only said what the Father was saying.

Chapter 19

DIVINE NATURE

By which have been given to us exceedingly great
and precious promises, that through these you may
be partakers of the divine nature, having escaped
the corruption that is in the world through lust.

—2 PETER 1:4

YOU PROBABLY WILL not hear many sermons about the divine nature. Many people do not understand that we were made in the image of God from the beginning, and we are a lot closer to the image of God than we know. The Spirit of God wants us to bring this back into the Church and back into the Body of Christ. This Scripture verse in Second Peter is hardly ever quoted because it is troubling to most people to think that we can be partakers of the divine nature.

When God made man in His image, He then gave man authority and dominion over all the earth (see Gen. 1:26). The authority that Jesus Christ bought back for us through the cross has been given to us in His name and through His blood. The demons understand that when we use the name of Jesus in addressing demons, we can drive them out. They have to go because they know that man has been restored.

If you are a born-again, Spirit-filled Christian, you are walking in the power of the Spirit of God. When you are born again and believe in Jesus Christ, you can speak to demons, and they have to listen to you. If you are baptized in the Holy Spirit, you are empowered by the Spirit with the evidence of speaking in tongues. That gives you even more power in the Spirit, and you will have supernatural strength and boldness to witness and to address demons at a greater level.

Two occurrences in the Bible empower us—the born-again experience and then the empowerment of the Spirit by the in-filling of Holy Spirit demonstrated on the day of Pentecost Acts 2:1-4. However, there is an even greater anointing and greater empowerment than that. It is the sons of God being revealed in the last days. Romans 8:19-25 talks about the fact that all creation is groaning and waiting for the sons of God to be revealed. We have the Holy Spirit, the Spirit of adoption inside us, by whom we cry out *"Abba Father"* (see Rom. 8:15).

As Christians, we ought to be focusing on the power of the divine nature. We need to focus on the fact that we can be partakers of the divine nature and yield to the Spirit in an even greater manner. The next step that God is revealing in these last days is that we can walk in the divine nature and be partakers of that nature.

When we partake of the divine nature, what does that manifest in our lives? Certain things can happen in our souls that will cause us to yield to the devil. Then Paul reminds us not to give any place to the devil when he tells us *"not to let the sun go down on"* our wrath (Eph. 4:26-27). If we can get angry to the point where we yield to the devil, then what if we yielded to joy? We could start to yield to the divine nature. We could become partakers of the divine nature to where we manifested God in our lives. That was what happened to Moses.

Moses spent so much time with God on the mountain that Moses' face became transformed, and the way he looked became fearsome. When Moses came down off the mountain, the people could not look at him because his face was glowing. They asked Moses to cover his face because they were afraid to come near him, and so he covered his face with a veil (see Exod. 34:29-35). What happened? Moses' face started to transform back into the pure stock of Adam—the way that Adam looked before he fell, which was in the perfect image of God. Just as a son would look like his Father, so we can look like our Father God in Heaven.

When Adam and Eve sinned and fell in the garden, it had terrible consequences for humankind, but through Jesus Christ, we are restored spiritually. Moses encountered a physical manifestation of being close to God, and his face began to transform back into the image of God. That is what is going to happen in the last days. The revealing of the sons of God in the last days will include the faces of God's children beginning to shine.

WHERE WE ARE HEADED

Hebrews 12:22-24 talks about where we are going:

But you have come to Mount Zion and to the city of the living God, the heavenly Jerusalem, to an innumerable company of angels, to the general assembly and church

*of the firstborn who are registered in heaven, to God
the Judge of all, to the spirits of just men made perfect,
to Jesus the Mediator of the new covenant, and to the
blood of sprinkling that speaks better things than that
of Abel.*

Accordingly, we are going to a place where there are myriads of angels, and there is a general assembly of the Church of the firstborn. We are all registered in Heaven, and God will be there, and Jesus, the Mediator of the new covenant, will be there. We are to concentrate on these things in Hebrews 12.

Once you are born again, God has sealed you with His blood, the blood of Jesus. From now on, the life that you live down here in the flesh is by faith in the Son of God. You do not yield to the flesh, because those who yield to the flesh cannot please God (see Rom. 8:8). We want to please God and yield to the Spirit of God.

*But without faith it is impossible to please Him, for he
who comes to God must believe that He is, and the He is
a rewarder of those who diligently seek Him.*
 —HEBREWS 11:6

When you have faith, you can have such a pleasing walk with God that like Enoch, God could take you, and you could disappear. Because Enoch pleased God so much, God just took him!

You should concentrate on the fact that you are going to Mount Zion. We are going to be on the mountain of God. Before lucifer fell, he was cast out of Mount Zion, the mountain of God. We can now take our rightful place through Jesus Christ on that mountain.

There are spirits of just men made perfect there. There are angels there. We should concentrate on the promise that we have.

There is not a day that goes by where I do not think about Mount Zion, because I have set my face like flint, just like Jesus did. Jesus told the disciples that He was going to Jerusalem and that He would suffer many things and be killed (see Matt. 16:21). Jesus set His face like flint toward Jerusalem. You must set your face toward Mount Zion, where you are going to be honored. God has wonderful plans to honor you there on Mount Zion, and that is where you belong, and that is your home.

GET UNDER AUTHORITY

Most of the demon problems will go away in your life when you get under authority. When you are under authority, you are under the covering of the gifts that God has set in the Church—apostles, prophets, pastors, teachers, and evangelists (see 1 Cor. 12:28-31). God set all of these people in the Church. When you have a pastor, and you are under authority, then a lot of the demon problems that you have will go away. Dealing with the demonic is not just about your rebuking the devil and resisting the devil because it also has to do with authority.

God has placed people who walk in these offices that we call the *fivefold ministry of the Church.* When you have those people in your life, then you are under them, and a lot of your battles go away. That is why it is very important to honor the fivefold ministry of the Church. I am talking about legitimate fivefold ministry. I am not talking about people who are self-appointed to those positions. I am talking about people who have a track record and have been honorable—ones whom God has set in the Church.

A pastor will be a teacher and someone who will help you in times of trouble. He will be there to feed you and give you an opportunity to minister in the local assembly. Everyone needs to have a pastor, and God has set this office in the Church, and it was His idea from the beginning.

Jesus stood up in the synagogue, as was His common practice, and taught. Jesus did not teach all the time, but He was still there at the synagogue. I have been in that synagogue in Capernaum, where Jesus taught. It is a wonderful thing to know that even Jesus sat in church and that He might not have even been speaking. Jesus probably knew more on the subject than the rabbi or the head of the synagogue did, but He still went there. You need to go to church and get under authority. When I am under authority, a lot of the demonic cannot touch me because I am under authority.

Another aspect of the divine nature is that all your needs are going to be met, and even your wants as it says in Psalm 23:1—*"The Lord is my shepherd; I shall not want."* You shall not want or lack anything. God is going to provide all your needs. Remember that part of walking in the divine nature is that God is your Provider. You have authority and dominion on the earth, and you can use your authority in prayer to release finances in your life. You do that by speaking out the Word of the Lord through your spirit. Part of the divine nature is prosperity, and part of that is causing you to triumph over your enemies.

DIVINE NATURE WITHIN

What if there are demonic forces all around you that are stopping the supply from coming? You have to use your authority. You can use your authority as you speak from your spirit. There is a divine nature inside you of the almighty God. You need to speak and release your finances. You need to speak against the demonic that might be holding up your flow, your supply.

When I was in Heaven, I saw that the demonic can hold back your healing. It can hold back your finances and can hold back relationships. The demonic activity works all around you in a circumference, and as you push them out and drive them out, they go further out from you. Until you completely push them out and stop them from coming back or operating, you are going to have resistance in the spirit. You are going to experience a lack in certain areas because that demonic activity is still working. You need to drive out the devil and reinforce it continually, and eventually, he will be so far gone that he will not be able to influence you in any way. God puts a hedge around people, and it is mentioned in Job 1:10. The demonic could not touch Job until God allowed it to happen.

Here is another way that you can meditate and think upon the divine nature. I saw the river of life that was coming out of the throne of God in Heaven. It was flowing through paradise, and out into this place where it fell onto the earth. Then I saw that the river of life comes up through a believer's spirit. If you are born again, there are rivers of living water coming out of you; you should meditate on this. Jesus said, *"He that believeth in Me, as the Scripture hath said, out of his belly shall flow rivers of living water"* (John 7:38 KJV). The power that raised Jesus from the dead is in this living water; the same power that heals the sick comes up through your belly and out of your mouth when you pray in the Spirit.

Just because you do not see your healing coming, it does not mean it is not coming. Just because your finances are not responding, it does not mean that water is not coming through your belly and up out into your mouth. You have to yield to it, and you have to speak it continually. Your finances will be released. Your healing will be released. Your deliverance will be released.

Jesus told me that eternal life is flowing through believers constantly. He told me that at any one moment, the Spirit of God is ready to move. The Spirit of God is activated by the words of our mouths, by expressing our faith. Our faith is spirit-born, and it is not from our souls. Faith is a spiritual thing. You can agree mentally, but that will not get it done, because mental agreement is not faith. Spiritual faith comes from your spirit. It comes from that living water that flows out of you from the eternal life.

Speak into the Realm of the Spirit

The Spirit of God is always available, and He is always ready to act, but He needs you to yield to Him and speak. You speak out of your spirit, and the words of life that come out of your mouth activate the Spirit of God. Just like at the time of creation, the Spirit of God was hovering and brooding over the waters at creation in Genesis 1. As soon as God started to speak, the Spirit started to form and create, and that is exactly what we were born to do. We were born to speak, and when we are born again in our spirits, we speak life. When you speak from that river of life, you will see your whole world change.

God told me that we can frame our worlds by our words. Our words can cause us to triumph over our enemies. The Holy Spirit, at any one moment, wants to engage us, and He wants us to speak into the realm of the spirit from the Spirit. Then suddenly, we are no longer physical, carnal people but spiritual people. We transform to the image of God, just like God created us to be. That is what Adam did when he spoke the names of the animals as they are named to this day.

You were made in God's image, and you have to deny the flesh and yield to the Spirit. You have to love when you do not feel like loving, and you must yield to love. You have to go the extra mile with people and not give up on them. You have to decide beforehand that God is correct, and you are not, and that God's will is better than your will. As you do these things, you are going to start to yield to that river, that eternal life that is in you.

The Spirit of God is already in your future, and He is already getting you prepared for eternal life in the millennial reign of Christ. The Spirit of God is ready to have you walk into your future right now because He knows more than you do about your future, and He wants to tell you. Jesus said,

> *When He, the Spirit of truth, has come, He will guide you into all truth; for He will not speak on His own authority, but whatever He hears He will speak; and He will tell you things to come.*
>
> —JOHN 16:13

The Holy Spirit is going to remind you of the things that Jesus said, and He is also going to tell you about the future.

It is your body that limits you down here. We still die at a certain age, and we have not overcome that. God gave us eternal life in our spirits, but one day we are going to shed our earthly bodies. Your body is going to limit you in many ways, and that is why you need to implement the power of the Holy Spirit. That same power that raised Jesus from the dead will quicken our mortal bodies and bring resurrection power from within us (see Rom. 8:11). We can allow the Holy Spirit to come out of our born-again spirits and to influence our bodies, and that is how we receive healing.

Men and women of God stand up, and they take their authority, and they yield to the Spirit. Then they start to speak from that other realm, and this physical world responds, and it is by faith. *"Faith is the substance of things hoped for, and the evidence of things not seen"* (Heb. 11:1). You do not see God, but you believe in Him.

You do not see the Spirit of God change your spirit and be born again, but you know that you are changed. It is the same as receiving from God through the divine nature. You yield to the Spirit of the eternal God, and you let that river of life flow up from your belly. Then from out of your mouth, you start to speak wherever you are going. You should not be speaking where you are, but you should be speaking where you are going as you receive from God through the divine nature.

Chapter 20

ABSOLUTE TRUTH

*And you shall know the truth, and the
truth shall make you free.*

—JOHN 8:32

BSOLUTE TRUTH IS a power word that people do not even
understand, and if they do, they do not realize that absolute
truth is missing. Absolute truth is starting to disappear from
everyone's thinking. As I have looked into this, I noticed that in
our educational system in the United States, things have changed.
Things have gotten to the place where there are all these different
views and opinions, but there is no absolute truth.

Today anyone can believe in what they want to believe. Even in
Christian circles, your theology seems to mean your accommoda-
tion of whatever circumstances you are experiencing. If you do not
receive your healing, then you change the truth about healing and
believe that God does not heal all the time. The only reason that
you say this is because you have not experienced healing.

God is a healer, and He wants to heal all the time. God has already said, *"He sent His Word and healed you"* (Ps. 107:20). Jesus is the healer and has taken stripes upon His back, and *"by His stripes, you were healed"* (Isa. 53:5). And that is absolute truth! It does not matter if you do not experience it.

It is the same thing with your finances. If you do not experience supernatural financial provision, it does not mean that you have to change the way you believe. You do not change your theology to accommodate what you perceive as the inactivity of God. God is not inactive because He has already spoken His truth. We must believe that and reinforce it.

What if the demonic is holding back your provision and making God look like He is being mocked? That is what is truly happening. God says, *"Do not be deceived, I cannot be mocked; for whatever a man sows, that he will also reap"* (Gal. 6:7). If you sow toward something, it is impossible not to receive a harvest from it.

God's absolute truth in Heaven is established in His throne.

> *Righteousness and justice are the foundation of your throne. Unfailing love and truth walk before you as attendants.*
>
> —PSALM 89:14 NLT

There are layers in the foundation of God's throne. God's righteousness and justice, and His faithfulness and truth, are found there. God is seated on His throne, and everything is established from His throne. From His throne, God makes righteous judgments based on absolute truth, which is His truth. When I was in Heaven, I saw that everything is absolute, but down here on the earth, there are all these opinions.

Everyone has their opinion and their interpretation of what God is saying. "This is what I believe," they say. You will see that they have accommodated the fact that what God said has not happened in their lives, and therefore, they have changed their beliefs. What they now believe is incorrect. Absolute truth must come back into our vocabulary. We must realize that there is a war against absolute truth in our society.

REINFORCING GOD'S ESTABLISHED TRUTH

People are trying to educate our children and reeducate us, telling us we can choose what we believe in and can have our own view on everything. We are supposed to choose what works for us, according to them. God has already established truth in Heaven! God has established truth, and we need to reinforce what God has already spoken. We must begin to reverse what is happening in our school systems. We need to educate our children properly, and we do that by teaching them the Word of God. The Word of God has already established the truth that God has from His throne.

Moses was told to take the people of Israel out of Egypt, and he obeyed God. In the desert, the people were constantly rebelling against him and dragging their feet. God had already spoken to Moses and told them about the Promised Land and that the people of Israel must go into this Promised Land. However, the people resisted, and they stayed in the desert for forty years, until a whole generation had died.

God had already offered the Israelites the absolute truth about His plans. God had already provided for them in the Promised Land, but the people of Israel refused to go in. The truth about God is that He determines what He wants, and then He speaks it, and we must obey it. If we do not obey it, then we do not encounter it. So it is with everything that God has said because He has already spoken it.

God says the Word that He has spoken goes out and accomplishes what He pleases, and it does not come back to Him void (see Isa. 55:11). It always comes back, producing the result of what God said. God's Word is absolute. God sits on His throne and waits for His Word to come to pass. God does not change His Word because it is taking too long. What happens to us is that we begin to accommodate God's inactivity by changing what we believe because we have not waited on God. We do not realize in faith that if we stand firm, it is going to happen.

We have to be taught God's Word, and every day we have to repeat God's Word from our spirits. We have to say to God, "Father, this is what You said." Not because God is forgetful, but because in this realm, we have the demonic, and we must reinforce everything that God has said.

Every day you have to quote the absolute truth. God is not going to revoke His Word, and He is not going to go back on what He has already said. The demons want you to back off, but if you keep reinforcing what God has already said, they must obey. They will try to make it hard on you, but if you start to reinforce what God has said in your life, the demons will be pushed back.

Paul told Timothy to wage war with the prophecies that he had received (see 1 Tim. 1:18). When you start to quote the prophecies that you have received by the Spirit of God, demons will start to come against you. They know that if you continue, you are going to get what God has spoken over you. The demons know that they cannot do anything about it if you continue with persistence.

God does not need to be convinced by you repeating prophecies. It is you reinforcing in your environment what God has already said so that God will have His way. God will have His way because you have agreed with Him. God wants a relationship with you, and He wants you and Him to work together to wrap it up down here. He needs you to stand in dominion and authority on the earth, and this is part of the absolute truth.

TRUTH RESISTS THE ENEMY

If satan can take out the absolute truth, then you have nothing to stand on in authority. However, if you establish in your own life and your own mind that God's Word is true, then you are not going to back off. It is satan who will have to back off. I see those demons all the time testing to see if I am going to back away. When you can stare at them and say, "No, this is the way it is going to be," you will see them blink. That is when demons will start to back off because they know they cannot take you. Those demons have no choice but to run in terror, because you have submitted to God and resisted them. You have pushed them back, and they have to obey.

Jesus has all authority, but He gave us His name and gave us authority on the earth. We are co-heirs with Jesus, according to Romans 8:17, and we can experience the same ministry that Jesus experienced on the earth. When Jesus walked on the earth, the devils would cry out and flee as He approached them. That is the walk that we are supposed to be walking in. Jesus understood His authority because He understood that His Father had given Him authority. Jesus never did anything unless His Father told Him to do it, and that is the way it is with us.

Absolute truth has been established in Heaven. Jesus was pre-existent with the Father. When He came down to the earth, Jesus was fully confident in who He was and why He was sent. The demons knew who Jesus was, too. It is the same way with us now that Jesus is our Mediator (see 1 Tim. 2:5). Jesus has opened up a new and living way into the Holy of Holies so that you can enter in there as well (see Heb. 10:19-20). You need to go in there and get the confidence that you need by establishing your relationship with God in the Holy of Holies. Then after being in that secret place in the Holy of Holies, you can go out into the world, and the demons will know that you are one with your Father. They will know that you are convinced that God is the absolute truth. From His mouth, God speaks, and that is the end of it. God's people who walk in authority are ones who understand absolute truth.

When a police officer holds up his hand for you to stop, you stop. You stop not because he is a big person, but because he has authority. Authority does not have to do with how big you are. It has to do with the fact that you are submitted to authority and have been given a badge. Every officer has been given authority as a police officer. You need to obey that police officer, not just because he can physically hurt you, but because if you rebel against authority, there are consequences to that. The demons know when a believer understands their authority.

As a believer, you know that God has chosen you, called you, and sent you. You did not choose Him, but He chose you, and you are a sent one, and you have been given authority (see John 15:16). Jesus gave the seventy authority, and they went out and drove out demons and healed the sick (see Luke 10:1-12). When they came back, and they were surprised, Jesus said, *"Do not rejoice that the spirits submit to you, but rejoice that your names are written in Heaven"* (Luke 10:20). That is absolute truth. Your name is written in the Book of Life in Heaven right now, and that is why demons must listen to you.

HOLY AND SET APART

Absolute truth has to do with boundaries as well. There are boundaries that God gives you, and they are not to restrict you. God knows what He is doing, and He loves you and creates boundaries for your safety. God calls us to be holy and set apart. He tells us, *"Come out from among them and be separate"* (2 Cor. 6:17). God does not want to ruin your fun. God is saying that You are part of His family. He has given you authority on the earth, and so you are in leadership. Christians all over the earth, regular believers, are in authority and leadership.

A Christian who walks with God is in full authority on the earth. You have been restored back to the way it used to be before the fall. Other people in the world, because they are not born again, have not been restored back and are under the power of the devil. Paul explained this in Ephesians 2:2. He said, *"You once walked according to the course of this world, according to the prince of the power of the air."* Paul was basically telling the people at Ephesus that they used to do the desires of the devil because they were submitted to the god of this world and could not resist him. When they became born again, they were translated into the Kingdom of light and are now the light in this world.

No Provision for the Flesh

You are in the full authority of God, and He wants you to walk in dominion. The reason that you walk in dominion is that you have established certain truths in your life, but with those truths, there are boundaries. There are certain things you do not do, and God lists those in Galatians when He talks about the works of the flesh (see 5:19-21). God goes as far as to say that those who do these things will not inherit the Kingdom of God.

God wants you to manifest the fruit of the Spirit and the character of the Holy Spirit.

> *But the fruit of the Spirit is love, joy, peace, longsuffering, kindness, goodness, faithfulness, gentleness, self-control. Against such there is no law.*
> —Galatians 5:22-23

If you do these things and yield to the Spirit, that is absolute truth, and it creates God's boundaries. You need to decide what you are going to manifest, remembering that those who walk in the flesh cannot please God (see Rom. 8:8). And those who walk in the Spirit are sons of God (see Rom. 8:14).

We are not to give any provision to the flesh (see Rom. 13:14), and we are not allowed to let the flesh manifest. Paul talked about all of these carnal desires with the Corinthians (see 1 Cor. 6:9-11). The Corinthians thought that they were very spiritual because they were using all the gifts of the Spirit. There was so much going on in the services that Paul told them that they were carnal and babes in Christ because they had so many manifestations of the flesh (see 1 Cor. 3:1-10).

You do not want to be carnal because you cannot please God when you are in the flesh, and it all has to do with boundaries. Being in the flesh is happening more than ever with believers. If you want to stand out and be separate from the world, then you have to allow God to establish these boundaries in your life.

When I was in Heaven, I saw that people who had yielded to the flesh were very weak and did not have any confidence. Your relationship with God is hurt when you walk in the flesh. When you yield to those desires, you cannot access the spiritual power and authority that you have inside you. It does not manifest, so you are always having trouble. You have one foot in the world and one foot in the Spirit, and you are just like the Corinthian church. You have to start to seal it up by honoring the boundaries that God has told you.

God told me that I cannot do certain things anymore, many of which other Christians still do. The Lord told me to separate myself. For me to be able to do what I am doing on the earth, I have to stand out and be separate. My time, my life, and my body are not my own anymore. Everything that I do is based on absolute truth about my particular situation and my calling. You have to honor what God is telling you to do. You may not be able to do the things that others seem to allow and accept in their lives.

I spend most of my time studying and being in prayer and doing the work of the ministry because that is what I am supposed to be doing now. That might change, and God might take me in a different direction, but I must follow the Spirit. The Spirit of God is the Spirit of truth, and He understands absolute truth. What you want to know is what God is saying to you in your situation. The best way to find out is by praying in the Spirit and then allowing God to bring it into your understanding.

As it says in Jude 20, you pray in the Spirit, and you build yourself up in your most holy of faith. Then you meditate on the Word of God day and night as it says in Joshua 1:8, yielding to the Spirit. As your spirit is built up, you start to hear the voice of God because you have the Word of God in front of you. The Spirit and the Word will develop you to where you will walk in absolute truth. Suddenly, you will be able to discern when evil is happening in your life. You are going to know when there is something wrong because your discernment will start to develop.

I can see through many things now, and I know when people are saying things and when evil is happening. I never used to be that way, but now I can see. I know what is going to happen even when people tell me differently. You start to know things like that. I cannot even pray in certain ways anymore because the Spirit will not side with me when I pray.

The Holy Spirit comes alongside you to help you pray, but what if the Holy Spirit wanted to be your prayer coach? When you start to pray in a certain direction, you may feel that the Holy Spirit is not siding with you. That is a sign that maybe God's will is in another direction. Now I pray for wisdom first, and that is to eliminate wrong prayers. I only pray one prayer all the time now, and that is Ephesians 1:17-23. It is a prayer that Paul prayed for the church in Ephesus.

If you remember in the book of Acts, the city of Ephesus was steeped in witchcraft. When the Ephesians repented and came to the Lord, they brought their spellbooks worth over $50,000 to the fire there and burned them (see Acts 19:19). Paul prayed that the eyes of their hearts would be enlightened and that they would know the hope to which they had been called (see Eph. 1:17). There is the absolute truth that is in Heaven about your calling, and you must know the glorious inheritance that you have in the saints.

God has given all of us saints a huge inheritance, but many of us do not understand that or even know it. You have a hope and a calling from God Almighty. Paul prayed that the Ephesians would know the hope to which they have been called, but it is for you, too! Then Paul asked God that the Ephesians would understand and encounter the power that raised Jesus from the dead, and that is the absolute truth that needs to be revealed to you as well. And just as important for you to know is the river of eternal life in Heaven is flowing from the throne of God, and it is coming up through you, and that is absolute truth. The Spirit of God wants to coach you to pray in the direction of God's will.

GENERATIONAL INFLUENCE

The Holy Spirit already knows where you are going. It is so important in this power word of absolute truth that you understand God has already written a book about you (see Ps. 139:16). That book has your days written in it before any of them have come to pass, and that is the way it is. Jesus did not ask for your opinion, and He wrote your book without you ever being there to give your input. Jesus never asked you what you wanted, because He wrote the truth based on what *He* wanted for you.

What God wants involves plans for a whole generation, even though you think that you want to know what God has just for you to do. What you do not understand is that when you pray the Ephesians prayer, you are going to be shown that you affect everyone else around you. That is why it is important to find out what is written about you. If you do not do what is written about you, then you affect your friends, and you affect your whole generation.

God inserted you into the environment you are in with a powerful calling, an election that is sure, through absolute truth, so that you start to influence your generation. You begin with your friends and your family, and you find out what God has for you, and you do not bend. You find out what God has already spoken, and you speak healing. God speaks healing over you, and He sings songs of deliverance over you because He wants you to be delivered (see Ps. 32:7).

There should be no demonic activity in your life. And that is the absolute truth. Now, for most people, they have demonic activity in their lives. That is because we are in a fallen world that has demons in it, but that does not mean that you change your theology. You do not change what you believe because you are not encountering a demon-free zone. God has ordained for you to be free from demon activity, and He sings songs of deliverance over you.

> *For the Lord your God is living among you. He is a mighty savior. He will take delight in you with gladness. With his love, he will calm all your fears. He will rejoice over you with joyful songs.*
> —Zephaniah 3:17 NLT

God is a warrior, and He sings songs of deliverance over you. There is a wall of fire that surrounds you, and He protects you. That is the truth, but if you do not encounter that every day, it does not mean that God is not true. It means that you need to reinforce what God has already said in your life. Absolute truth has to do with these boundaries that God has already established for you, and you need to honor those even if you do not know what they are. You need to pray the Ephesians prayer. God wants you to walk in your authority, but your authority stems from the fact that you are under authority, and that is the absolute truth in Heaven.

There is strength and power of God's voice. *"The voice of the Lord splits the mighty cedars; the Lord shatters the cedars of Lebanon"* (Ps. 29:5 NLT). In the Old Testament, there were many times when God spoke audibly, and one of them was in the desert on Mount Sinai. When the Israelites heard God's voice, they were afraid (see Exod. 20:18-19). They heard the Lord thundering up there on the mountain, and the earth quaked. They felt that God was terrible and that He was too much for them. They were so afraid that they told Moses to go up and speak to God himself and come back and tell them what God said. They were afraid because they did not have a relationship with God, but Moses knew God and was not afraid.

The Lord is speaking to you, and His voice is very loud. You do not always hear God's voice loudly because, in this world, there are all kinds of voices speaking. There are demonic spirits and soul power, and many things being spoken contrary to the Word of God, and this physical realm is cursed. However, you are blessed in your spirit, but to be able to receive that into your mind and body, you need to realize that God has already spoken on your behalf. You need to start quoting God's Word. You need to begin reinforcing what God has already said, and then God's voice will become louder to you.

It is when you eliminate all of the demonic influences and smaller voices around you that hearing God will begin to turn in your favor. I know this because I have seen this happen in my life. I have seen the demonic clear out because they could not withstand the absolute truth that was coming through me. That is what I want for you, and I want you to walk in this absolute truth.

I want you to know that God has already ordained you and sent you into this world. He has already written about you in Heaven. From God's throne, He has given out the command, and He is speaking very loudly to you. You need to meditate on His Word and pray in the Spirit. You must have confidence that God loves you and that He has ordained you to be in this world at this time to influence your whole generation. This generation may see the return of the Lord Jesus Christ.

Chapter 21

REVELATION

That the God of our Lord Jesus Christ, the Father
of glory, may give to you the spirit of wisdom
and revelation in the knowledge of Him.
—EPHESIANS 1:17

R EVELATION IS ONE of those power words that we need to be careful that satan does not take out of our vocabulary. Revelation is something that the Spirit of God takes from His realm and gives to us. Down here in this realm, we encounter times when things are veiled, they are hidden from us, and they are a mystery. God has clearly said through the apostle Paul, that the Spirit of God wants to reveal those things that are not seen.

> *But as it is written: "Eye has not seen, nor ear heard,*
> *nor have entered into the heart of man the things which*
> *God has prepared for those who love Him." But God has*
> *revealed them to us through His Spirit. For the Spirit*
> *searches all things, yes, the deep things of God.*
> —1 CORINTHIANS 2:9-10

Revelation is part of the inheritance that God has given to us through Jesus Christ. The Spirit of God was given to us on the day of Pentecost so that we can be empowered and that our eyes can be open (see Acts 2:1-12). As Christians, we pray the prayer that Paul prayed, asking God for the eyes of our hearts to be flooded with light (see Eph. 1:18 NLT). You ought to pray Ephesians 1:17-23 for yourself daily because the Spirit of God wants to get some of the hidden things of God over to you.

While I was out of my body when I died during my operation, I received revelation from the heavenly realms, and I was taken up by Jesus. I was able to look back at the earth, and I could see that things were veiled, and they were hidden spiritually. Being out of my body and with Jesus, I was able to see clearly the things that were hidden from me.

I was so surprised at what was going on, and I remember thinking that if I could come back, I would be able to do so much more for Jesus. I could do so much more because I saw how I could have had the Spirit of God in my life in a much stronger way. I saw that if I had prayed in the Spirit constantly and meditated on the Word of God, the Holy Spirit would have gotten more things over to me. There were so many more things available to me, but I had not been persistent.

SPIRIT BEINGS IN A PHYSICAL REALM

Jesus sent me back, and I want to show you that the Spirit of God is the Spirit of revelation, and that revelation is an unveiling. God wants to unveil to you His plans for you, and He wants to show you the spirit realm. He wants you to learn how to operate as a physical being on this earth while having a spiritual part of you called your *spirit*. Your human spirit is a spiritual being that is born again if you believe in Jesus Christ.

The spirit realm is real, and what I found out was that your spirit inside you has a shape just like your body has a shape to it. Your spirit has a human form to it, and it has arms and legs, and you have a head and a face. You have this ability in the spirit to hear with your whole body. When I was out of my body, I could not just hear with my ears, I could hear through my whole being. It is the same way with seeing; you can see with your whole being a full 360 degrees. Your spirit man can see and hear in any direction.

When you are born of the Spirit, revelation comes in through your spirit, but it is not limited to just what your eyes see and your ears hear in the physical. Your spiritual senses are so much more profound and greater than you realize. You can hear things and see things in the Spirit that your physical eyes or ears would not pick up in the natural. Revelation comes in through your spirit and is not limited to the physical realm.

To develop this ability, the first thing that you have to do is establish the fact that the Spirit of revelation is inside you. That you, as a spiritual being, have the ability between your own spirit and the Holy Spirit to work together to encounter God in the physical realm.

God is going to communicate with you, but He is *not* going to communicate with you physically. God is going to communicate with you spiritually, and it is Spirit to spirit. This is because, as Jesus said, *"God is a Spirit, and those who worship Him must worship Him in spirit and truth"* (John 4:24). You can communicate Spirit to spirit with God because when you were born again, your spirit became a new creation (see 2 Cor. 5:17).

ROMANS REVELATION

You become a new species in Christ who can hear and see in the spirit, and not just in the physical realm. You are not going to be able to see angels with your physical eyes unless God takes you into the Spirit. Then your spirit-being takes over, and even though you have physical eyes, everything physical will disappear, and you will go into a vision. That can happen because the Holy Spirit has come and allowed you to see with your spirit being.

The Spirit of God came into you when you were redeemed, and when you confessed, "Jesus is Lord," and you became born again. The Spirit of God is a Spirit of adoption of acceptance (see Rom. 8:15). You have been accepted into the family, and your spirit joins the Holy Spirit and cries out, "Father, Father!" You become one with God. Can you imagine being one with God? God sees everything and hears everything, and so there is this part of you now that can see and hear by the Spirit of God.

You are an heir of God and a co-heir of Jesus Christ (see Rom. 8:17). You start to participate in the supernatural and in the divine nature. *"Yet in all these things we are more than conquerors through Him who loved us"* (Rom. 8:37). You become more than a conqueror. As you read the Word of God, this revelation starts to come through. You start to realize that because you are one with God, you are one in the family, and that revelation starts to increase and multiply. As it multiplies throughout your whole life, you are going to get to a place like Enoch did. Remember he walked so close to God that God took him. That is God's goal for us as we have already discussed. He wants us to walk so close with Him, and this is true revelation.

I am recommending that you walk through Romans 8, reading it verse by verse and focusing on each one individually. You should be able to get through it in just about a month. As I go through Romans 8, I read one verse per day, and I slowly meditate on each verse. When I finish the chapter, I repeat it all over again in a cycle. This chapter in Romans is representational of your spiritual life.

The revelation that you receive from Romans 8 will confound you. Reading each verse and meditating on it will greatly increase your spiritual life. Paul gave us this chapter as the way that we are supposed to walk in Christ. The revelation that you will receive from this is something that you can live off of for the rest of your life. You can eat it every day like bread from Heaven.

In Romans 8:35-39, Paul asks, *"Who can separate you from the love of Christ?"* Paul shows us that no one can and then names all the things that cannot separate us. One day, I read that and realized what God had set up for me. He wanted me to walk in intimacy with Him. That intimacy with God means that He is going to share secrets with you. This power word—revelation—and the Spirit of revelation, and all the things that pertain to revelation cannot slip from your life. Satan wants to steal revelation from you, but God wants to reveal Himself to you, and He wants you to know His ways. God's ways are His pathways.

PLEASING GOD

Moses knew God's ways (see Ps. 103:7). God's ways have to do with His personality, and it has to do with the ways that He likes to do things. I want to know what God likes, and if you look in the Scriptures, there are keys. There are certain things that God does that will reveal what He likes, and He reveals those things to us.

I know that God wants us to seek Him diligently and that He rewards us for doing that (see Heb. 11:6).

I saw that Jesus marveled at only two people in Scripture, the centurion for his faith, and the Samaritan woman at the well. They were both Gentiles and were not even part of Israel. God sent Jesus to reveal the Father's heart, and Jesus revealed the Father's heart when He said, *"I have not found anyone in Israel with such great faith"* (Matt. 8:10). If we would become more like that, then we would see more happen in our lives. The Spirit shows us that Jesus marveled; this is revelation. I want Jesus to marvel at me based on what He has shown me in the Word of God.

When I was in Heaven, Jesus showed me that there are certain things that the Father likes, and He told me some of them. Jesus said, "Every day before you go anywhere, say to the Father, 'Unless you go with me; I am not going anywhere.' He loves to hear that." I now know that God loves to hear that without Him, we can do nothing, but with Him, we can do everything.

God loves to hear that even though we feel weak, we know that He can make us strong. God loves to hear you ask Him what is on His heart, and I ask Jesus this every day. What is it that you are doing, Lord? What would you like me to do today? God loves to hear things like that, and you will start to see the Spirit of God begin to unveil the hidden things of God. There are going to be characteristics of God that you never thought existed, and God is going to show you a part of Himself that you have never seen.

Moses had an intimate relationship with God, and this is what happened with the apostle Paul, and it was why God caught Paul up to Heaven. Before Paul became born again, he was a Pharisee who was being trained to be the leader of all the Pharisees. While persecuting the believers, Paul was knocked off his horse by a bright light from Heaven, and Jesus appeared and introduced Himself to Paul (see Acts 22:6-8). One day, after Paul accepted Christ, he was caught up into the heavenly realms, and he saw things that he could not even speak of. However, he was sent back to tell us what he could share.

Jesus Himself came and revealed all these truths to Paul (see Gal. 1:12). And he was able to write about them to the churches. Through Paul, we have all the Epistles, which are the letters that were written by the Spirit of God through Paul to the different churches. These letters are Paul's revelation of Jesus Christ. If we did not have Paul's letters, we would not know the things we know today. We would have the Gospels, and that would be an account of all the things that Jesus said and did, but Paul, through the Spirit, unveiled the secrets. These were deep secrets that were held back until they were shown to Paul, and he was permitted to write about them.

You need to pray the prayer in Ephesians 1:17-23, declaring over yourself that you are going to live by the righteousness of God. Say aloud that you are going to have eyes that see and ears that hear. Declare that you are going to allow the Spirit of God to come upon you and that He is going to lift you up and cause you to see. As you speak the things in this prayer, you will begin to see and hear in the Spirit. Speak out that you are going to know the hope to which you have been called and the inheritance that has been given to you. Declare that you are seated with Christ in the heavenly realms. Declare that you will know the authority that you have seated with Him and that you will have the power of the resurrection revealed to you. You must confess these things in prayer.

When Samuel was a little boy, he was placed in the temple of God and grew up there. Samuel's environment was restricted to the godly things that were in the temple. He grew up and heard the voice of God and became a prophet. At the end of Samuel's life, it was said that not one word in prophecy that he spoke fell to the ground (see 1 Sam. 3:19). They all came to pass.

How would you like to be 100 percent correct in everything that you prophesied? The Lord showed me this was true of Samuel because Samuel was kept from the world. He lived in an environment where God dwelt in the Holy of Holies. The Lord showed me that if you want to receive revelation, and you want to have that unveiling happen in your life, you have to have an environment that is conducive to revelation. You must separate yourself and make time to spend with God.

MYSTERIES REVEALED

When the revelation of God comes, then people practice restraint, but when there is no revelation, it says in Proverbs 29:18 that *"people cast off restraint."* People cannot stay within their boundaries without revelation, and this shows how important it is for the revelation of God to come forth. As Christians in this world, we need to have restraint so that we can be the example of Jesus Christ to those around us. We need to practice restraint, and we cannot allow our boundaries to be moved in any way.

Jesus brought light with Him to *"bring revelation to the Gentiles, and the glory of* [God's] *people Israel"* (Luke 2:32). When He walked on the earth , it was revelation even to the Gentiles. *"And we beheld His glory"* (see John 1:14). Jesus was Emmanuel, God with us (see Matt. 1:23). Jesus was a light in the darkness, and we have become that light also, and it all happens through revelation that is received from the Spirit of revelation.

Paul said,

> *Now to Him who is able to establish you according to my gospel and the preaching of Jesus Christ, according to the revelation of the mystery kept secret since the world began.*
>
> —ROMANS 16:25

Paul received this revelation when he was in the area of Sinai, where he was caught up by the Lord. Paul had disappeared for about fourteen years, and people did not know anything about him for a long while. All that time, Paul stayed separate and was taught by the Lord. He said that no man taught him except the Lord Jesus Christ. When he returned, people did not understand what had happened to him. Everything about Paul's revelation was from Jesus, who taught him personally.

Moses, when he ran from Pharaoh after he had killed the Egyptian, spent forty years in the desert being a sheepherder. Moses was humbled by being alone in the desert, but he also learned the desert life. When he was told to go back to Egypt and tell the Pharaoh to let God's people go, he was humbled to the point where he could not speak.

In Egypt, Moses, having been brought up in Pharaoh's court as his son, had been trained and groomed to be the next Pharaoh. Moses was a great orator and had learned all of the knowledge and wisdom of the greatest university in the world, which was in Egypt at that time. But, after forty years in the desert, Moses was so humble and had spent so much time sheepherding that he could not speak. When God called him to return to Egypt, Moses asked God to send his brother Aaron with him to help him.

That is what happens to a lot of us when we are humbled. We get into a situation where we are in a desert experience, but God has not given up on us. We needed to be humbled, and we go into these solitary places where we feel alone, but it is all part of God's plan. God is not doing this to hurt you; He is doing it to form your character. Revelation will come as it did for Moses when he turned aside to see the burning bush. God was then able to use Moses because he was humble, but Moses did not understand that at the time.

There was no one as great as Moses, who saw the glory of God. He was on the mountain with God twice that we know of for forty days at a time. Moses was in that glory to the point that his face shone, and the Israelites were afraid of him, and he had to cover his face. The mystery of God was revealed to Moses on the mountain. Moses wrote the first five books of the Bible, and Genesis was a book that occurred before Moses was even born. So, Moses received the book of Genesis on the mountain, given to him by angels. Moses wrote the whole book of Genesis, and he did not even live during that time. That was a mystery revealed to Moses, and it showed how much God trusted him.

Moses also had a revelation of God's glory when God put Moses in the cleft of the rock, and God walked by him (see Exod. 33:22-23). Moses got to see God's goodness coming off of Him as he walked by. God called Moses a friend, and there are very few people in the Bible to whom God refers as friends, but Moses was one of those people.

If you want to do something for God in this life, it is going to be because of your relationship with God. It is not going to be because you go out and you do something for God by choosing what *you* want to do. The revelation that comes to you is that you are sent. All these people had an experience with God. They encountered God, and they received a revelation, and out of that revelation came their ministry, and they changed history.

If you want to change history, you have to focus on the Spirit of revelation and the Word of God, and you have to pray out God's mysteries. Paul said that when you pray in the Spirit, you are praying out the mysteries of God and that you are speaking to Him (see 1 Cor. 14:2). This language that you are speaking is not known to you, because it is a mystery, but your spirit is praying it out for you. When you pray in the Spirit, you are praying out your book that is written in Heaven. The Holy Spirit is praying out the perfect will of God for you, and He is causing you to triumph over your enemies.

God is helping you and participating in this powerful mystery, which is praying in tongues. You need to pray in tongues every day as much as possible. When I first started, I prayed for ten minutes a day. It was such a war because the demonic does not want you to pray in tongues. The demons will try to get you to delay praying in every way possible.

Set yourself in an environment where you will not be disturbed and refuse to let yourself get out of it. Then increase your time praying by ten minutes each day until you get to one hour or more a day. Soon two hours praying in the Spirit will seem like nothing to you. The demonic does not want revelation to come because they want you in the dark. When you have no revelation, that is where the enemy can beat you. The demons do not want you to know the mysteries of God, but they will have to back off when you pray in the Spirit. As you yield to the Spirit of God, the Spirit will light up your path, and He will light up your understanding, and the Spirit of revelation will come.

When I was in Heaven, I saw that the best thing we could do is pray in the Spirit, meditate on the Word of God and then walk away and refuse to doubt. Reconfirm that the Spirit of God has spoken through you, and reconfirm that what God has written in His Word is true. You pray under your breath in the Spirit all day, and you do not back off. Never back off of what God has already spoken through you and what He has spoken in His Word. Trust in God because He is with you in a mighty way.

Chapter 22

VISITATION

Thou hast granted me life and favour, and
thy visitation hath preserved my spirit.

—JOB 10:12 KJV

W E ALL LOVE to hear about times of visitation when the Lord has visited people or sent an angel. Those are times when the Spirit of God comes in a powerful way, and we have the visitation of the Spirit of God. It is so important to have visitations. God deals with us mostly by the visitation of His Spirit, because the Holy Spirit has been given to us. Jesus said, *"It is to your advantage that I go away, for if I don't go away, the Divine Encourager will not be released to you. But after I depart, I will send him to you"* (John 16:7 TPT). Jesus was telling His disciples that after He left earth, the Holy Spirit was going to come and take His place.

> *But the Helper (Comforter, Advocate, Intercessor—*
> *Counselor, Strengthener, Standby), the Holy Spirit,*
> *whom the Father will send in My name [in My place,*

to represent Me and act on My behalf], He will teach
you all things. And He will help you remember every-
thing that I have told you.

—JOHN 14:26 AMP

We now have the Holy Spirit with us on the earth, and He is the one who was sent to us after Jesus ascended to Heaven. He is the Comforter, our Counselor, the Revealer, the Advocate, our Standby, and He is the Power of God. We can now have the visitation of the Holy Spirit. Just before Jesus ascended to Heaven, He had commanded His followers not to leave Jerusalem but to wait for the Promise of the Father (see Acts 1:4-5).

On the day of Pentecost, 120 people, including the disciples, gathered in the upper room in prayer and were in one accord (see Acts 2:1-16). Suddenly, the rushing mighty wind of God came into the room, and they had the visitation of the wind of the Holy Spirit. Then they experienced the visitation of fire, as divided tongues of fire appeared over each person's head. Even more, they were all filled with the Holy Spirit and began to speak with other tongues, as the Spirit gave them utterance.

As Jesus' followers came down from the upper room, they were all speaking other languages that were not their own. In Jerusalem that day, there was a multitude of people from every country celebrating Pentecost. When they heard their own languages being spoken by these Galileans, they were amazed and marveled. They knew that the Galileans did not know their languages. The Lord visited that day with the manifestation of utterance.

The final manifestation that they had was public drunkenness. The believers all appeared to be drunk during the middle of the day. Peter got up and said, *"These are not drunk, as you suppose, but this is what was spoken of by the prophet Joel"* (Acts 2:15-16). They appeared to be drunk because the Holy Spirit had that effect on them in the power that was manifested.

The 120 were all in one accord on the day of Pentecost. The power of the Holy Spirit manifested with a mighty rushing wind, flames of fire, utterance, and public drunkenness. These are all manifestations of the Spirit of God. That is the way the Spirit of God first visited those people, and today, even two thousand years later, the Holy Spirit has not changed in any way. He is still the same Person, and He has the same power and manifestation. The Holy Spirit can come into your life in a very powerful way and reveal Himself to you, and we can enjoy the Spirit's visitation.

ANGELIC ACTIVITY

We enjoy the fact that when we pray, the Holy Spirit comes, and that we have a Helper, an Advocate who comes alongside as a Standby. When we do not know what we should pray for, and we do not understand the will of God, we can yield to the Spirit.

> *Likewise the Spirit also helps in our weaknesses. For we do not know what we should pray for as we ought, but the Spirit Himself makes intercession for us with groanings which cannot be uttered.*
> —ROMANS 8:26

The Spirit of God will pray out the mysteries of God, and the will of God, and help us to pray. The Holy Spirit causes our spirits to pray out the mysteries of God in another language, and this is part of visitation.

You can be visited by God in your dreams and visions. God can pull back the veil and show you in a dream what is going on in the future, or what is going on in your life right now. God can give you a vision to where your physical senses are suspended, and you can see into the spirit realm.

Angels are another way that God can visit you. You can have an angel visitation when God wants to give you a message. God can send an angel to help you in your daily life, and sometimes you see them, and sometimes you don't. Most of the time, God's angels do not want to be noticed. They do not want to get credit for what they are doing because they want God to get all the credit. So you could be visited by an angel on assignment. However, everyone has an assigned angel, and you are being visited by your angel every day. There is angel activity going on in a believer's life all the time, but you do not always see it. As you develop spiritually, you will begin to develop a sensitivity to the shifting and the changing in the atmosphere around you.

My favorite type of visitation is when Jesus shows up and visits with you. It is an amazing thing to see Jesus and to have Him talk to you and to be able to encounter the Lord Jesus, your Redeemer. He can come and visit you and talk to you. As extraordinary as this visitation is, it is very rare. This kind of visitation is not something you can pray and fast for because it is divinely appointed, and it is something that the Trinity decides beforehand.

I have had some visitations from Jesus, but I know this was something that was determined long before I was born. It was something that God had ordained to help a generation understand what He was doing and saying. These types of visitations are God-ordained and are things that God determines beforehand.

You are one with God in your spirit because you are joined with the Lord in Spirit. Jesus prayed that we would know the unity that He has with the Father and that we would encounter the glory that they share.

> *That they all may be one, as You, Father, are in Me, and I in You; that they also may be one in Us, that the world may believe that You sent Me. And the glory which You gave Me I have given them, that they may be one just as We are one: I in them, and You in Me; that they may be made perfect in one, and that the world may know that You have sent Me, and have loved them as You have loved Me.*
> —JOHN 17:21-23

Jesus prayed these things for everyone who believes. He asked the Father for the same love that They shared would be shared with us as well. Jesus prayed that we would be one as They are one and that we would encounter that oneness. These are all considered visitations of God.

The move of God in the last days is symbolized as a type of rain—the early rain and the latter rain. There are all kinds of visitations of God that are symbolized by certain elements like fire and water and wind. We have the wind of the Spirit, the water of the Spirit, and the fire of the Spirit. There is even the anointing oil of the Spirit. Where you can feel the anointing oil of the Spirit upon you, and you receive an anointing. That is a visitation of the Spirit, as well.

There are all these many different manifestations of the Spirit of God. Encountering God on these different levels will become more common in the last days. You develop your spirit by eating the Word, reading the Word, meditating on it, and then praying in the Spirit. You will then start to encounter the manifestations of the Holy Spirit, which are veiled. Your eyes need to be opened to the visitation, which is happening around you all the time.

Chapter 23

HABITATION

*I love the habitation of your house and
the place where Your glory dwells.*
—Psalm 26:8

H ABITATION IS SOMETHING that is spoken of in many different ways in the Bible, especially when it has to do with God's temple and His tabernacle. When God came and stayed in the Holy of Holies, that describes one type of habitation. In the New Testament, God does not dwell in buildings anymore because He is dwelling in man. In the New Testament, God comes to human beings and indwells them and inhabits them.

Jesus spoke about the Holy Spirit coming as the Comforter. He said,

> *And I will pray the Father, and he shall give you another Comforter, that he may abide with you forever; even the Spirit of truth; whom the world cannot receive, because it seeth him not, neither knoweth him:*

but ye know him; for he dwelleth with you, and shall be in you.

—JOHN 14:16-17 KJV

The Holy Spirit is not going to leave you. He is going to be with you forever. The Holy Spirit indwells you. You then have the Trinity living inside of you. When you are obeying God, and you want and desire to walk with Him, He comes to live with you, and it is called *habitation* (see John 14:23 TPT). And God will never leave you.

You have visitations where Jesus comes, and He talks to you, and you have angels coming, and you have the Holy Spirit manifesting Himself in visiting with you. When you begin to experience habitation, you begin to synchronize with Heaven. You start to walk with God in a place where Enoch walked—where God stays with you all the time, and there is a manifestation of God's presence with you and a manifestation of His angels working with you. This life of habitation with God is possible, but it is not taught about very often.

GOD'S PLAN FOR HIS PEOPLE

It is very important not to let go of *any* of these power words that we've been discussing. Habitation is God's plan and His plan for the Church, but we must gather together corporately for that to happen. Jesus said, *"For where two or more are gathered together in My name, I will be there in the midst of them"* (Matt. 18:20). When you get two or more people together, then you have habitation, and Jesus will be there. It is the same way with the Holy Spirit. When you get agreement and unity within a body of believers, then God will inhabit their praises when they worship (see Ps. 22:3 KJV).

David loved to worship, and he understood habitation. He said, *"Lord, I have loved the habitation of Your house, and the place where Your glory dwells"* (Ps. 26:8). David loved the tabernacle, and he helped institute worship there with all of the instruments and all the singers; worship involves habitation as well. When Solomon dedicated the temple, he had prepared all of the sacrifices, and he prayed, and fire came down from Heaven and consumed the sacrifices. Then the people worshiped, and the glory of the Lord came and filled the temple. Not one could stand there in God's presence, and they bowed their faces to the ground and worshiped and praised the Lord (see 2 Cor. 7:1-4).

INHABITED BY GOD

You can be preserved by visitation: *"Thou hast granted me life and favor, and they visitation has preserved my spirit"* (Job 10:12 KJV). But when habitation comes, then you have God dwelling with you all the time. That is God's goal for you, especially in these end days that we are living in now. The sons of God are going to be revealed in these last days, and all creation is groaning for this manifestation (see Rom. 8:19).

In the book of Exodus, when the people came out of Egypt, there was a pillar of fire. There was a cloud by day and fire by night. It was the angel of the Lord, and God was with His people the whole way through the desert, even though they disobeyed and rebelled. The people did not want to meet with God on the mountain, but God was still there with them. That fire of God would even go into the tent of meeting with them. When Moses and Joshua entered in, the fire and cloud would be right there in the

Holy of Holies. It is the same within you; He is in your heart right now, because God inhabits you, and He has fire.

This visitation turns into habitation when we continually yield to it. God will never leave us. The manifestation of the Spirit of God in habitation is possible in these days, and it does not have to wane or go away. You can experience God's presence and His power all the time, but it is really up to you. It is you who must yield to it.

In Exodus 24:9-11, God came down to visit with Moses, Aaron, and the seventy elders who came halfway up the mountain. Moses wrote that under God's feet was a paved work of sapphire stone, and it was *"like the very heavens in its clarity"* (Exod. 24:10). When God came down, He could not stand on the mountain. God had to have His own platform made of sapphire stones from His throne room in Heaven. The reason God had to have His platform was that God is so awesome in power that if He had touched the mountain without the platform, it would have started to quake and burn. God wanted to visit with the people who were chosen, and Moses was told to bring them up, and God showed Himself to them. God's whole purpose was not just to visit His people; God wanted habitation.

Later, God wanted them to come into the tent of meeting and meet with Him (see Exod. 33:7-11). When you read the account, only Moses and Joshua went in there, but God had invited all of Israel to come and meet with Him in the tent of meeting. God was hurt that the people did not want to meet with Him. The Israelites did not want God to be that close to them; it was too much for them.

We, as Christians, want God to be that close to us. We want to experience His power and His glory, and we want to encounter

Him. We want to know God intimately. God has spoken this forth because He wants to inhabit us. His whole goal was to restore us back to before the fall of man. God wants us to come back to that place in relationship with Him, where He can walk with us in the garden of Eden, just like He did with Adam and Eve. Jesus fulfilled His mission, and everything has been bought back, and the price has been paid. In Second Corinthians 5:18-21, the apostle Paul talks about us being given the ministry of reconciliation, whereby we are to go out and compel people to come in and choose life this day because God has bought them back.

God has already spoken over your life. God's Word goes forth from His mouth, and it does not return empty but accomplishes what God pleases. His Word prospers in the thing which God has sent it (see Isa. 55:11). You were God-breathed, and you were sent to this earth. A book was written about you, and your spirit was breathed into your mother's womb (see Ps. 139:16). Now, God wants you to walk out your life according to what was written. God ordained your days before you even were born.

ENCOUNTERING THE SECRET PLACE

God has already caused us to be able to enter into the most intimate place, into that Holy of Holies (see Heb. 10:19). It is a secret place, and you can go in there and encounter God in habitation. When you encounter God this way, it becomes more intimate, and you will not want to leave. You will never want to stop worshiping, praying, and seeking God. You can get addicted to the secret place, to the power of God in that Holy of Holies, where you feel clean because the holiness of God is so strong. Holiness is a characteristic of God, and it is part of His personality. His holiness gives you a clean feeling, and it involves knowing that God is God and He is all-powerful.

There is a revelation that comes from habitation, and you realize it when you leave the secret place. When you go out into the world and go to work, or do whatever you need to do, God goes with you. You will get to a place where you can feel comfortable walking in this world while not being a part of it. You are in this world, but you are not of it because you know that you are just visiting (see John 17:16). God has sent you to this generation to change a generation, but it all happens in habitation. It all happens in the secret place, and it is from there that you can go out.

He who dwells in the secret place of the Most High shall abide under the shadow of the Almighty.
—PSALM 91:1

In this psalm, the word *dwells* is relational; it speaks of habitation. You are not just sitting there and not saying anything. It is referring to a relationship where you talk to each other and communicate. When the psalmist refers to the secret place, he is describing you sitting with God and sharing intimate secrets with each other. That is the relationship that God wants with you; He wants habitation. You must stay very close to God in the shadow of the Most High. You must stay in the shadow to qualify for the secret place.

I saw that the cherubim that are on either side of God cover His face because the glory is so strong. God is seated on the mercy seat, just like it is depicted on the ark of the covenant. The mercy seat is on top, and there were the cherubim, one on each side that cover with their wings. God sits on His throne in Heaven, and the cherubim cover Him with their wings. There is a place where the cherubim's wings shield you from the glory that is coming from God's face.

As you read Psalm 91 with this in mind, you can see that if you are that close, then you are right in the shadow of the wings of the cherubim. You will then realize that you qualify for all the things that are spoken of in Psalm 91. Nothing evil will come near you, neither will you even stub your foot against a stone because angels will be assigned to you. You can read about all of the benefits of dwelling in the secret place. No disease will be able to touch you. God spoke this psalm through Moses.

Moses wrote Psalm 91 from the cleft of the rock when he encountered the glory of God passing by him. Moses saw that in that shadow, in that place, there was no demonic force or disease that could touch him. Be encouraged when you read Psalm 91, and make sure that you understand it had to do with the proximity of you to God. In that secret place, no demonic force can touch you.

People have asked me, "Why did God let this happen to me?" or "Why did my friend die of cancer? Why did this car wreck happen?" I have to tell them that God is not a liar, and Psalm 91 is true, but they have to stay within that secret place. You must stay in that proximity, in the closeness of God with relationship, and that is habitation. Habitation is when you never leave the secret place, but that takes discipline, it takes maturity, and it takes your being diligent.

God will qualify you, and His angels will not allow you to be hurt. You will never be in another car accident, never have another disease, and that is all possible in habitation. If you are just visiting God, then there is an in and out to it, and you are left exposed at times. I do not want that because I want to be in the secret place all the time, and I want to be protected.

PEACEFUL HABITATION

Isaiah prophesied, *"My people will dwell in a peaceful habitation, in secure dwellings, and in quiet resting places"* (32:18). God wants us to be in a peaceful habitation. God wants us to have a secure dwelling, and He wants us to have a quiet resting place. You can meditate on this as well, *"A father of the fatherless, a defender of widows, is God in His holy habitation"* (Ps. 68:5).

In God's habitation, He is your Father, He is your Defender, and He is with you. You only need to come in and be with Him, and you need to stay in there with Him. You need to tell your Father every day, "I want to stay close to You, Lord. Help me. Send your angels to help me stay in the secret place." Satan will try to attack you, and he wants you to worry and get out of the faith realm and into his realm. Satan wants you to be in his realm so that he can beat you, but if you stay in God's realm, satan cannot get in there. Satan would never go into the secret place, he would never go into the Holy of Holies, and it is not even possible for him to get there. In the secret place, you are safe with God.

Chapter 24

WAITING ON THE LORD

*I wait quietly before God, for my victory comes
from him. He alone is my rock and my salvation,
my fortress where I will never be shaken.*

—PSALM 62:1-2 NLT

WAITING ON THE Lord is one of my favorite power words, and it is essential. A lot of people today are in such a hurry that they do not know how to wait or how to be patient. The psalmist here in Psalm 62 is convinced of several different things, and if you can understand this, it will take you to the next level spiritually. You will be very effective, not only in your own life, but in the lives of others. You can be a history maker if you can grasp waiting on the Lord.

The psalmist says, *"I wait quietly before God because He is my victory."* While the psalmist waits, the victory comes from God. The psalmist goes on and says, *"He alone is my rock and my salvation. He is my fortress."* These are things that you need to meditate on as you wait on God. I learned how to wait on God because the Lord instructed me that people were not waiting on Him.

One morning I woke up and looked out through the darkness in my room, and I saw someone standing there. As I looked closer, and more clearly, it looked like an angel, but he did not have wings. He was very big, but he was dressed differently than I have ever seen before. He explained to me that he was sent to show me and instruct me on waiting on the Lord. Then he grabbed me, and he took me. I do not know where we went, but we went very fast.

THE ROOM OF REVELATION

I found myself in this place where there was a large room that I needed to walk into with him. When I entered, Jesus was there, and Jesus and the angel started to instruct me on how to wait on God. They showed me that people were not waiting on the Lord, and they were missing out on a lot of things that God had for them. At the time, I did not see this as clearly as I do now. Jesus and the angel showed me how effective waiting on God was. I realized that a lot was missing from, not only my life, but from others' lives as well as we were not effectively waiting on God.

Jesus told me that the room we were in was the room of revelation. As I waited on God, the revelation, which seemed to be a substance of the Spirit of God, began to permeate my being. I consciously bowed my head and waited on God right there in the presence of this angel and Jesus. I felt the whole room start to move upward and accelerate. The longer I waited on God, the faster the room of revelation started to move upward. It got to a point where I felt we were so high that I lifted my head and looked at Jesus. He just smiled at me, and the door opened, and we had gone into the heavenly realms.

The earth was below us, and I could see the lights of the different cities. Jesus said, "You see, your perspective changes when you wait on Me. Now you are so high up that you see things the way that I see them. From here, all of your problems are very small, and this is what people need to do. They need to wait on Me." Then Jesus said, "If they wait on Me, their problems will become very small, and they will be able to resolve things because they will see it from My perspective." This revelation was very powerful to me, and then the angel of the Lord took me back to my room.

Ever since that day, I have seen God do many miracles in my life. I started to wait on God in these periods, and I would not do anything other than waiting; I would not even pray. I would sit and meditate on His Word, and the power of the Holy Spirit would hit me. One day I started to notice that my eyesight was getting better, and it got to the place where I do not need to wear contacts anymore. It was all because I waited on God and let the revelation of the Spirit of God permeate my being, and then something happened to my eyes physically.

There is a substance in the Spirit that can permeate you, and it will cause you to manifest physically, even healing. Your body can be healed without anyone touching you, and without you doing anything besides waiting on God. My physical eyes responded to a spiritual substance that came into me by waiting on God. This is very important. God changed my perspective that day by taking me above the world and showing me the world from His perspective. I realized then that God has always wanted me to come up higher with Him.

Jesus has always wanted me to sit with Him in the heavenly realms. We are all seated with Him in the heavenly realms united in Christ Jesus (see Eph. 2:6 NLT). I saw the plans and purposes of God from His perspective. I began to realize that my involvement in this world had been too intense at times and that I needed to have a perspective only He could give me.

BEYOND HIS PRESENCE

You can only have God's perspective because the Spirit of God lifts you up. There is a lifting up by the Spirit, a catching away by the Spirit. There is a breath of God that causes revelation to come, and the mystery of the ages can be revealed to you. The mysteries of God can be revealed in these times of waiting on the Lord.

Jesus told me that there is a synchronization that happens in your spirit with Heaven when you wait on God. That synchronization happens in your spirit, and then it starts to permeate out into your soul and your understanding. After a while, you will start to encounter understanding that is beyond your physical ability. You can start to encounter the revelation of God in a greater way. If you lack in understanding, if you lack in revelation, it could be that you are not waiting on the Lord, and you just might be too busy.

It is time to slow down in your time with God, and it will never be wasted time. I was so used to praying or fasting, and I had all these different things that I wanted to do, and it can become a system. It can get to the place where you are no longer waiting on the Lord. You can become way too busy in your process of seeking God.

At first, waiting will feel uncomfortable. I told the Lord that I felt like I wasn't doing anything. He said, "Waiting on Me is not wasted time." We get busy at times to where we have this process we go through when praying, and the Lord almost wants to wreck that. He wants you to wait on Him and sit at His feet and listen to what He has to say. What happened to me was that the Word of the Lord started coming to me. The Word of the Lord was so strong that it began to transform me every day just by waiting on Him.

If you remember, Moses wanted God to be with Him because the people were hard for him to handle. He did not know how to deal with all those millions of people who were in rebellion with God. At the end of Moses' conversation with God on the mountain, God said that the Israelites were Moses' people (see Exod. 33:12-14). Moses disagreed and told God that they were His people, and they would not go anywhere unless God went with them. Moses was telling God that he would not do anything without Him. God answered and said, *"My presence will go with you, and I will give you rest."*

Moses then asked God, *"Please, show me Your glory"* (Exod. 33:18). When Moses asked this of God, he used the Hebrew word *glory,* which Moses knew was different than the Hebrew word for *presence* used earlier. This difference infers that Moses knew that there was much more to receive from God, and he knew that God was holding back from him. Moses knew that there was more beyond God's presence; there is His glory.

In that time of Moses being diligent and waiting on the Lord, the Lord said,

> *So it shall be, while My glory passes by, that I will put you in the cleft of the rock, and will cover you with My*

hand while I pass by. Then I will take away My hand,
and you shall see My back; but My face shall not be seen.
—Exodus 33:22-23

These are the types of things that happen when you wait on the Lord. There is much more about God than is even written. Did you know that God could show you something that no one else has ever seen before? Did you know that God could do something in your life that you have not believed for, and He could give you something that is beyond what you have asked? These kinds of things happen to people who wait on the Lord and who realize that God still has more that He has not shown them.

Many of us get to the place where we want to feel God's presence. What if that happens, and then you want it to be permanent? That is when it will become permanent, and then you will want to know more and more about God. There is so much of His character that has not been revealed. What we have in God's Word is sufficient, but God could show you something that is beyond your ability to even think of asking. God wants to give you more. *"To Him who is able to do exceedingly abundantly above what we could ever ask or think"* (Eph. 3:20).

When you wait on the Lord, God starts to cause you to walk in dominion, and He exalts you, and you are going to inherit the land.

Wait on the Lord, and keep His way, and He shall
exalt you to inherit the land; When the wicked are cut
off, you shall see it.
—Psalm 37:34

Our land, our inheritance, is the Lord Himself. We are going to obtain more of Him; there is always going to be more of God.

I saw things in Heaven that I am not allowed to talk about, and they are beyond our comprehension. I cannot even form the words to talk about them, but I did see that we can never know God completely.

There will always be a part of God that is beyond our ability to understand unless He reveals it. Waiting on God causes Him to show parts of Himself and His personality, and I want to know His personality. I want to know what God likes and what He does not like. God's plans and purposes can be revealed in your life, but there are also His characteristics that you want to know, and He can show you things about Himself.

Job said that when you wait on God, He brings justice on your behalf.

> *But it is wrong to say God doesn't listen, to say the Almighty isn't concerned. You say you can't see him, but he will bring justice if you will only wait.*
> —JOB 35:13-14 NLT

God can come in as you wait on Him and correct everything. I have seen this happen daily, where I have waited on God, and everything is corrected even before lunchtime. I did not have to do a thing, not even make a phone call. God had taken care of it all because I had waited on Him. There will be times when God will tell you not to make a call or not tell people anything, only wait on Him, and then He fixes it all. That is the kind of inheritance you have, where God wants you to encounter His power as you wait on Him.

God is faithful, and if you wait on Him, it may not always happen right away, but He is faithful.

Therefore the Lord will wait, that He may be gracious to you; and therefore He will be exalted, that He may have mercy on you. For the Lord is a God of justice; blessed are all those who wait for Him.

—ISAIAH 30:18

After you have waited on God in prayer, you go on about your day. If what you needed to happen does not happen right away, be encouraged. According to this verse, you have to wait for God's help, but He is going to come and show Himself to you. God is going to show His love and compassion to you, but you must wait, knowing that He is a faithful God.

When I was in Heaven, I saw the warfare that goes on down here on earth. God will speak, and He will reveal Himself in a situation, but Christians do not wait. They do not understand warfare—that there is a fight that goes on.

Initially, when you pray, God hears you, but immediately, satan comes to steal the word. He tries to talk you out of it, to get you to compromise or back off or renege on your prayer. You cannot back off. You have got to stay in there and be persistent.

SUBMITTING YOUR WILL

The key to this power word is this: When you wait on the Lord, you are not only doing yourself a favor, but you are doing everyone you know a favor. You are doing a favor for everyone in your church, all your friends, your family, and everyone in the generation you live. When you wait on God, there is something that happens inside you, and it is a kind of breaking. You have a will, and that will can work for you, or it can work against you. Your will must be yielded to God's will, and when you wait on God, there is a breaking that has to happen. Human beings are like horses that want to run, yet they are being held back. They need to have their will broken to where they are submissive.

Once the Spirit of God has accomplished that in your life, and you have become submissive and broken, He can use you. Waiting on the Lord causes you to have that submission in your spirit. Then God's angels will start to work with you all the time because you are submitted to God, and you are not grieving the Spirit of God any longer. Did you know you can grieve the Spirit of God? It happens many times because we do not wait on the Lord. If you want to stop angelic activity in your life, then grieve the Holy Spirit by being rebellious.

Participate in waiting on the Lord until you become submissive. Always be willing to act under the impulse of the Holy Spirit, and that will increase the angelic activity in your life. Everyone wants to have angels active in their lives. There are often angels around me, and they are strong, but the reason they are around me is that my will had to be broken.

I had to decide that I would not do a thing until God speaks to me and tells me to do it. Many people want me to call them, but I will not call them until the Lord tells me to. The Lord will not let me talk to a person until I have the word of the Lord for them, because that is what they want to hear. They want to hear what God is saying to them through me, but I have to wait on God. I can't just call them and make something up or encourage them from the soul. I want to hear from God for them, but I have to wait on God to hear.

You should not be pulled in every direction. Wait on the Lord, and then the Holy Spirit will be pleased with you. Then the angels will be pleased with you and will want to work with you because you are moving in the Spirit. If you are working in the flesh, if you are manipulating or doing your own thing, then the angels will back off. Angels can be your friend as long as you are God's friend and as long as you are doing what God wants you to do. If you are grieving the Holy Spirit, if you are holding back, if you are doing your own thing, they do not like that. The angels will back off, and you do not want that to happen because they are sent to minister to you and for you.

There is a process to your will being broken, and it is not fun, but there are some shortcuts. When you wait on the Lord, you need to tell God that you are not interested in your own will. You must say to God, "This is not about me. This is about You, Lord. Whatever desires You have for me, for this world, and my family and friends, that is what I want. Lord, what is it that You want me to do? If Your will is for me to do nothing, I will do nothing." You have to be willing to do nothing. You are going to have pressure from people to perform and pressure from situations to act, but do not do it. You must wait on the Lord.

Moses spent seven days waiting when he went up on the mountain to meet with God (see Exod. 24:15-18). It says that the Lord called Moses up into the mountain, and he waited on the Lord right there on the mountain. The glory of the Lord was like a consuming fire where Moses stood outside the glory cloud. Moses waited there for seven days, and then the Lord called to him from out of the midst of the cloud. And Moses went into the midst of the cloud and was on the mountain forty days and forty nights.

Moses waited seven days. Could you do that? God calls you up, and He says, "Wait right here." You have a mountain on fire, and you are outside of a glory cloud for seven days. Moses waited seven days outside of that glory cloud, and then God said, "You can come in." What do you think was going on during that time? I will tell you. Moses' will was being broken. Moses had to stand there and watch what was right ahead of him. He had to be patient for seven days. Could you have done that? We all have an element inside us that needs to be broken. We need to be broken and humbled.

Here is a shortcut, and it is a secret.

For thus says the High and Lofty One
Who inhabits eternity, whose name is Holy: I dwell
in the high and holy place, with him who has a con-
trite and humble spirit of the humble, and to revive the
heart of the contrite ones.
—ISAIAH 57:15

God does not want you to stand and talk about yourself. That is what the rich young ruler did with Jesus (see Matt. 19:16-30). He asked Jesus what he could do to inherit eternal life. Jesus told the young man that he had to obey all the commandments, to which the rich young ruler explained that he had been obedient to since birth. The young ruler stood there, telling how good he was to the Creator, Jesus Christ, who breathed him into his mother's womb. That rich young ruler was full of pride. Jesus loved him and said, *"You lack one thing; sell everything you have."* In other words, Jesus was telling him how he could be fixed because Jesus knew that he needed to be broken. He needed to give away everything he had to have treasure in Heaven and follow Jesus.

That young man could not do that because his wealth was his crutch and his strength was his riches. Jesus was trying to help him, and he needed to be broken. That rich young ruler was not perfect, and he was not righteous because it was all works. That is why waiting on God is so important, because it breaks you.

Here is the shortcut: If you can humble *yourself* under the mighty hand of God, then God will not have to humble you (see 1 Pet. 5:6-7). God will lift you up in due time when you cast all of your cares upon Him. There is a process of the Spirit that works in your inner man. It begins in your spirit where it works outward into your soul—into your *mind, will*, and *emotions*.

Adam and Eve had the ability to not eat of that tree in the garden. God had told them not to eat from that tree or to touch it (see Gen. 3:1-7). They could have stayed away from it, but they allowed themselves, through reasoning, to be deceived, and they ate. The problem was that they were given everything, but they felt like God was holding something back from them. That was not the truth, and God was not holding anything back from them. Adam and Eve did not need to eat from that tree. They could not handle knowing the knowledge of good and evil. They only needed to know good, and they did not need to know about evil. God is the only one who can eat of that fruit and know the difference between good and evil and still choose good.

We do not have the ability to have our eyes opened to evil and still choose good. We are made in the image of God, but we are not God. This problem has surfaced over and over again throughout the Bible, and it is the problem of our wills. God has given you free will. You have to understand that how far you go into God depends on your ability to humble yourself and to walk with Him in sober-mindedness.

> *For the grace of God that brings salvation has appeared to all men, teaching us that, denying ungodliness and worldly lusts, we should live soberly, righteously, and godly in the present age, looking for the blessed hope and glorious appearing of our great God and Savior Jesus Christ, who gave Himself for us, that He might redeem us from every lawless deed and purify for Himself His own special people, zealous for good works. Speak these things, exhort, and rebuke with all authority. Let no one despise you.*
> —TITUS 2:11-15

A PROPHECY

As You allow the Mighty Holy Spirit to fill you to overflowing, you will see My special will for you. And from that seeing, you will understand My ways. Stand on the foundation of the Absolute Truth that has been established and speak boldly. Speak to your mountains and speak to the powers of darkness and see them move out of your way. I have established your way before you were born. Speak from the place of being seated with me in the heavenly realms by Christ Jesus.

SALVATION PRAYER

Lord God,
I confess that I am a sinner.
I confess that I need Your Son, Jesus.
Please forgive me in His name.
Lord Jesus, I believe You died for me and that You are
alive and listening to me now.
I now turn from my sins and welcome You into my
heart. Come and take control of my life.
Make me the kind of person You want me to be.
Now, fill me with Your Holy Spirit who will show me
how to live for You. I acknowledge You before men as
my Savior and my Lord.
In Jesus' name. Amen.

If you prayed this prayer, please contact us at
info@kevinzadai.com for more information and material. Go to
KevinZadai.com for other exciting ministry materials.

Join our network at Warriornotes.tv. Join our ministry and training school at Warrior Notes School of Ministry.

Visit KevinZadai.com for more info.

ABOUT DR. KEVIN L. ZADAI

Kevin Zadai, Th.D., was called to ministry at the age of ten. He attended Central Bible College in Springfield, Missouri, where he received a bachelor of arts in theology. Later, he received training in missions at Rhema Bible College and a doctorate of theology from Primus University. He is currently ordained through Rev. Dr. Jesse and Rev. Dr. Cathy Duplantis.

At age thirty-one, during a routine day surgery, he found himself on the "other side of the veil" with Jesus. For forty-five minutes, the Master revealed spiritual truths before returning him to his body and assigning him to a supernatural ministry.

Kevin holds a commercial pilot license and is retired from Southwest Airlines after twenty-nine years as a flight attendant. Kevin is the founder and president of Warrior Notes School of Ministry. He and his lovely wife, Kathi, reside in New Orleans, Louisiana.